THE STORY OF JANE

THE STORY OF JANE

The Legendary Underground Feminist Abortion Service

Laura Kaplan

THE UNIVERSITY OF CHICAGO PRESS

Reprinted by arrangement with Pantheon Books,
a division of Random House, Inc.

The University of Chicago Press, Chicago 60637

 Originally published 1995
University of Chicago Press Edition 1997
Printed in the United States of America
12 11 10 09 6 5 4

Library of Congress Cataloging-in-Publication Data

Kaplan, Laura.
The Story of Jane : the legendary underground feminist abortion service / Laura Kaplan.
p. cm.
Includes bibliographical references and index.
Originally published: New York : Pantheon Books, 1995.
ISBN 0-226-42421-9 (alk. paper)
1. Jane (Abortion service). 2. Abortion services—Illinois—Chicago. 3. Abortion—United States—History. I. Title.

HQ767.5.U5K37 1997
363.46—dc21 96-39768
CIP

∞ The paper used in this publication meets the minimum requirements of the American National Standard for Information Sciences—Permanence of Paper for Printed Library Materials, ANSI Z39.48—1992.

FOR OUR CHILDREN

Liberty will not descend to a people, a people must raise themselves to liberty.

Emma Goldman

INTRODUCTION

During the four years before the Supreme Court's 1973 *Roe* v. *Wade* decision legalized abortion, thousands of women called Jane. Jane was the contact name for a group in Chicago officially known as The Abortion Counseling Service of Women's Liberation. Every week desperate women of every class, race and ethnicity telephoned Jane. They were women whose husbands or boyfriends forbade them to use contraceptives; women who had conceived on every method of contraception; women who had not used contraceptives. They were older women who thought they were no longer fertile; young girls who did not understand their reproductive physiology. They were women who could not care for a child and women who did not want a child. Some women agonized over the decision, while others had no doubts. Each one was making the best decision about motherhood that she could make at the time.

Organized in 1969, Jane initially counseled women and referred them to the underground for abortions. Other groups offering the same kind of crucial help took shape at this time throughout the country. But Jane evolved in a unique way. At first the women in Jane concentrated on screening abortionists, attempting to determine which ones were competent and reliable. But they quickly realized that as long as women were dependent on illegal practitioners, they would be virtually helpless. Jane determined to take control of the abortion process so that the women who turned to Jane could have control as well. Eventually, the group found a doctor who was willing to work closely with them. When they discovered that he was not, as he had claimed to be, a physician, the women in Jane took a bold step: "If he can do it, then we can do it, too." Soon Jane members learned from him the technical skills necessary to perform abortions.

As members of the women's liberation movement, the women in Jane viewed reproductive control as fundamental to women's freedom. The power to act had to be in the hands of each woman. Her decision about an abortion needed to be underscored as an active choice about her life. And, since Jane wanted every woman to understand that in seeking an abortion she was taking control of her life, she had to feel in control of her abortion. Group members realized that the only way she could control her abortion was if they, Jane, controlled the entire process. The group concluded that women who cared about abortion should be the ones performing abortions.

None of the women who started Jane ever expected to perform abortions. What they intended was to meet what one member called "a crying need." That need gradually led them to radical actions. Their work was not based on a medical model, but on how they themselves wanted to be treated. When a woman came to Jane for an abortion, the experience she had was markedly different from what she encountered in standard medical settings. She was included. She was in control. Rather than being a passive recipient, a patient, she was expected to participate. Jane said, "We don't do this to you, but with you." By letting each woman know beforehand what to expect during the abortion and the recovery stage, and then talking with her step by step through the abortion itself, group members attempted to give each woman a sense of her own personal power in a situation in which most women felt powerless. Jane tried to create an environment in which women could take back their bodies, and by doing so, take back their lives. When I joined Jane, the group had managed to give women not only psychological control, but also freedom from the financial extortion that illegal abortionists subjected them to. Jane charged only the amount necessary to cover medical supplies and administrative expenses. And no woman was turned away because of her inability to pay.

Whenever individuals gain access to the tools and skills to affect the conditions of their own lives, they define empowerment. Our actions, which we saw as potentially transforming for other women, changed us, too. By taking responsibility, we became responsible. Most of us grew stronger, more self-assured, confident in our own abilities. In picking up the tools of our own liberation, in our case medical instruments, we broke a powerful taboo. That act was terrifying, but it was also exhilarating. We ourselves felt exactly the same powerfulness that we wanted other women to feel. We came to understand that society's problems stemmed from imbalances in power, the power of one person over another, teacher over student, doctor over patient. The weight of the authority and the expert was inherent in the position, no matter who held it. Jane, through the group's practice, challenged institutionalized authority and tried to redress these imbalances of power.

But the politics of power, which we recognized so clearly in the larger society, were ironically mirrored in our own internal dynamics. While Jane succeeded in giving control to the women in need of abortions, the group was not as successful in sharing control among its own members. A hierarchy of knowledge developed—knowledge of medical technique, of crucial problems and critical decisions. Those who withheld the knowledge frequently justified their actions by citing the need for secrecy to protect the group from exposure. This was a valid argument in an era in which simply providing information about abortion was a criminal act. But necessary caution was not the only explanation. We discovered how difficult it was to resist reproducing those ordering structures which shape our society, even as we challenged many of their manifestations. Sometimes it seemed that our determination to empower the individual could find consistent expression only in our interactions with the women who turned to us for help. To them, we gave as much information as we could uncover about the workings of their bodies and what they could do to foster their own health.

Jane developed at a time when blind obedience to medical authority was the rule. There were no patient advocates or hospital ombudsmen, no such person as a health consumer. Few women understood their reproductive physiology or had any idea where to get the information they needed. The special knowledge doctors had was deliberately made inaccessible, couched in language incomprehensible to the lay person. We did not have a right to it.

It was only in late 1970 that *Our Bodies, Ourselves*, the first in a wave of self-help health books, was published. Now many of us know that we can get the medical information we need in a library or bookstore, but this was unheard of twenty-five years ago. Still, finding health care that is not only adequate and affordable, but also respectful, is, for most of us, a continuing struggle.

In the late 1960s others outside the women's liberation movement were working to change abortion laws. There were legal scholars and organizations like the Association for the Study of Abortion in New York; population control groups like ZPG (Zero Population Growth), and NARAL (then, The National Association for Repeal of Abortion Laws) that supported legislative change and challenged the constitutionality of laws in the courts. They directed their efforts at the established channels of institutionalized authority, but their gains were only modest until the women's liberation movement mobilized women across the country who accelerated the struggle with their anger.

Women's liberation groups organized speak-outs at which women testified to their own illegal abortions. They marched and demonstrated and disrupted legislative hearings on abortion that excluded women. They demanded that women, the true experts on abortion, be heard and recognized. They brought abortion out of the closet, where it had been shrouded in secrecy and shame.

But the women's liberation movement did more than place abortion in the realm of public discourse. It framed the issue, not in terms of privacy in sexual relations, and not in the neutral language of choice, but in terms of a woman's freedom to determine her own destiny as she defined it, not as others defined it. Abortion was a touchstone. If she did not have the right to control her own body, which included freedom from forced sterilizations and unnecessary hysterectomies, gains in other arenas were meaningless. These issues were addressed not only in political terms, but also in moral terms. To force a woman either to carry an unwanted pregnancy or to venture into a dangerous underground was considered morally indefensible. Women were dying because they were denied the ability to act on their own moral decisions.

While the public struggle was underway, every day women who tried to find abortions put their lives at risk. Their suffering could not be ignored. Women's groups and networks of the clergy organized to meet these women's immediate needs. Based on a moral imperative, Howard Moody, a Baptist minister, founded the first clergy group, the New York Clergy Consultation Service on Abortion. He encouraged clergymen throughout the country to set up similar networks to help women get safe abortions. These clergy groups, with the moral standing of organized religion, played a public role, announcing their work in the newspapers, framing the issue in moral terms and advocating for legislative change.

Both the clergy and women's liberation groups sought out competent abortionists, negotiated the price, raised money to pay for abortions and counseled thousands of distraught women. Not only did they help women but, by breaking the law, they also undermined it. They followed the tradition of the Underground Railroad which defied another immoral law, the Fugitive Slave Act, and helped to undermine the institution of chattel slavery. Like the scores of people who were part of the Underground Railroad, the stories of those who participated in these referral services are part of our hidden history.

Starting in 1973 with Lawrence Lader's *Abortion II: Making the Revolution*, the history of the struggle for reproductive rights has been written from the perspective of the legislative and court battles. Few have documented the grassroots efforts of feminists and of those who formed the abortion underground.

A few years ago I was asked to speak to a class of first-year teachers in a Master's of Education program. The professor hoped that Jane's example would help her students understand empowerment. After my talk we broke into discussion groups. I tried to describe to these young teachers the position women were in before the women's movement. The message that women received was that they were less intelligent, less capable, less valuable than men. They weren't the heroes. They were the ones rescued by heroes. The issues that directly affected women's lives were rarely framed by them, but rather by institutions and authorities dominated by men, such as legislatures and the church.

A young man in the group asked, seemingly astonished, "You mean the women's movement was about options for women and not about women becoming lawyers?"

I thought, is that what the younger generation thinks? Where do they get their information? Who is defining our history? If we who were directly involved do not speak out, what we struggled for will be lost.

For those of us who came of age in the 1960s, the arguments for our sexual freedom are still fresh. For those born after that time it may all seem like ancient history. But it was not until 1965 that the Supreme Court guaranteed even the right to acquire contraceptives, and then for married people only. Before that some states still had laws, stemming from Anthony Comstock's nineteenth-century "moral purity" campaign, prohibiting the sale and distribution of contraceptives. Not until 1972, less than a year before its decision in

Roe v. *Wade*, did the Supreme Court in *Eisenstadt* v. *Baird* extend the right to contraception to single people. Before that, access to contraceptives for unmarried people varied from place to place, doctor to doctor. Some women bought cheap wedding rings at the Five and Dime to convince physicians that they were married. One woman I know went to her doctor for contraceptives just before her wedding. He told her to come back after the honeymoon.

For young women in the 1960s control of our bodies and control of our sexuality were central concerns. It was at a time when segments of society were breaking out of the cultural and political repression of the 1950s. The civil rights movement, the student and antiwar movements, challenged accepted norms and authority. Out of those upheavals the modern women's movement was born.

When I moved back to Chicago in 1971, two years after graduating from college, I knew I wanted to participate in the women's liberation movement, but abortion was not my primary interest. I had just moved from New York state which had, in 1970, enacted the most liberal abortion reform in the country, a law that legalized abortions by physicians up to twenty-four weeks of pregnancy. The legislative victory was high drama. Just as the vote tally was about to be announced, Assemblyman George Michaels, representing a heavily Catholic upstate district yet overwhelmed by his conscience, switched his vote from no to yes, dooming his political career. The bill passed by his vote. At the time I did not think about what it meant that one vote was all that protected women's lives, nor was I aware of the ongoing battle between reformers and radicals that the New York legislation had highlighted.

When New York's legislature debated legalizing abortion in 1969 and 1970, radical feminists passed out a copy of their ideal abortion law—a blank sheet of paper. They advocated repeal and repeal meant no laws on abortion. They argued that any reform, no matter how liberal, was a defeat since it maintained the State's right to legislate control over women's bodies. With that control codified, as in New

York's liberal law, the door was open for further restrictions. These radicals could foresee a time when abortion was legal but relatively inaccessible, perhaps as inaccessible to most women as it had been before reform.

The Supreme Court's *Roe* v. *Wade* decision of 1973 stated that abortion in the first two trimesters of pregnancy was a medical decision to be made by a woman and her doctor. Four years later Congress passed the Hyde Amendment, which banned the use of federal Medicaid dollars for abortion. Only seventeen states continue to fund abortions for poor women. Eighty percent of counties in the United States have no abortion services. Half of medical schools do not teach doctors abortion techniques. Because of harassment and intimidation by anti-abortion forces, few doctors are willing to perform abortions. The Supreme Court's decision in *Webster* v. *Reproductive Health Services* (1989), a Missouri case, upheld a ban on the use of public funds and public hospitals for abortions and allowed a number of other restrictions that the Missouri statute included. Although the Webster decision did not overturn *Roe* v. *Wade*, as some had predicted it might, it was a signal that the Court would consider a variety of restrictions on abortion, state by state. Justice Harry Blackmun, who had written the *Roe* v. *Wade* decision, noted in his dissent in Webster that the future seemed ominous "and a chill wind blows." It seems that the radicals' prescient warnings have come true with a vengeance.

Those of us who remember what it was like before *Roe* v. *Wade* know that restricting abortion will not end it. For every woman, abortion as a decision is not a theoretical abstraction, but is rooted in the concrete conditions of her life. She will weigh her decision and then try to act on it. This is what women have always done, irrespective of the law or even of the risks to their own lives. In 1988 in Indiana, a state that requires parental notification, a teenager, Becky Bell, died from an illegal abortion because she felt she could not tell her parents she was pregnant. In Texas in 1977 Rosie Jimenez died from an illegal abortion because she could not afford a legal one. Newspapers still print accounts of the lengths to which women are driven in order to do what they feel they have to do.

For those of us who participated in the struggle for abortion the growing threats to a woman's right to control her own body are more than a chill wind blowing. In the public discourse the fetus has been elevated to an equal status with a living, breathing human being. More and more, women are viewed as the enemy of children, requiring the State's intervention to protect their developing children from them. But, in reality, women still conceive, nurture, give birth to and, in most cases, are the primary caregivers of children. Women are being reduced, once again, to the incubators of future generations with total responsibility but no power. That is the same oppressive view that the women's movement sought to challenge. It is not just abortion, but women's power to control their destinies that is at stake.

For feminists in the late 1960s the issues were clear. We were not bombarded with the false emotionalism of fetal images. The "unborn" were just that, not yet born, not yet human beings. The decision of when or whether to carry a child to term belonged to only one person, the pregnant woman. That very moral decision had to be hers. She was the one to bear the consequences. It was the basis of the freedom women were trying to gain. Abortion referral groups saw themselves as facilitating each woman's decision-making power.

I consider myself lucky that a friend's IUD failure led me to Jane. After her abortion she came to see me, excited and surprised that her illegal abortion had been not only medically safe, but a positive and educational experience. I had just moved back to Chicago and was looking for a way to participate in the movement. Here was a group that was doing something concrete that was also risky, daring and secret, all of which appealed to me. I decided to join.

The group I joined in the fall of 1971 had already evolved to the point at which the members were performing the abortions themselves. Jane was an established organization, with defined procedures and a track record. I started out as a counselor, then took on administrative and medical tasks and worked with the group until we folded in the spring of 1973 when the first legal abortion clinics opened.

Jane taught me about more than abortion or women's liberation. Its history presents a fascinating example of what happens when people organize to do something and how they are changed by the actions they take. Since my time with Jane, I have drawn on those experiences as a way to understand personal power. We in Jane were fortunate that we were able to create a project that met an immediate, critical need and, at the same time, put into practice our vision of how the world ought to be.

For me Jane was the most transforming project I have had the privilege to be part of. I could never pretend to be objective about it, nor do I think it is possible to tell an intimate history objectively. The point of view, the biases of the storyteller, must intrude. I was a direct player, not an observer. I took sides; I formed alliances; I filtered events through my particular history and personality. My truth, too, is multilayered.

As history Jane presents a challenge. The group deliberately kept few records. What we were doing was illegal—details about individual women, highly confidential. In case of a raid, it was essential that documentation be minimal. We did not take minutes at meetings, nor did we write about what we were doing. In constructing this history my primary sources have been our recollections. How accurate are memories twenty years later? For instance, of the hundreds of women I counseled, and the thousand whose hands I held during their abortions, I can remember only the few who had problems. But even if more than twenty years had not elapsed, how accurate was our assessment at the time, colored as it had to be by each of our positions in Jane and what we were going through in the rest of our lives?

What I have written might be called a collective memoir. The book has been woven from hundreds of hours of interviews with somewhere between a third and a half of the more than one hundred women who were at one time or another members of Jane. I have also been able to draw on the interviews sociologist Pauline Bart conducted in the mid 1970s with group members, which were the basis for several studies she published in sociological journals, and on a series of articles "Jane" wrote for a Chicago neighborhood paper in the summer and fall of 1973. One former member let me draw on excerpts from unpublished vignettes she had written about her experiences. Along with the women who were in the group, I interviewed some of the men they lived with, as well as a few supportive doctors. And I sought out women who had had abortions through Jane.

As I read over my interviews I was amazed at how open people were. Of course, many of the women had worked with me; they knew me personally and trusted me. But even those who had never met me before were forthcoming. It was our common understanding that enriched their memories. Some had never talked with anyone about what we did. Most of us have not kept in touch with each other over the years.

Although I am not unbiased, I have aimed for fairness. I have weeded out secondhand anecdotes and rumors and have tried to corroborate events and interpretations, trusting the memories of the actual participants. I cannot say that this book represents The Truth about Jane, only how we remember it—or rather, how I have chosen to portray what we remember.

For the purposes of this collective memoir, I have given all the members of Jane, including myself, and everyone who had direct contact with Jane, a pseudonym. Since some people were comfortable using their real names while others, to protect their privacy, did not want their identities disclosed, I chose pseudonyms for everyone for consistency. But there is another reason I decided to use pseudonyms, even for myself. This book is about a group of women anonymously subsumed under the code name Jane. It is a story of a group, how it came to be and how it evolved. More than an anatomy of any individual, it is the group's anatomy.

Those of us who were members of Jane were remarkable only because we chose to act with women's needs as our guide. In doing so we transformed an illegal abortion from a dangerous, sordid experience into one that was life-affirming and powerful. In the process we ourselves were transformed. This book is the story of that group, a group of ordinary women with weaknesses and strengths who saw something that needed to be done and did it. It is Jane's story.

THE STORY OF JANE

CHAPTER 1

The first voice Jenny heard as the anesthetic lifted was the surgeon's, "The sterilization procedure was a success, and congratulations, you're eight weeks pregnant." That was the news Jenny dreaded most. "All I wanted to do was roll off the table, pull the IV out of my arm, and bleed to death right there," she recalls. Jenny was twenty-six, the mother of a two year old and a three-year-old and had been suffering from lymphatic cancer, Hodgkin's disease, for the past two years. Her health had deteriorated to such an extent during her previous pregnancy that she had every reason to believe another one would kill her.

It was while she was pregnant with her second child that the disease surfaced. She was having chest pains, difficulty swallowing, and chronic low-grade fevers. An X ray revealed the small, localized tumors of early Hodgkin's. Her doctors decided not to begin treatment, since medication and radiation could harm the developing fetus. By the time she went into labor she had chronic nosebleeds and was coughing up blood. During the birth she hemorrhaged so severely she barely survived. In the three months since the initial diagnosis, the disease had spread through her lymphatic system. She had huge masses of visible tumors, the size of golf balls, from her neck to her armpits. Her prognosis was poor; she wasn't expected to survive. She spent the next two years in and out of the hospital, undergoing massive radiation and drug therapy. Given how quickly the disease had progressed while she was pregnant, she was terrified of what would happen if she got pregnant again. She begged her doctor to sterilize her but he refused. He could not endorse elective tubal ligation for a woman as young as she.

Instead, her doctor prescribed birth control pills, which were considered the most effective method for preventing conception short of sterilization. At that time, in 1968, the medical profession was still experimenting with the hormone levels in birth control pills; little was publicly known about their side effects. As sick as Jenny already felt, taking birth control pills made her feel worse. Her doctor tried different pills and dosages. On one she menstruated all the time; on another she never menstruated at all. Then he put her on a brand that was later discontinued because of its high failure rate. A few months later she suspected she was pregnant. She went back to her doctor, hysterical. He couldn't confirm her pregnancy but, fearing for her emotional stability, he agreed to schedule the tubal ligation. It was after that operation that the surgeon told her what she already knew: she was pregnant.

If she had felt trapped by her illness and by her battle over sterilization, now that she was pregnant the trap tightened. It wasn't only her own health she worried about, but also, given the amount of radiation and drugs she'd be given, both she and the doctor recognized that there was little chance the child would be born normal. But abortion in Illinois in the late 1960s was illegal except when necessary to save the mother's life. That decision was in the hands of the hospital board. The doctors, including the oncologist, the radiologist and the gynecologist, who had been caring for her, asked the board for permission to perform an abortion, but the request was denied. The board noted that at present her life was in no imminent danger. It was only after she convinced two psychiatrists she would commit suicide if she didn't get an abortion that the board relented and agreed to it.

She came out of the hospital after her abortion infuriated. It was one thing to be helpless in the face of a deadly illness; it was another to feel powerless before medical authorities. Adding to her frustration and anger was her realization that "through that whole experience there wasn't one woman involved. It was men—the doctors, the hospital board—controlling my reproductive rights and condemning me to death."

Even though Jenny was used to taking action for political causes and had even worked with Illinois Citizens for the Medical Control of Abortion (ICMCA), she viewed abortion and women's health as medical problems. Then, two weeks after her abortion, she went to the February meeting of Voters Committed to Change, an organization of both men and women working within the electoral process. They were holding a series of educational sessions and, for their February meeting, after a heated interchange about whether it was even a relevant topic, the group decided to discuss women's liberation.

During the discussion another member of Voters Committed to Change, Claire, a longtime Movement* activist, talked about abortion as a women's liberation issue. Claire noted that it was essential to frame the problem of abortion in terms of women's powerlessness, in terms of women having the right to control their reproduction. What was needed, she said, was to organize people to address abortion as a women's issue.

Even with her recent experience so fresh in her mind, Jenny had never considered abortion in a political context. As Claire presented her position, Jenny thought: No way. There are much better things to organize around. Abortion is too medically controlled to be made into a political issue.

It wasn't that Jenny was unaware of the need to cast the problems that women faced in terms of women's liberation. In fact, it was she who had suggested they discuss women's liberation in the first

*The Movement is the term used in this book to denote involvement in the Left social movements of the sixties—the civil rights, antiwar and student movements.

place. But she had never viewed abortion as a rallying point for women. Abortion was so hidden; the word itself had a seamy, negative connotation that she feared might alienate women from women's liberation.

Jenny had been an advocate of women's rights for most of her adult life. She was raised on the stories of her great-aunt Lillian, a suffragette, who had once chained herself to the gates of the White House. When Jenny entered Michigan State University in 1959 she tried to join the college golf team but was rejected because she was female. That sparked her commitment to address the discrimination that women faced through her role as an editor of the college newspaper and as a public speaker. In college she was active on civil liberties and civil rights issues and later, when she attended graduate school in constitutional law at the University of Chicago, she joined the board of the Chicago Civil Liberties Union. As a board member she lobbied to set up a women's committee but was voted down. The rest of the board did not think there was a separate agenda worthy of civil rights attention.

As she participated in the discussion of women's liberation at the February 1969 meeting of Voters Committed to Change, Jenny began to appreciate Claire's perspective. She thought, yes, abortion can be seen as a political issue that affects a huge segment of the population oppressed because of their reproductive ability, which is almost as bad as oppression based on skin color. Reflecting on the trauma of her own medical experiences with sterilization and abortion, she realized that "it wasn't just the power of the doctor. It was me, my existence as a woman, that left me vulnerable to this terrible oppression."

After the meeting, Jenny discovered that Claire's comments weren't just theoretical. Claire was actually referring women for illegal abortions. It was not something Claire had actively chosen. She did it because women asked her to help them find safe abortions. The first time someone approached her she was in her second year of college at the University of Chicago. It was a few months after she returned from Mississippi, where she was a student volunteer with SNCC (the Student Nonviolent Coordinating Committee) for their 1964 Freedom Summer project, registering black voters and setting up Freedom Schools. The people of Mississippi inspired her. She had never witnessed such grueling poverty or such courage.

One incident that summer clarified her thinking about government institutions as a force for social change. Late one night, while she was working at a Freedom Center, someone phoned threatening to bomb the building. The volunteers called the Justice Department for help but were ignored. All night Claire and the others lay on the rough wood floor, terrified, out of range of any possible gunfire. Claire learned a valuable lesson: We can't rely on the government; we can only rely on each other. But that summer taught her something else too: ordinary people, acting together, can change history.

A few months after Claire returned to Chicago a friend called her. His sister, who was also a student at the university and active in the civil rights movement, was pregnant and needed an abortion. Neither of them knew where to turn. Could Claire try to find someone willing to perform an abortion? Claire doesn't remember "even thinking about abortion before that call, but I admired her and she was distraught, so I tried to help her."

She asked everyone she could think of, but no one knew how to get an abortion. Eventually, through her civil rights network, she found a black doctor on Sixty-third Street in Woodlawn, the black community just south of the university, who could help. He was also involved in the civil rights movement and routinely performed abortions at his South Side clinic. She sent her friend's sister. The abortion was successful and they were all elated.

A few months later she received a call from another frantic young woman needing an abortion. This time the call came from Mississippi, from someone she had met during Freedom Summer. She had turned to Claire in Chicago because she couldn't find an abortion in Mississippi that she thought wouldn't kill her.

. . .

Claire's decision to help these two women was based on values modeled by the civil rights movement, which included working to build a just society in which everyone had options. She believed those ideals weren't only goals for some future time but had to be incorporated in whatever she did in the present. She thought that vision of justice and equality applied to women, too. Beyond that, she genuinely cared for each of those women: one, a middle-class white woman with a bright future ahead of her, and the other, a black woman in great poverty, struggling to overcome it.

In the next few months Claire got three or four calls from women desperate for abortions, which was, to her, mind-boggling. It began to dawn on her that abortion wasn't something that only a very few women needed once in a great while. In 1965 women were not talking openly with each other about abortion or any "women's" problem. Only people who had direct knowledge of abortion, like doctors or the police, had any idea how common it was, so it was not surprising that Claire was astonished by the number of women calling her for help.

Late in 1965 women in the Movement began raising the issue of women's second-class status in the Movement and in society in general. Since Claire's return from Mississippi she had spoken at universities around the Midwest about her experiences in Freedom Summer. By 1966 she was speaking about women's subservient role within society. As a result, she became known as a Chicago contact for issues pertaining to women. At that point, Claire believed that women's liberation was not a separate struggle but was subsumed under a greater struggle for human freedom and justice being waged on many fronts: in the South, among the urban and rural poor; in the universities, and in Vietnam.

By the fall of 1967 radical women, whose attempts to force the Movement to explore women's role had been either ignored or greeted with derision and hostility, realized they needed to form their own movement. In Chicago Claire was one of the founders of the first autonomous women's liberation group, known as the Westside Group. A few months later she was instrumental in organizing the first campus women's liberation group at the University of Chicago, the Women's Radical Action Project (WRAP).

Meanwhile, from 1965 to 1968, desperate women needing abortions continued to contact Claire. At most, only a few women a month called her, but every one of them was terrified. Claire realized that a telephone conversation wasn't enough to calm them. The only way she could figure out how to do that was to meet with each woman face to face. Claire, for all her radical ideas, was a neatly groomed young woman who dressed conservatively. She hoped her appearance would be reassuring.

Claire called her discussions with women counseling sessions. She learned what to say by trial and error and by checking back with the doctor performing the abortion. With each woman she described the medical procedure, explained how to arrange payment, where to go, and how to take care of herself afterward. After the abortion Claire called the woman to make sure she was all right. She asked how each woman felt about the experience and what the abortion was like and incorporated the responses into what she said to other women.

She asked only the essentials that she knew the doctor needed—the date of each woman's last menstrual period and her general health. She never asked why anyone needed an abortion, or pried into intimate details. She felt her primary function was to help women handle their fears: Will I live through it? Will anyone find out? Will I be able to get pregnant again? Will it hurt?

Each woman Claire met with felt isolated and frightened; each one was wrestling with guilt and self-blame. Often women apologized and cried while expressing gratitude for Claire's help. To lessen the heightened emotions of the situation, she tried to be supportive and, at the same time, businesslike: This is a matter of fact. This is what happens; this may hurt a little. She wanted to create an emotional detachment so that, as she says, "in addition to the social and psychological horrors being inflicted on them, and the medical uncertainty, they wouldn't feel there was an additional moral trip being done on them. Some came nearly suicidal. The key for me was to learn to empathize with their feelings but not become so overwhelmed by the grief and the tragedy that I was immobilized."

Several times Claire's doctor on Sixty-third Street stopped performing abortions because he feared legal repercussions. The first time he was unavailable she considered suspending her referral work, but women kept calling her for help, so she searched for other doctors and managed to find two. She heard rumors that one was often drunk, so she didn't send women to him. The other worked out of hotels in the suburb of Cicero.

When she called the doctor in Cicero she spoke with a woman who had an Italian accent. Claire mentioned her new contact to a friend who casually responded that Cicero was known as a Mafia neighborhood. That possibility had not entered Claire's mind. In any case, if she pursued this option she would no longer be working within the safety and moral purpose of the Movement. It had never occurred to her that her work could lead to a criminal underworld. For the first time she realized that she was acting as an accessory to criminal activity. She had no idea what she might be getting into. She'd seen the movies. Was this going to be one of those situations where the Mob does you a favor and forever after they expect horrible favors in return? She worried, could she depend on them to treat women right? Would the doctor feel any accountability? If not for moral principles, exactly why were these people involved in abortion?

Stifling her own fears, she agreed to meet the woman at a restaurant downtown. A friend dropped her off. As Claire opened the car door, trembling, she turned to her friend and said, "If I don't come back . . ." She steeled herself and joined the dark-haired woman in a back booth. Claire's questions tumbled out: Is the person who does the abortions a doctor? Why is he doing abortions? How many abortions has he done before? She marshaled all her courage and even asked whether he was connected with the Mob.

The other woman reassured her. The doctor, she said, had years of experience. The well-being and health of the women they saw was his primary concern. She gave Claire the number of an answering service through which the doctor could always be reached. The woman's responses seemed honest and straightforward. Claire began to relax. Maybe she could trust these people, so far removed from the world she was used to.

She explained to Claire how they operated. They met women at a public place in the city and then drove them to a hotel where the abortions were performed. Afterward they dropped the women off where they'd been picked up. To protect the doctor's identity they blindfolded the women, but only during the operation.

The women Claire sent to this new doctor confirmed her sense of things. Although they were blindfolded, they were always treated well. Whenever any minor problem arose, the doctor was responsible and helpful. As she sent more women to him, Claire came to believe that he was someone she could trust.

Claire's South Side doctor charged $500. After a certain number at full price he would occasionally do one free. This new doctor, too, was willing to make a financial arrangement: so many at $600 and then one for less. Claire charged each woman the full $600. She put any excess in a fund for women who could not manage even the reduced fee. She pressed people to pay. They had to. The doctor had to be paid. It was never easy for people to come up with $600.

In those first few years the range of people calling for abortions surprised her. There were college students of all races, which she expected, and black women from the neighborhood and her Movement contacts. But there was also a growing number of white working-class women, wives and daughters of city workers, many of whom were Catholic. She remembers one, a mother with a very large family, who had a heart condition and had been warned that the pregnancy would add fatal stress to her weakened heart.

She always asked women if they were sure they needed an abortion or did they want to think about other options. She remembers only one person who seemed unsure; Claire encouraged her to take the time she needed to decide. For the most part, the last thing these women wanted was time. When she asked if they were sure, they looked at her aghast. Sure? Why would they put themselves in a stranger's hands if they weren't? Why would they be risking their lives if they weren't desperate?

As time went on Claire became aware that there was a group of policemen who were sending their wives, daughters and girlfriends. So many police officers' families were calling her that Claire had a certain sense of security even though she knew what she was doing was illegal. If the police were sending their children and wives, then, logically, they weren't going to arrest her; they might actually be protecting her. But she wasn't naive about the risks she was taking. Helping someone obtain an abortion was a criminal act, according to Illinois law.

While she never intended to set up a formal organization to handle abortion referrals, by 1968 she was getting more requests for help than she was able to handle on her own. She was married, pregnant, a graduate student, had a job and was involved in many other projects both on and off campus. For a while Claire depended on the women in the Westside group and WRAP to help her.

By the fall of 1968 the women she had recruited to help were moving in different directions. A few were leaving Chicago. Some were uncomfortable in the counselor's role or couldn't handle breaking the law; some were more interested in other projects in the women's movement. Her loose network was not sufficient or committed enough to manage this work. And Claire herself was more interested in political organizing than counseling women. She knew that if she wanted this serious work to continue she would have to take aggressive steps to organize something substantial.

It seemed to Claire that in 1968 there was an explosion of political activism. Opposition to the Vietnam War had spread through every strata of society. On college campuses dissent turned into resistance. Alternative institutions such as free health clinics and free universities proliferated. Authorities and once-accepted truths were challenged. People who had never identified themselves as protesters were marching and sitting in. Some radicals believed a revolution was imminent. Activists suspected they were being watched, assumed their phones were tapped and worried about the presence of police informers.

While these social upheavals were occurring, women were beginning to organize to challenge their limited role in society. Groups of women began meeting to discuss what Betty Friedan, in her 1963 book *The Feminine Mystique*, had referred to as "the problem that has no name." In 1966 Friedan and a small group of professional women founded NOW (National Organization for Women), a reform-oriented women's rights organization. Women's liberation groups, like the Westside Group and WRAP, with a more radical stance, were forming in many cities.

Claire and other women traveled around talking about women's liberation. They left in their wake groups of women who began the process of revealing the personal as political. These groups would meet to discuss a range of topics such as: What messages about women's roles did you get from your parents? From your religion? What messages did you get about puberty? Have you ever considered an abortion? Most women were articulating for the first time the vague notions buried in their thoughts. They were amazed to discover that they had each internalized the same messages. Their experience was being repeated in ever-widening circles. Abortion was a natural topic of conversation. Through these discussions women realized that, without control of reproduction, their other freedoms were limited.

Women were beginning to understand that the individual problems they had faced separately fit a pattern that was common to all of them. They were a class and, as such, could organize themselves to address their common concerns. Since the barriers to their full participation in society had gone unrecognized, it was natural for them to feel that once they had named and analyzed these obstacles they would be able to create their own solutions. At women's liberation workshops yellow legal pads with specific topic headings, such as abortion or day care, were passed around so that women could sign up to work on issues that interested them.

Claire, by now a skilled organizer, took notes at each meeting, documenting the ideas that emerged and listing who said what. She believed that the social change that was now in progress was critical, so she followed up on her notes, connecting people with similar interests and perspectives. It was from these sign-up sheets and the people who approached her whenever she spoke, like Jenny at the Voters Committed to Change meeting, that Claire attempted to build a group to continue her abortion referral work.

CHAPTER 2

Once Claire realized she needed an organized group, it came together quickly. A few months before she talked with Jenny, she compiled a list of women who had expressed interest in the abortion issue and invited them to a meeting. One of those women was Lorraine.

Although Lorraine had attended antiwar demonstrations and worked on Eugene McCarthy's campaign, she did not consider herself a political activist. Lorraine was a clerical worker at the University of Chicago, where her husband was pursuing his doctorate. She had recently realized that women like her, at the bottom of the employment heap, kept the university afloat, so she went to a workshop on women's issues hoping to learn more and signed her name to one of Claire's abortion lists.

When, in the fall of 1968, Lorraine walked into Claire's apartment for the first abortion meeting, she had no idea what to expect. Claire's living room was packed. Women were sitting on the couch, on chairs, cross-legged on the floor.

Claire described what she had been doing for the past few years. She said she hoped to start a group that would take over her work, build on it, and get it better organized. In Illinois, helping someone find an abortion was illegal, so anyone who got involved would be breaking the law. That, she explained, was the practical end of it. The political piece was to create a bond between women. Beyond providing a service, they should use this service to raise women's consciousnesses.

From the questions asked, Lorraine sensed that some of the women weren't exactly thrilled with the idea of breaking the law. Lorraine, who had had an illegal abortion herself six years before, was not bothered by that prospect. But she was not surprised when, at the next meeting, a few weeks later, only about a dozen women showed up.

At the second meeting Claire described what she did in more detail. She explained that women needing abortions called her at home. The minute she picked up the phone and heard a pause in the person's voice she knew what the call was about. Claire told the women at the meeting that she herself checked out the doctors and, if they didn't suit her in any way, they were out. She mentioned one doctor she had rejected who, in lieu of examining-table stirrups, tied women's legs to the bed.

Through that fall and early winter the group met sporadically. For Lorraine, those early sessions blended with other political meetings she and her husband, Stan, were attending: "It seems like we were going to meetings all the time. Oh, God, boxes and boxes of Oreos and pots of coffee and tea were consumed."

Claire wondered about lanky, brown-haired Lorraine. She seemed to be a middle-class housewife and not the kind of person Claire usually met through the student culture or in the Movement. To Claire it was an indication that the women's liberation movement was broader than the student movement. It was drawing in people from different backgrounds, like Lorraine. What bonded them wasn't a common culture but rather their shared concerns and the work.

By the time Jenny began attending the meetings a few months after Lorraine, she no longer viewed abortion as a medical problem but as a political one. It seemed to her that Claire was determined to organize this group in such a way that it would be firmly grounded in a political analysis that, if not the same as Claire's, was compatible with it. Claire led discussion after discussion on the politics of abortion: why women needed abortions, what it meant to women that they couldn't control their ability to reproduce, and what that indicated about society's attitudes toward women. But Jenny felt she understood as much as she needed to; she was ready to begin the work. She kept pressing Claire to get to the point: Who were these doctors she used and how could they be contacted?

Other new members had none of Jenny's impatience. One of them was Karen, who had also joined after the Voters Committed to Change meeting. For several years she had worked for independent candidates but, as had been true for so many others, the brutal police response to the demonstrators at the Democratic National Convention the previous August, and the nomination of Hubert Humphrey, had left her disenchanted with electoral politics as a vehicle for social change. "We were all radicalized, frustrated, miserable," she remembers, "and ready to do something."

She had recently seen a group of radical feminists on the David Susskind television show. Women, they said, had been denied independent identities and were valued only through their relationships with men: someone's daughter, someone's wife. As a feminist act, a few of the speakers had adopted the last name X, in order to dissociate themselves from the patriarchal system in which women were treated as the property of men. Since her marriage, Karen had felt her own identity disappearing in her husband's. She was uncomfortable being referred to by his name and having her mail addressed to Mrs. ________, but she hadn't been able to put a name to her feelings until she heard these women on TV. Listening to them transformed her instantly into a feminist.

After the Voters Committed to Change meeting, Claire explained to Karen that her experiences in political work had led her to believe there was a need for separate women's groups to deal with women's problems. As one of the first feminists in Hyde Park, the university community, Claire was acting as an informal network for just about everything connected with women, including abortion referrals. Lately there were more calls for abortions than she could handle. She told Karen that she thought abortion referrals would be an important project for a group of women to take on, but right then she needed help and one of the best ways to help her was to raise money for women's abortions.

Abortion had never been an issue in Karen's life. In fact, for the past year she had been trying desperately to get pregnant and had begun a fertility workup. She had had several medical procedures and more aggravation than she had believed possible. She felt "like an absolute victim. I had no control over what was happening to me. I was furious at the medical authorities and furious about all these reproductive issues. That anger really fed my fires and I identified with those on the other side who didn't want to be pregnant. I felt they should have the same control over their bodies that I needed."

That was her personal and emotional connection to abortion, but there was another aspect that made the project even more appealing. From her disillusionment with the electoral process after the Democratic National Convention, she now felt that substantive societal change could be accomplished only if masses of people took political action. She thought that Claire's project had the potential to turn large numbers of women into activists, and that was something she wanted to do.

At Claire's suggestion, Karen got to work raising money to lend to women who could not afford abortions. Karen determined to expand and organize Claire's idea into an abortion loan fund. Through her electoral political work and community contacts, Karen knew women who had money to donate to worthwhile causes. She called them and asked for money to help pay for abortions. To Karen "it seemed like the most serious, necessary and easy work we could do: to link these women up, the women who had money to give with the women who needed the money for abortions."

While Karen was busy raising money, Jenny grew increasingly impatient with all the talk at meetings. She considered Claire a strict ideological teacher and felt reined in by her methodical training process.

Almost as quickly as Jenny involved herself she disinvolved herself. She had made a commitment to raise money for the defense of the Chicago Eight, who had been charged with conspiracy to incite a riot at the Democratic National Convention. "But the feeling of male domination in and around the conspiracy trial was just . . . ," Jenny remembers. "I felt like I was being ground into the ground. It got to a point where I couldn't take it anymore. I wanted to get into a strictly, completely, totally women's issue, even if it wasn't the perfect politics, even if it didn't represent the working classes. I wanted it to be by, for, and about, and because of, and at the will of women."

She returned to Claire's abortion group determined to control her impatience. In her absence, a few new people had joined. One of them was Miriam, a disheveled-looking woman Jenny had never met before.

Miriam had heard about Claire's group at a house in Hyde Park that had become a center for the women's liberation movement. Consciousness-raising groups and work groups used the house for meetings. There were sign-up sheets for a variety of projects, such as a women's newspaper and a day-care center, that were being organized. Miriam added her name to a list of people interested in abortion counseling. Although she was a full-time housewife, caring for two small children, she had earned a master's degree in social work, and thought, I've been trained as a social worker, I can counsel women and that's how I'll participate in the women's movement.

"I always believed that people are responsible for the world around them and I wanted to play my part," Miriam says. In college she read Saul Alinsky's *Reveille for Radicals* and realized there were two ways she could put that sense of responsibility into practice: Either she could be one of the people who change the world, the political organizers, or one of the people who take care of those who are hurt because the world hasn't changed, who do the Band-Aid work. She consciously decided on the latter because she wanted children and she didn't think it was a good idea to be an organizer and try to raise children at the same time because she wouldn't have enough time to do both well.

Miriam had been working with a peace organization. When the peace group planned a demonstration against the war in Vietnam that involved civil disobedience and Miriam decided against being arrested, she thought, If I'm not willing to put myself on the line for this, then I don't have enough of a commitment. There must be something I'd be more committed to. "I was looking for some place that was my place," she recalls. "It was like I was waiting for the women's movement to come around so I'd have something to participate in that was my life."

Miriam remembers the discourse at those early meetings of Claire's group in-training as powerful. From their own experiences they knew that even if contraceptives were readily available, which they were not, they sometimes failed. They talked about the different reasons women needed abortions, the economic, emotional, social, medical and personal reasons. They were as varied as women themselves. No one but a pregnant woman could weigh those considerations and decide what she wanted to do.

They explored the social constraints that women were under: Women were valued for their ability to attract men, encouraged to be sexy, and then damned for being sexual. They were stuck between two opposites—the Madonna or the whore—neither of them of their own creation. Women had a right to be sexual beings, to sexual pleasure. They had to free themselves from those oppressive definitions. They had to gain control of their lives and they could not control their lives without having control over their bodies. If they did not have the right to regulate this basic biological function, their reproductive ability, what chance did women have to control any aspect of their lives? It was women who got pregnant, bore children and raised them, but men—husbands, fathers, clergymen, legislators and doctors—had the power to judge women and to punish them.

Women were oppressed because they did not have the power to control their lives. They had to take back that control to ensure their own liberation.

Claire's group wasn't going to promote abortion. They would help women who had no other options. Abortion was a last resort. A woman who felt she had to get one was stuck in a horrible situation. She was forced to beg and plead with unsympathetic hospital boards who most often denied her request, or she had to find her way through an uncertain underground. Illegal abortionists charged exorbitant rates, demanded sexual favors in return, degraded, injured and even killed women. It was an outrage that a woman who did not want to have a child was economically, physically and emotionally exploited and forced to risk her life.

They discussed how much more difficult the situation was for poor women, who were the least likely to have access to medical care or contraceptives and could not afford the high prices that competent abortionists charged. As much as society supposedly honored motherhood, it offered no help, such as day care or flexible work hours, to enable working mothers to support their families. Society offered only a punitive welfare system; demeaned women for needing assistance; blamed them for getting pregnant and labeled them immoral.

As to the question of whether abortion was murder, murder was a legal term applying to human beings, and a fetus, in their view, was not a human being. To give it the same or greater value than a living woman was an indication of how little women were valued, as if their only worth was the children they produced. The moral decision of whether to have a child or seek an abortion had to be left to the pregnant woman. It was her body; it was her life. As a human being, she had to have the power to make those moral decisions. She was the one who would bear the consequences.

Claire led discussions on every aspect of abortion so they could understand it from as many perspectives as possible and be able to speak convincingly about it. Jenny, on the other hand, felt Claire was withholding important information, the names and numbers of the doctors she used. "We went through this whole political indoctrination," Jenny recalls. "Claire wanted it to address economic issues and feminist issues. I think it was important for her to stamp her political view of abortion on this group that she was forming."

They discussed how to talk about abortion strictly in terms of women's liberation and not as either a population question or a medical problem. The necessity for women to control their bodies as a condition for women's liberation was a central tenet of the movement. But earlier in the decade others had begun speaking about abortion as a woman's right. Pat Maginnis, an abortion activist in California, organized the Society for Humane Abortion and, in 1965, stated, "We say . . . that a woman's body is her own and she has a right to it." NOW (National Organization for Women) had been established to fight discrimination in employment and education. At its second national convention in 1967 NOW drafted a Bill of Rights for Women which included the right of women to control their own reproductive lives by removing laws restricting contraception and abortion. The inclusion of abortion law repeal caused dissension within the organization. Some in NOW questioned whether abortion was a women's rights issue, while others, who were committed to abortion rights, worried that taking such a controversial and radical stand would damage NOW's image and alienate potential supporters.

In the years before the rise of the women's liberation movement, a number of professionals, primarily doctors and lawyers, worked to liberalize abortion laws. Whether or not they personally recognized abortion as a woman's right, to gain credibility they based their arguments in state legislatures and in the courts on a doctor's right to exercise his medical judgment.

The need to reform laws that limited abortions to those necessary to save the life of the mother had been brought to the public's attention by two events earlier in the decade. In 1962 in Arizona Sherri

Finkbine attempted to get an abortion after she read a report on the grave birth deformities associated with thalidomide, a drug she had taken early in her pregnancy. Although hospital authorities initially agreed to the surgery, once the case was publicized the hospital backed down, fearing prosecution. Finkbine was forced to travel to Sweden for a legal abortion. The second event was a rubella, or German measles, epidemic in the mid-sixties. Rubella was known to cause serious birth defects in babies born to mothers who had contracted the disease in the early stages of pregnancy, yet these women were not covered by the restrictive existing laws. Those two events provoked a spate of articles in the national media that highlighted the suffering incurred because of the legal strictures. Abortion was viewed as a medical problem, not as a women's rights problem. In this scenario women were passive victims of either a drug, thalidomide, or a disease, rubella, rather than active determiners of their lives who had a right to control their bodies.

By 1969 ten states had modified their abortion laws. These states based their new laws on the Model Penal Code that the American Law Institute (ALI) drafted in 1959. The ALI code called for "therapeutic" abortions if two doctors agreed that continuing the pregnancy would gravely impair the mother's physical or mental health; if the fetus was seriously damaged; or if the pregnancy was a result of rape or incest. This formula again relegated women to a passive role. Doctors determined whether a woman deserved an abortion. Although the earliest legislative changes in 1967 in Colorado, North Carolina and California seemed like a major breakthrough to reformers, they recognized that the new laws' limits would approve abortions for fewer than 5 percent of the women who wanted them. The vagueness of the health and mental health condition allowed wide variations in interpretation, at the discretion of doctors and hospitals. In Colorado's first year of liberalization only 289 abortions were approved by the hospital committees that had the final say in granting them. In 1969 Colorado's Richard Lamm, who had introduced the reform legislation, commented, "We have replaced one cruel outmoded law with another one." Reformers were moving toward a repeal position that would remove abortion laws completely.

In February of 1969, at the same time that Jenny and Karen connected with Claire, three hundred fifty people met in Chicago for the First National Conference on Abortion Laws. The conference was organized by Lawrence Lader, a leading abortion rights activist, and Dr. Lonny Myers, who had founded ICMCA (Illinois Citizens for the Medical Control of Abortion). The purpose of the conference was to sway people from reform to repeal and to create a national organization, NARAL (then NARAL stood for the National Association for Repeal of Abortion Laws; now it stands for the National Abortion and Reproductive Rights Action League).

Betty Friedan attended the conference. Lader and a few others drafted a preamble for their new organization's charter and presented it on the last day of the conference. As Friedan recalls in *It Changed My Life: Writings on the Women's Movement* (1976) the preamble addressed doctors' rights but said nothing about women's rights. She proposed adding, "Asserting the right of a woman to control her own body and reproductive process as her inalienable, human, civil right . . ." In her book Friedan remembers that "some of the leading abortion reformers and Planned Parenthood types were aghast at that. Protesting, they took the mike: 'Abortion is not a feminist issue.' 'We have nothing to do with feminism.' 'What has women's rights got to do with abortion?' " Over those objections, Friedan's proposal was approved.

Jenny knew about NARAL's founding conference and had decided not to attend. She thought the focus of the conference was too conservative, too much attention on doctor's rights and population questions. She felt that "politically we were so far from them that it was a different world. They were content to inch forward and we wanted to do it right now, but it was great that NARAL was happening."

Population control groups with an ominous eugenics slant joined the ranks of those lobbying for reform. They raised the specter of a dangerous global population explosion among the poor. In that view women were again, as in the medical model, the objects, not the subjects, of the abortion debate. Since their arguments supported the power of professionals to determine what was best for women, abortion was potentially a weapon used against women, rather than a tool for women's liberation. Population control groups were attacked as genocidal by Third World activists and communities of color. The first massive trials of birth control pills were carried out on poor women in Puerto Rico and Haiti. Although hospital boards approved far fewer abortions for women of color than for white women, reports of sterilization abuses in Puerto Rico and among women of color in the United States were beginning to surface in the media. In fact, while Jenny was begging for a tubal ligation, she had heard from her contacts in the radical medical community that poor women in public hospitals in the city were being sterilized without their consent. Their women's liberation abortion group had to reframe the arguments for abortion in terms of the control over their lives that individual women had a right to, regardless of their economic status or race.

They spent hours on the nuts and bolts of what they might do. How would they handle medical emergencies, such as a women with serious complications from an abortion? What if someone died? What would they do if one of the doctors they used was arrested, or one of them was arrested? How would they handle a police investigation? Claire cautioned them to maintain only minimal records so that, in the event of a raid, the police would find nothing incriminating. For security reasons they decided to keep their two main functions—contacts with the doctors who performed abortions, and contact with the women—separate. One group member would initially speak with each woman and put her in touch with a counselor in the group. Someone else would be responsible for contacting the doctors and arranging for her abortion. Each counselor would follow up with the women she saw. Claire had the names of a few doctors but they knew they would have to expand on that list. How were they going to find new doctors? And how would women who needed abortions find them? They joked about handing out flyers on street corners.* They tried to explore every logistical question they could think of, but they knew the answers would have to come from actual experience.

Claire had learned all she knew about abortion from the doctor on Sixty-third Street. If they planned to expand the operation, they needed more information. When they researched abortion in the library, they discovered that not only was there almost nothing on abortion but there was almost no information about women's bodies and women's health written for lay people. What each of them knew about her body she had found out through her personal medical problems—Jenny's Hodgkin's disease, Karen's fertility work. From one study of legal abortions in Sweden that they were able to locate, they learned that the basic procedure was fairly simple and, when performed by a competent practitioner, had few complications.

Since abortions in most states in the United States were illegal except to save the mother's life,† most doctors knew little about them. The group suspected the accuracy of what they read in American journals, since those were likely to be tainted by lack of experience and the authors' biases. They realized they would have to get the information they needed from other, possibly unofficial, sources and one source was going to be women who had abortions.

They continued meeting through the spring, but now, at Claire's direction, rather than holding philosophical discussions, they practiced counseling techniques and sat in on counseling sessions. From Claire and a few women who had been working with her, they learned

*Unknown to any of the Chicago women, three women in San Francisco—Pat Maginnis, Rowena Gurner and Lana Phelps, the Army of Three—had been passing out flyers listing referrals on street corners.

†In the few states that had reformed their abortion laws, the circumstances under which abortions were permitted were still quite limited, and, as a result, the number performed was very small.

to describe the abortion procedure and to answer the questions women were likely to ask. They talked about ways to deal with the various emotions, like shame and self-blame, that women expressed in counseling sessions. Along with the medical information Claire wanted them to address the political dimensions and give each woman a sense that her personal predicament was part of the larger socioeconomic-racial-sexual struggles that were going on at that time.

Throughout those months of preparation Jenny kept thinking, Just give me the names and the numbers and we're ready to go. "Powerless, we were powerless," Jenny says, with the same impatience she felt then. "We didn't even have the name of a person who could do abortions. We had this strict ideological teacher who insisted on our learning our lessons before she was going to give us any telephone numbers."

Late in the spring, they picked a name for their group: the Abortion Counseling Service of Women's Liberation. But they also needed a simpler code name. As they worried over the details of their work, Jenny said, "It looks like we're creating a monster." Lorraine answered, "Well, in that case, I like my monsters to have sweet names, like Fluffy or Jane." * Jane seemed a good choice. No one in the group was named Jane and Jane was an everywoman's name—plain Jane, Jane Doe, Dick and Jane. The code name Jane would protect their identities while protecting the privacy of the women contacting them. Whenever they called a woman back or left a message for her, they could say it was Jane calling. No one else would know what the call was about. And having someone to call by name might make women more comfortable.

At the end of the training process Claire had them write a pamphlet to use for outreach and education. Jenny thought of it as their final exam. The pamphlet, "Abortion—a woman's decision, a

*Although the four original members remember selecting the name Jane, Claire recalls using Jane as her code name in the years before the group was organized.

woman's right," begins with the question: What is the Abortion Counseling Service?

> We are women whose ultimate goal is the liberation of women in society. One important way we are working toward that goal is by helping any woman who wants an abortion to get one as safely and cheaply as possible under existing conditions . . . .

After a few words about the Abortion Loan Fund and a section describing the abortion and follow-up, the pamphlet continues:

> . . . the current abortion laws are a symbol of the sometimes subtle, but often blatant, oppression of women in our society . . . Only a woman who is pregnant can determine whether she has enough resources—economic, physical and emotional—at a given time to bear and rear a child . . .
>
> The same society that denies a woman the decision not to have a child refuses to provide humane alternatives for women who do have children . . . .
>
> The same society that insists that women should and do find their basic fulfillment in motherhood will condemn the unwed mother and the fatherless child.
>
> The same society that glamorizes women as sex objects and teaches them from early childhood to please and satisfy men views pregnancy and childbirth as punishment for her "immoral" or careless sexual activity especially if the woman is uneducated, poor or black.
>
> Only women can bring about their own liberation. It is time for women to get together . . . to aid their sisters . . . and make the state provide free abortions as a human right . . .
>
> There are currently many groups lobbying for population control, legal abortion and selective sterilization. Some are trying to control some populations, prevent some births—for instance

poor people and black people. We are opposed to these and to any form of genocide. We are for *every* woman having exactly as many children as *she* wants, *when* she wants, *if* she wants.

It's time the Bill of Rights applied to women . . . ."

Throughout the winter and spring, attendance at meetings ebbed and swelled from five to fifteen women. By late spring, when they were ready to begin the actual work of counseling and referring, the group had winnowed down to a handful of committed women.

The months of meetings had given the core group a sense of each other and a cohesiveness. They were prepared. Karen remembers their exhilaration: "This was our issue, not our men's issue, not our kids' school, but ours. For the first time we had something that was our own and that was exciting."

Their last task was to divide up the work. Lorraine took the phone contact. She would be Jane; her home phone number was listed in their pamphlet. Karen continued to contact women with money to donate to the loan fund. Jenny and Miriam volunteered as the doctor contacts, the people to deal directly with the abortionists. Since the group was so small, every member, on top of her other duties, would be responsible for counseling women. For the time being they kept what they were doing word of mouth and grass roots, notifying other women's liberation groups around the city, using their pamphlet to get their message and phone number out. Claire handed Jenny and Miriam the contact names and phone numbers for the doctors and then she was gone.

It was, in Claire's memory, a remarkable group. She loved being with women who were going to take this problem seriously and do something about it. They were clear thinking and goal oriented and there was little of the internal bickering that Claire was finding so wearing in student and Left politics. These women seemed decent and caring, both about each other and about the women they were going to be helping. "That group of women," Claire muses, "whether we were made that way because of the struggle and the things we had to face, or whether we were that way and therefore attracted to it, I don't know. Jenny was so sensitive and insightful and straightforward and truth telling. You had to be both inspired and carried along by working with her. Lorraine and Karen were efficient and methodical, and Miriam, the oldest of us, with more experience in the world, brought a kind of mothering instinct to the group. No one was pretentious or b.s."

CHAPTER 3

When Lorraine told her husband, Stan, what she planned to do, he was appalled. He couldn't believe she was going to go off and do something insane like that without checking with him first. He couldn't have his wife running around breaking the law. He had to finish his Ph.D.; he had his career ahead of him. Lorraine wasn't completely surprised by his response. Her friends often complained about the strict segregation of roles in their marriages. Their husbands wouldn't be caught dead wheeling baby carriages or changing diapers. Wives were supposed to manage the household and care for the children, not go off and do any crazy thing they wanted to, especially without their husband's permission. But it had never crossed Lorraine's mind to clear it with Stan.

After he realized that tack wasn't having any effect on her, he warned, "You're going to wind up in jail. You'll be a felon."

It had not occurred to Lorraine that she could be arrested. She knew she would be breaking the law, but she didn't think she would be punished. Once Stan raised those concerns, Lorraine simply decided, We'll cross that bridge when we come to it. She felt that "if we do it right, if we do it well, and if we provide a 'service to the community,' we'll be left alone."

From the grapevine and articles in newspapers and magazines,* the group had found out that in Chicago, and probably in every major city, there were at least a half-dozen abortionists who were tolerated as long as nothing went wrong. An abortionist was closed down if his morbidity rate went up. Lorraine says, "We figured we would see to it that we would not have a morbidity rate."

Being arrested was a minor worry compared with their overriding concern that women come out of their abortions physically and psychologically healthy. Although they talked about what it meant to be breaking the law, they weren't bothered by the morality of breaking this one. "Why should we respect a law that disrespected women?" Jenny asks. Miriam and Karen, young Jews raised in the shadow of the Holocaust, framed the issue in terms of the lessons learned from the Nuremberg trials. There was no justification for obeying an immoral law. They would not be "good Germans" who stood by and did nothing while others suffered.

Now that the Abortion Counseling Service was trained and organized, Claire referred callers to Jane's number. Soon Lorraine's phone started ringing. The person on the other end would hem and haw and finally ask timidly, "Is Jane there?" When Lorraine answered, "This is Jane," the relief was almost audible. Then she asked, "How can I help you?" It was essential that the person calling ask for what she wanted. Rule number one was never to suggest an abortion to anyone. They weren't promoting abortion. The service was for women determined to find an abortion. Lorraine knew how important that first phone call was. It set the tone for all future contacts. After she took a brief medical history, Lorraine ended the conversation by saying that a counselor would call within the next few days to explain everything. Part of Lorraine's job as Jane was to match up

*With state legislatures continuing to debate abortion law reform and several prominent cases involving doctors and abortion (primarily Milan Vuitch in Washington, D.C., and Leon Belous in California), in the courts, the press paid growing attention to the abortion controversy.

group members as counselors with women to be counseled, which she did either by phone or at the next weekly meeting.

Women who had the ability and the means were referred to London where abortions were legal, Mexico or Puerto Rico, to doctors the group knew about from Claire or from women they knew who had used those sources. In neither Mexico nor Puerto Rico were abortions legal, but a few doctors there performed abortions in hospitals and clinics. They charged anywhere from several hundred dollars to over a thousand. Most of the women who contacted Jane either could not come up with the money for travel and the abortion or could not leave the city. Their local sources were reserved for these women.

No one in the group was totally comfortable calling strangers on the phone and inviting them over for counseling. Neither the counselor nor the woman being called knew who or what to expect.

Once a woman arrived for her counseling session, the first step was to ascertain whether the person was absolutely sure she wanted an abortion. If she was at all conflicted, she was encouraged to go home and think about it. Once that was established, a description of the abortion followed, not just the technical/medical part, but, based on what they knew of each doctor's method of operating, how the entire day would proceed, the phone calls, the contact with the doctor's people. The intent was to lessen the fear through giving detailed information, to make the unknown known.

Most women they counseled lacked basic knowledge of reproduction or even their own physiology. Although counselors were disturbed by the women's lack of information, that was not unusual, since, as the group had discovered while researching abortion, there was almost nothing written for women on women's health. The general public was insulated from medical knowledge. In particular sexuality and contraception were shrouded in secrecy. It was as if there were something inappropriate, if not indecent, about a woman wanting to understand her body.

~

Some states still had statutes, dating from Anthony Comstock's nineteenth-century obscenity laws, which banned contraceptives. Those bans were lifted for married people in 1965 when the Supreme Court in *Griswold* v. *Connecticut* found a constitutional right to marital privacy, overturning a state law that made it a crime for a woman to use, or for a doctor to prescribe, contraceptives. It wasn't until 1972, that the Court, in a case in which Bill Baird, a birth control and abortion activist, was arrested for handing Boston college students contraceptive foam during a public lecture, extended the right to sexual privacy to single people,* so access to birth control information in 1969 was limited.

To counteract that, the counselors explained everything having to do with abortion and contraception as simply and thoroughly as they could, so that the counseling session would educate the women. They gave everyone they counseled a free copy of *The Birth Control Handbook,* from Montreal. The handbook, printed on newsprint and illustrated, was written in 1968 by a group of students at McGill University who were running for student government. Outraged that disseminating birth control information was illegal, they pledged that, if elected, they would make sure it was available to students. To fulfill their pledge they published the handbook, the first of its kind, in the fall of 1968. It quickly found its way onto campuses throughout Canada and the United States. In lay person's terms, it described human reproduction and the different methods of birth control.† Not only was the information detailed and accurate, but the pamphlet was written from a feminist perspective that was especially appealing to the Chicago women. In the introduction the authors

*Before the Baird decision the availability of contraceptives for single people varied from one locale to another, from one physician to another. It was easier to obtain birth control through a sympathetic private doctor than through a public clinic. Unmarried women often pretended to be married in order to obtain contraceptives.

†A few years later, the group evolved into the Montreal Health Press which is in existence today, still publishing *The Birth Control Handbook*. For their address, see resource list.

state: "We see the handbook and contraception in general as playing a major role in the liberation of women. Once child-bearing becomes one option among many and [a] woman has some power to control her destiny, she may well be less ready to accept subservience as an inevitable part of her condition." The handbook was something tangible and positive that women could take home and use as a reference.

As had been the case when Claire was counseling, each woman they met with asked, "Will it hurt?" Since no one in the group had seen an abortion, and only Jenny and Lorraine had had abortions, their response was based on what Claire said and what women reported back after their abortions. They used words like discomfort or pressure and described the pain as similar to severe menstrual cramps, adding that the level of discomfort varied from woman to woman, but it wasn't anything a woman could not handle.

In describing the technical steps of the procedure, the group members emphasized that an abortion was not a complicated operation. The basic method, a D & C (dilation and curettage), entailed opening the cervix, the muscle at the neck of the uterus, with a dilator, so that instruments would be introduced, then removing the fetal and placental material with small forceps and scraping the wall of the uterus clean with a curette. People were surprised to find out that it was simpler than a tonsillectomy, and, if it was done properly, the problem rate was lower than it was for tonsillectomies. No one they counseled was aware of how common abortion was. Instead, most women thought that once in a while a woman had one by someone who butchered her and left her to bleed to death. "And despite all that," Lorraine says, still amazed, "how many women came through our service? This was their concept of abortion, yet they wanted abortions so badly they were willing to risk that same thing happening to them."

Each counseling session was different, as each woman and girl was different. With each one, the counselors would try to explore what effect pregnancy and the decision to seek an abortion were having on her life and relate the situation to her attitudes about contraception and her relationship with her boyfriend, husband or parents. However each counselor approached the information that had to be covered, the underlying message was always the same: It's up to you to take charge of your life. You have to make your own decisions. You control your body, no one else does.

What they were doing wasn't charity. It wasn't some do-gooder project meant to lift up the less fortunate. They were working for the liberation of women. They wanted every woman who called them to see herself as an active participant, to take responsibility for her decisions. One way she could participate was by paying for her abortion. If they lent a woman money, they expected her to repay it so that another woman, as much in need as she, would be able to get an abortion. They developed a form for the loan fund which they distributed at counseling sessions and at women's meetings they attended:

> I,__________, am willing to contribute $ _______to the non-interest Abortion Loan Fund. I fully understand that my contribution implicates me along with all others in the Abortion Counseling Service of Women's Liberation.

The high cost of the abortions (between $500 and $1,000) made it possible and logical to talk about abortion in terms of economic oppression, that coming up with the money added greater stress for women whose resources were minimal. Part of the counseling session was spent helping people figure out where to get money. Women were encouraged to tap the guy, tap their parents, sell their radios. "You say you can't come up with six hundred dollars. This is something that's going to affect your whole life. What do you have that you can sell: a stereo, a coat, a toaster? Do you have a sister, a cousin, a brother? Go to them and explain, or don't explain, just tell them you need money. Go to your parents, rob your piggy bank, because this may be the most important decision you'll make in your life."

The most difficult task was to counteract the guilt and self-blame that women carried. Even if there was no way they could afford or care for a child, they still internalized society's judgments that women who sought abortions were selfish, immoral, denying their female duty, and stupid or careless for getting pregnant. Black women, as usual, were under a double bind. They were not only burdened with society's attitudes, but also, by the criticism of black nationalists who identified abortion with genocide. Within those circles any woman seeking an abortion was considered a traitor to her race. It was the counselor's job to try to lift the guilt, validate each woman's decision, and put the entire experience in the context of women's liberation. Jenny always came on strong, "You wouldn't be in this situation if you weren't being exploited. Facing this situation is one of the ways you are oppressed and, in this case, oppression is really physical." For some women, as she remembers, the response was: Yeah, that's fine, let's get on with it. But with others she could almost see a bulb light up.

The final step was in the hands of the doctor contacts, Miriam and Jenny. After a woman was counseled, Miriam or Jenny called the doctors and negotiated the price. The process of matching women with doctors was based on the calculation of number of weeks pregnant and money available. One doctor took only women who were under 10 weeks lmp,* while another was inflexible in his price. Once the doctor had the woman's number, his people made the specific arrangements regarding appointment place and time directly with her. From the moment a woman left home to meet the doctor until she safely returned, the group was out of it.

The women in the group decided which of a handful of doctors they referred women to and what information they gave each

*lmp: (from the) last monthly period.

woman, but when it came to the abortion itself, they had no control over what went on. All they could say was, "We've sent women before and they all came back alive." Not much of a recommendation but really all they could give. They had to trust the doctors not to mistreat women; the feedback they got from women after their abortions was their only control.

With all of Jenny's impatience and frustration with the process, she realized that those months of discussion had raised her understanding of abortion to a level to which even her own personal experiences couldn't bring her. She came to see it this way: "We, as women, are biologically the way we are, but that doesn't mean we don't deserve power. We deserve power and shouldn't be deprived of it because we were pregnant and didn't want to be, because we didn't have control of our own reproduction. We were entitled to that control and had to get that control."

Control was the key. It was a lesson Jenny had learned from her own struggle to get the sterilization and abortion she desperately needed. She had come out of her own abortion with loose, unchanneled anger, and the discussions Claire led had given her a framework through which to understand it. But she took what she learned from Claire one step further. It wasn't enough to locate and refer women to competent doctors willing to perform abortions. The group had to be able to call the shots and make demands. They had to create a situation in which they could treat the doctors as merely the technicians they were. They had to be able to monitor the abortion procedures. That was the key. If they could find a doctor willing to let group members attend the abortions so they could guarantee good treatment, they and the women having abortions would gain more control.

By late spring of 1969, when they began counseling women, they had a short list of doctors. Two of the names came from Claire's network and the others came from the grapevine, from women who had used them or heard about them. Jenny hoped to convince the doctors to meet with her, rather than limit contact to the phone. She knew enough about business to know that to get the control they wanted they had to negotiate from a position of strength. If they could offer these doctors volume, they'd have some leverage. She called each one and said, "Look, we're a powerful organization and we've got a lot of business. If you want a piece of the action you're going to have to do some things our way rather than your way." It was quite a shock for some of the doctors, who were used to dealing with helpless women one at a time, to be faced with an organization that was giving orders. But Jenny felt that was critical: "We wanted women to go in there with a feeling of power, knowing they were backed by an organization, knowing they could voice complaints and make demands, knowing they had the right to be treated fairly. It gave women more strength and made them feel like they were part of the organization, too."

Their short list did not offer much in the way of choices. Some of the doctors, Miriam and Jenny discovered, were either sloppy practitioners or, more often, displayed attitudes and behaviors that were offensive. For instance, one doctor presumably paid police protection, because his name was on the door of the medical office where he performed abortions. He was medically competent, but he was often drunk and demanded sexual favors as a condition for the abortion.

The doctor Claire had used on Sixty-third Street was not interested in the kind of close working relationship Jenny had in mind. His abortion business was as busy as he wanted it to be; the last thing he needed was the kind of volume Jenny wanted to offer. He had never met Claire and had no intention of meeting any of them. And he had two prices: one for black women and almost double for white women.

Another doctor worked in a suburban high-rise apartment. To conceal his location, women were picked up on street corners and had to put on opaque glasses so they could not see where they were going. In his all-white neighborhood, black women and Latinas waiting on street corners were uncomfortable and conspicuous. He performed abortions only on women up to 10 weeks lmp and there was no way to get in touch with him if there were problems or complications.

A local doctor's receptionist recommended a foreign-trained doctor she said she had used herself. He charged only $150 for a "painless European technique" with which he could perform abortions up to 12 weeks lmp.

When they heard about him the loan fund was depleted and there were a few women waiting who couldn't possibly scrape together even $150. Two women, knowing that the group had no firsthand experience with him, decided to use him anyway. The first woman was fine, but the second one, a young black woman, wound up in the hospital with a lacerated cervix. Her parents were calling for "the blood of the Nazi who did it." The police were pressuring the woman and her parents to talk. In operation less than a month, the group's future looked bleak.

They were rescued by a young black civil rights worker who knew Jenny and had referred the young woman. He interceded on the group's behalf, telling Jenny, "I'll take the heat on this one. I can do my work from jail, but you can't." He convinced the parents not to talk, but it was the young woman's full recovery that ultimately saved them.

There was one other option, Dr. Kaufman, Claire's Cicero contact. He worked with a team, including a front man and a woman assistant, performing abortions either in a woman's own home or in motel rooms. Motel rooms, he said, were clean and safe. In her own room, a woman could rest as much as she needed afterward. He performed D & C abortions up to 13 weeks lmp and, with more advanced pregnancies, induced miscarriages. From what they had heard and read, 13 weeks seemed dangerously late in a pregnancy for a D & C and none of them knew anything about induced miscarriages, so they were wary.

But Dr. Kaufman offered them something no one else had. He

agreed to send his middleman to meet with them, but only with one person at a time and in a public place. More than two people talking could be considered a conspiracy, he warned. Then he added, as if Jenny needed to be reminded, never talk to the police. They arranged to meet on a night early in the summer, on a street in Hyde Park.

As Jenny prepared for the meeting, she swore to herself that she would do and say whatever she had to to get the control they needed, even if it meant using all her feminine charms. She put on a skimpy tan miniskirt, a sleeveless tank top, long dangling earrings and sandals. She had picked her outfit carefully, thinking, If women are stuck with the victim/whore dichotomy, I'll be the whore because we've had enough victims.

She met him on the sidewalk under the trees and leaned against a parked car. He stood facing her, one foot on a low railing, his arm braced against a huge tree. For a moment the two of them eyed each other suspiciously. Her face, framed by dark hair, all planes and angles, contrasted with his pale sensual features. There was something slick and self-confident about him, she thought, like a used-car salesman. His eyes, in constant motion, scanned the street.

He broke the silence first, launching into a warning about conspiracies. She cut him off. "I don't want to hear any of that bullshit. We both know why you're in this. You're in this to make money. We don't care about money. We're in this to help these women, and it's as important to us as your money is to you, so let's start right now and find some way we can make it better for you and you can make it better for us.

"You're doing one or two cases a week for us now at six hundred to a thousand dollars per case. We have the wherewithal to deliver a lot more people to you, which means you'll have to work harder, but you'll make a shitload more money than what you've been making. But, in order for us to do that, we want some concessions too."

"Sounds interesting," he said. She had his complete attention now.

She continued, "You know, people like you are available all over the place, but if you want to be something special and relate to our needs, we'll take a special interest in you." She saw a smile dart across his face. He nodded at her to go on.

"The first thing is that we have to know where people are and what's happening with them," she said. She wanted some control over women's safety while they were helpless, which was how she thought of their situation when they were in the custody of the abortionists.

"We might be able to work something out," he responded tentatively. "But the doctor's identity has to be protected."

She played her first card: "We'll guarantee a certain number of cases a week if we have some control. The other thing is that the price is too high. These women are desperate and most of them don't have that kind of money. If we're going to supply you with volume, you'll make more money in the long run, so let's lower the price."

For a few minutes he was silent. "Okay. Here's my offer," he countered. "If you can guarantee at least ten cases a week, we'll lower the basic price from six hundred to five hundred dollars and we'll do one out of every five or so free if it's a real desperate case, but we want to be able to charge more for the ones that are twelve weeks and over."

"That's ridiculous," she shot back. "Let's talk about the total amount of money coming in over a week. Instead of doing five for five hundred dollars and then one for free, let's just lower the price to four hundred and skip the free ones."

"Out of the question. No way. An abortion is worth five hundred dollars and we deserve it."

She felt her anger rising. This wasn't about money or what he deserved. This was about women's lives. But he didn't want to hear any of that. He wasn't interested in politics.

She tried pushing for more but he was adamant. It was out of his hands. Without consulting his partners he had made all the concessions he was going to make. In exchange for a guarantee of at least ten abortions a week, they would lower the basic price to $500 with room for flexibility. He also agreed to call her immediately before and after the procedure and give her his home phone number so she could always reach him.

As she watched him walk away she felt pleased. Even if she didn't get every concession she wanted, at least the tone of their future interactions was set. They could deal.

In an apartment above the street, Miriam, Lorraine, Karen and a few other women waited impatiently. When Jenny finally appeared, they were amazed at her success and a bit taken aback. Where were they going to find ten cases a week? The number of abortions Jenny had promised entailed more work than they could handle. But Jenny was determined. If they were going to provide more than just an adequate service, if they and women needing abortions were going to be anything other than supplicants, they had to seize whatever advantage they could. They had to build their strength through numbers. Women were desperate for decent abortions. They had to go out and find those women. If that meant expanding the group, so much the better. The bigger the organization, the more women they served, the more power was going to shift from the doctors to women. Another motive was left unstated: If abortion was every woman's right, they had to take whatever actions were necessary to make that right a reality.

CHAPTER 4

To deliver ten cases a week seemed impossible. If two or three women called them, it was a busy week. But the others agreed with Jenny that it was vital to gain more control over the abortions, including negotiating to bring down the price. The Cicero doctor offered a chance to accomplish this. They decided to let more women know about their work by publicizing their service. To avoid attracting the wrong kind of attention, they had to do that selectively. Whenever one of them attended another women's liberation group, she handed their pamphlet out and announced: "There's an abortion service if you are in need or know anyone who needs an abortion. It might be a little cryptic but don't be afraid. These are people you can trust." Karen remembers making signs: "Pregnant? Don't want to be? Call Jane: 643–3844," which were posted at colleges and other places where women congregated in Chicago. It didn't take long for their pamphlet to find its way into the hands of doctors around the city who started referring women to them.

On Halloween weekend 1969 about one hundred Chicago feminists attended a retreat in Palatine, Illinois, to organize the Chicago Women's Liberation Union (CWLU). The first of its kind in the United States, CWLU's purpose was to create an organizing base through which to bring an army of women into the women's liberation movement. The union would serve as an umbrella for women's projects, as a central connector among these projects, and as a vehicle to create a mass movement. Women from every political stripe attended the organizing weekend—from members of NOW, representing the women's rights branch of the movement, to the most extreme Left groups, like the Yippies and Revolutionary Youth Movement II, for whom feminism was secondary to race and class issues.

Jenny, the only member of Jane at the retreat, was more than a little nonplussed by the group's reception. A vocal contingent believed the CWLU had to have a radical focus, i.e., to address the roots of the problems that women faced. Rather than reform the existing oppressive system, they should promote sweeping changes that would profoundly alter society. Abortion counseling, they argued, was not a radical activity but merely reformist social service work. How could an illegal, underground, service organization that referred women to male abortionists and charged hundreds of dollars, be considered radical? Jane was a Band-Aid that might help a few women but did not further or reflect the social changes they envisioned. Since abortions were so expensive, and therefore limited to women who could come up with money, how did this service meet the needs of poor people and black people, who were the most oppressed? How could this service fulfill the union's mission to bring large numbers of women into their movement and train legions of organizers?

Other women argued that creating alternative institutions, such as an abortion referral service, was exactly what the women's liberation movement had to do in order to address the needs of women. Claire, one of Chicago's first and leading advocates of women's liberation and one of CWLU's organizers, spoke in support of Jane. Although she had left the group months before, she knew this service was critical to women's lives. Not only, she argued, was it an essential women's liberation activity because it allowed women to take control of their lives, but also, feminist abortion counseling had the potential to raise women's consciousness, women the CWLU might not otherwise reach. It was Claire's outspoken defense of Jane that mollified what Jenny felt was outright hostility. Later, when Miriam heard about the discussion, her response was, "Sometimes I believed that abortion was a reform issue and sometimes I didn't. I guess I don't know what a radical issue is except that anything can be reform or radical depending on how you do it."

In any case, the link between Jane, officially known as the Abortion Counseling Service, or ACS, and the CWLU was forged, although uneasily. The ACS was now a member and a work group of the union, even if some of CWLU's members weren't completely comfortable with the group. Because the retreat brought together women representing many different strands of the movement, word of the service spread with a rapidity their individual outreach couldn't have duplicated. When, shortly after the retreat, the CWLU opened an office, the union's staff gave any woman who called looking for an abortion Jane's number.

After the CWLU retreat, the steady trickle of one or two calls a week increased exponentially. They had to recruit new members to meet the growing demand for their service, but they were worried about opening their tight little group. After months of meetings, their thinking had evolved to the extent that they could accept breaking the law, dealing with an illicit underground, and taking responsibility for other women's lives. But could they expect other women, coming into the group cold, without the benefit of those hours of discussion, to be willing to shoulder that kind of responsibility? Lorraine, whose home phone was ringing day and night with calls for Jane, responded, "Hell, yes. We don't have any choice."

Actually, the Jane calls were causing friction in her marriage. Stan was working on his dissertation; taking messages for Jane was a distracting irritation. They both led busy lives and frequently no one was home. The group secured an answering service to take messages when Lorraine was unavailable. Karen shared the phone duties with

Lorraine. It was Karen's job to call the answering service each day. "This is Jane," she would say, "I'm calling for my messages." She says, "We always thought it was a stitch that they never asked who we were or what we did." But the answering service made them uncomfortable. Suppose someone calling said too much or used the word "abortion." The answering service might catch on and who knew what could happen then.

It was tricky calling women back. Sometimes it required quick thinking to protect the confidentiality of the woman they were trying to reach:

"Hi, is Sharon there?"

"No, she's not. Who is this?"

"This is Jane. Do you know when she'll be in?"

"Jane? Where do you know her from?" The voice on the other end asked suspiciously.

"We work together." Whoever made the call crossed her fingers, hoping Sharon had a job.

"She doesn't have a job. Who is this?"

The only recourse was to hang up quickly and hope that Sharon herself answered on the next try.

During a similar call Jane acquired a last name. When the person on the other end asked, "Jane who?" Lorraine thought for a millisecond and said, "Howe. Jane Howe." It seemed appropriate: Jane could tell you how. When, months later, Lorraine and Stan got a different phone number for themselves, they listed their old number, Jane's number, under the name "Jane Howe."*

When Karen called women back she said, "Hi, this is Jane. I understand you have a problem. Why don't you tell me about it?" Karen walked a fine line. Some women wanted to turn the phone call into

*Although there were reports of sympathetic telephone operators giving out Jane's number, no one ever found Jane by looking in the phone book. In fact, hardly anyone in the group knew Jane had a last name.

a counseling session. Karen felt that "calling the women back was really tough, hearing their stories and trying to maintain a certain amount of businesslike detachment." Women were always asked where they got Jane's number, so the group could keep track of who was referring to them.

To protect their project, they turned to their friends, coworkers and classmates for potential recruits to the group. Karen thought that the group was "amazingly trusting of each other. One of us would say, 'I know a couple of women.' They'd come to the next meeting and automatically be part of the decision making. We looked for women who were ready to do something. 'You're pissed, your consciousness has just been raised. Here, join us.'" Over the next few months, through the fall and early winter, a few women joined. Most of them stayed briefly, deciding this wasn't what they wanted to do. The membership of the group remained under a dozen.

But the impact their work was having on women's lives was apparent and dramatic. Women sent thank-you's; they called after their abortions and offered to help.

That fall Susan, one of the women in Claire's original network, threw a surprise shower for Claire, who was pregnant with her second child. Among the guests were Jenny, Miriam and Karen. Susan wanted to give Claire a traditional suburban shower complete with decorations and ice cream in the shape of swans. In order not to arouse Claire's suspicions, Susan told her there was a Jane emergency and to come right away.

Claire hadn't been part of the group for months. What emergency can't be handled without me, she wondered? There could be only one answer: someone had died from an abortion. She always knew that was a possibility but she was not prepared for the wave of absolute terror that crashed over her. The blood drained from her face and her legs began to shake. Quickly she dug out whatever abortion notes she still had around the house and headed for Susan's, her pulse racing.

When she walked into the apartment her face was white. "Surprise!" they shouted, laughing, around the dining room table piled with pink-wrapped presents. One look at Claire and they realized they had made a mistake. Susan thought: Oh, no. What have I done? She's going to go into labor right now. It took Claire a few minutes to catch her breath, calm down, and start enjoying her party.

Claire wasn't the only pregnant woman at the party. Susan was pregnant, and, after almost a year and a half of painful fertility work, Karen had just found out that she was pregnant. There was nothing unusual in this group of middle-class, college-educated white women celebrating an impending birth except that these women were ardent feminists and most of them were or had been abortion counselors. As they ate cake and ice cream, they talked about their unique situation. Here they were, a group of women, many of them mothers, some of them ecstatically pregnant, who were more committed than ever to each woman's right to make that important decision herself—when and whether to bear a child.

CHAPTER 5

Before Karen found out she was pregnant, she had enrolled in Roosevelt University for the fall term as a graduate student in urban studies. With a graduate degree she would be able to get a community organizing job with more decision-making power than the social service casework she had been doing. Roosevelt's program allowed her to concentrate her studies on community and women's organizations. In an urban planning course she met Carol who was part of a small women's liberation group on campus and had volunteered as the group's representative to the CWLU. Carol seemed to have unlimited energy and was an outspoken feminist. Early in the winter Karen invited her to an Abortion Counseling Service meeting.

When Betty Friedan's *The Feminine Mystique* came out in 1963 Carol had been on her own for two years, working and struggling through college part-time at night. The book criticized society's message to women that they could find true fulfillment only as wives and mothers. Friedan had discovered that scores of suburban housewives who had accepted that limited role, rather than feeling fulfilled, were depressed and desperate. As a teenager Carol had decided that she wanted more than a life of devotion to husband and children. Friedan's analysis validated her own feelings and strengthened her resolve to lead a different kind of life.

Since 1961 she had been supporting herself on the only jobs she could get with a high school diploma. When she moved to Chicago in the mid-sixties she volunteered with the civil rights movement. She thought a degree in urban studies would give her the credentials to get paid for doing social change work. She applied to Roosevelt because it had a culturally diverse student body and a schedule of night classes that accommodated working students. By 1969 she had managed to save enough money to cut back to part-time employment, which left her time for outside projects.

Carol, the daughter of a watchmaker, was raised in a religious Lutheran family in rural West Virginia. Karen was her classmate, not her friend. She felt separated from Karen by the barriers of class. Everything about Karen spoke of privilege—her clothes, her home, not to mention her husband, a Harvard Law School graduate. She had never had to struggle as Carol had. But the two women, from such different backgrounds, shared a commitment to feminism and working for change.

In December Carol went to her first counseling service meeting at Karen's house. She was relieved that the handful of other women there seemed more like her than Karen.

Lorraine took it upon herself to explain what they did. Since abortion was illegal, women were forced to seek help from illegal abortionists and, if they were ripped off or treated badly, they had no recourse. For example, there was one doctor who demanded intercourse with women before the procedure. Another charged for an abortion he feigned but never performed. Lorraine said, "What our service tries to do is refer women who are determined to have an abortion out of the country, if they can afford it, or, if they can't, we guide them through the underground abortion market."

The others seemed so close-knit that Carol felt like an outsider looking for approval. Even though Karen vouched for her, Carol sensed she was being judged. She told them she had had her consciousness raised by trying to survive on a high school education. She had always had a strong sense of moral imperative that superseded any legal imperative, so the illegality of the work posed no problem. Then she told them about Mary.

In late 1961, when Carol was eighteen, she lived in a women's hotel in Gary, Indiana, working for the phone company and attending Indiana University part-time. In the winter of 1962–63 a friend at the hotel, Mary, an elementary school teacher, got pregnant. She was terrified she would lose her job if anyone found out. She needed an abortion and she wanted Carol's help. To Carol the whole idea was alien and frightening. What if they got involved with the Syndicate, since Gary was only a forty-five-minute train ride from Chicago and everyone knew the Mob controlled illegal activities there. What if Mary died, or they both got arrested? What would Jesus think? None of Carol's questions dissuaded Mary. Carol had to make a choice; she chose to help her friend. After days of circumspect asking around, Carol got the name of someone in Chicago.

Mary left on the train with $600. In Gary, Carol paced, praying, visualizing horrific headlines: "Woman's Body Found After Botched Abortion."

Mary returned after midnight. A catheter, a thin plastic tube, had been inserted into her uterus and her vagina packed with cotton to keep the catheter in place. Neither of them knew that catheters were the most common illegal abortion technique or that they were risky. The tube could puncture the uterus. It also opened a route for bacteria from the vagina into the uterus, often resulting in a serious, even fatal, infection.* Mary's instructions were to "pull the plug" when she went into labor. Neither of them knew anything about labor and Carol was petrified of blood. Together they midwifed the miscarriage. "It looked to me," remembers Carol, "like her whole insides were coming out." Mary was about four months pregnant and the fetus she miscarried was

*Because of the dangers associated with catheter abortions, Jane avoided referring to people who used them. From the women they counseled, the group learned that neighborhood "catheter ladies" were operating all over the city.

tiny but formed. Nineteen year-old-Carol thought, I've got to protect Mary from seeing it. She's been through enough.

She told the women sitting in Karen's living room that she carried with her, from that time, the feeling that women have to take care of each other. Sisterhood was literal. After she finished speaking, the others nodded and then went on as if she wasn't there, much to Carol's relief. She couldn't quite figure out what was going on but she kept hearing the name Jane. Finally she asked, "Who is Jane?" They laughed as Lorraine explained that Jane was their code name. By the end of the meeting, Carol was hooked.

•

Although their primary task was to increase the number of requests they got so they could lower the price for an abortion, the group continued to seek out other doctors. By late fall abortionists began contacting them. The same grapevine through which they learned about new practitioners brought their service to the attention of abortionists. It was a good thing, too, because, sometime late in November, just as their volume increased enough to implement their agreement with Dr. Kaufman, Jenny's contact disappeared. There was no answer at his home number. Jenny left messages for him with his answering service. They had to find other doctors and use the contacts they had, whether they were totally satisfactory or not.

At Carol's second meeting her outsider status evaporated. She remembers the meeting like this: One of the women said she had heard from a woman they had sent to Puerto Rico the previous week. In Puerto Rico the doctor demanded an additional $350, so she had returned to Chicago.

"We can't refer anyone there again. They always pull something, but it's never been money before."

"Now she's twelve weeks?" Miriam asked.

"Yeah, we've really got to do something for her. We sent her there," Jenny said.

That situation was left unresolved. Another woman reported: "We sent Gloria to the doctor on Sixty-third Street. She had a D & C at eight weeks for six hundred dollars. There was a little heavy bleeding but she's fine now."

"It's too bad he won't negotiate with us or take more than a very few women. He's really been the most reliable," Lorraine said.

"High price, though."

"Well, just the going rate."

"It's outrageous. Even if they pay protection, they still make big bucks."

Miriam turned to the first woman: "Go on."

"I counseled Marcia. She's thirty-nine, divorced with five kids. She was eleven weeks but real short of cash so we sent her to Dave on the North Side, since he's only five hundred dollars. The driver thought she looked like a cop, so he left her standing on a street corner for an hour before he picked her up. She said there were three men in the room telling dirty jokes and the place was filthy. She was running a fever yesterday, so I told her to see my gynecologist and say she's my friend. He put her in the hospital for a cleanup D & C and gave her some antibiotics. She's fine now."

"You know, if we have an MD for follow-up . . . "

"I can't send everyone to my own gynecologist. How many pregnant friends can I have in a week? He'll think I'm running an abortion ring or something!" That remark was greeted with laughter.

"Oh, a man called from Detroit. His name is Nathan. He's got a clinic set up and he's willing to meet with me. He says he thinks we could be useful to each other," Lorraine broke in.

"How does he know about us?"

"He says 'medical colleagues,' whatever that means. He said we might be able to work something out on price if the volume was high enough. What do you think?"

"Is he a doctor?"

"He says he's a doctor, but I'm skeptical. He sounds like an operator, kind of slick."

"For that matter, how do we know any of them are doctors?"

Since Lorraine had taken the original call from "Nathan Detroit," as he was instantly dubbed by the group, she agreed to see him when she visited her parents in Detroit over Christmas vacation.

Lorraine asked, "If I'm going to Detroit, who can take the Jane box?" The Jane box, a three-by-five-inch index card file, held the information on women contacting the group. Taking the Jane box meant handling the telephone work. Carol sat there, not quite sure of herself. Hesitantly she offered, "Well, if you can show me how, and, if it's okay, I'd like to try."

Jenny responded, "Great! I'll show you how to do it and I'll be here all vacation in case you have any questions." She sat next to Carol on the couch and began explaining what the job entailed. The meeting slipped into conversation.

Carol walked home alone, clutching the blue card box, the snow crunching under her feet, amazed that they were trusting her.

Nathan called several times before Lorraine went to Detroit. He seemed anxious for their business and was willing to make concessions he said he normally wouldn't make. After Lorraine arrived in Detroit, they arranged to meet. His driver would pick her up at a busy restaurant parking lot and, he added, she was going to see an abortion. Lorraine felt he was testing her to see if she could handle it. She had never seen an abortion. None of them had. For over six months she had been sending women off for a procedure that she was forced to describe based on hearsay. Now Nathan was giving her the opportunity she had been hoping for.

She waited in the parking lot. An unremarkable American car, a tan four-door sedan, pulled in next to hers. The driver identified himself as one of Nathan's people. She got in the car. He handed her a sleeping mask and sunglasses to put over it. As they drove, they chatted about the weather. He noted that what she was going through was exactly what "one of our girls" would go through. She was aware that they were making an unusual number of turns and she sensed they might be circling around. They stopped behind a building. He let her in a back door and then left.

Inside the building, a dark-haired man, over six feet tall and three hundred pounds, with a ruddy complexion, introduced himself as Nathan. He had on a vicuña coat. Lorraine thought he looked like a wealthy businessman. He ushered her into a room with a big desk and chairs that reminded Lorraine of her doctor's office except that the bookshelves were empty and extra furniture was stacked in a corner, like an office no longer in use. He asked again, "Are you sure you want to go through with this?" Then he took her into another room outfitted with an examining table with stirrups, shelves with linen in sterile packaging, instrument cases and an autoclave for sterilizing instruments, like every doctor's examining room she'd been in. Lorraine was impressed; the room was immaculate and neat. A nurse in a starched white uniform sat in a corner reading a magazine. A young woman was on the table. Then, another man, the doctor, came in, put on sterile gloves, and performed a D & C.

Afterward Nathan took Lorraine to a restaurant for dinner. The doctor joined them. Lorraine asked him why he did abortions. He was in the process of a divorce, he explained. His wife was taking him to the cleaners and he had two kids in college. He needed the money. He handed her his AMA membership card. Lorraine assumed these two men were trusting her because they were anxious for the increased business they thought her group could provide.

Nathan wanted $1,000 per case but Lorraine told him, "We can do better than that in Chicago." After some haggling he agreed to $600. When Lorraine returned to Chicago, she added his name to their list of sources.

As it turned out, Nathan Detroit proved not to be a useful resource for D & C abortions. Chicago women, unfamiliar with Detroit, were sometimes late for their rendezvous with his driver. When that happened, Nathan called Lorraine, furious. Lorraine did not want to have any more contact with these doctors, as Nathan was more of a headache than he was worth.

There were huge gaps in their knowledge they needed to fill. After what had happened with the European doctor the previous summer, they knew they couldn't trust what abortionists told them. They needed sympathetic medical sources not only for information but also for post-abortion checkups and medical backup. If someone they sent for an abortion had complications requiring medical care or hospitalization, she could avoid problems in the emergency room if a private doctor admitted her. Walking into an emergency room cold could be a nightmare. Often the police were called in; the woman was told she had been butchered and would die, and that medical treatment would be withheld unless she told them who had done it. Perhaps their own doctors could provide the medical information and services they needed.

Lorraine, like Karen before her, was in a fertility workup with a European specialist she liked and respected. She broached the subject by asking, "Could an abortion cause someone not to be able to conceive?"

"A woman could get a prolapsed uterus from too many abortions," he answered, using the same matter-of-fact tone as she.

"What's too many?"

"Let's see . . . 14 or 15 abortions are too many."

Fourteen or fifteen abortions! She was shocked, "But nobody has that many!"

He laughed at her naïveté. "In Latin America they do because it's the only form of birth control." He continued, "The problem you women have is that nobody does abortions in this country because the doctors are too rich." He went on to explain that in Latin America and some parts of Europe young doctors do abortions until their practice is established and they have paid off their medical school bills.

Gradually, over the next few months, she told him what she was doing. He was an excellent source for medical information but that was all he offered. His practice was quite specific and he was very busy.

Two of Jenny's neighbors were doctors. One lived down the street. They knew each other through their children, who were friends. He liked Jenny's kids and admired Jenny and her husband Glen's enterprising spirit. They were always working on one home business or another. They were politically active in the community just as he and his wife were.

His own feelings on abortion were unsettled. "I was kind of dragging my feet," he remembers. "I'm a vegetarian and the whole idea of killing is abhorrent to me. At the same time, I felt that women do have something to say about what's going on within them and I certainly was in no position as another human being to tell them what to do. These are very personal decisions and it rankled me that someone would have the audacity to go around telling people what they can and can't do." His attitude was beginning to shift when Jenny broached the subject by relating the histories of some of the women she was counseling. The inequity bothered him: the fact that women with money could get abortions but women without could not. He came to feel that "women have a right to have abortions when and if they want them and nobody has the right to make a law against them. It's strictly a private decision."

Jenny asked him for medical advice and diagnostic help. "She'd tell me some symptoms and I would try and tell her what I thought it was that was bringing on those symptoms: like a woman who was passing clots, having fever or pain or feeling faint," he recalls. Occasionally he prescribed antibiotics or admitted women to the hospital. She never flooded him with questions. "If she called me four times a year, that was a lot," he remembers. Whenever she called he always responded, but he had to be careful. He was known in the Chicago Medical Society for being "radically inclined." "Radical?" he snorts. "I wanted people to have more food, and better health care. But there were folks who would have loved to get some stuff on me. I didn't know if they were laying traps for me or what."

He wasn't the only doctor worried about traps being laid. One of the doctors with the Medical Committee for Human Rights,* who knew Jenny, Miriam, Claire and many of the other Hyde Park activists, had the same concerns. There had been at least one attempt to set him up for his antiwar work; his office had been broken into and his files rifled. He was helpful to the group, but from a distance.

What they were looking for was a network of people they could call in case of an emergency or for follow-up care. None of these backup doctors knew the details. They didn't ask and they weren't told. They agreed to help out of trust, trust for the individual women they knew in the group and trust for what the group was doing. Over time, they developed a list of helpful doctors. Next to Dr. X's name might be a note: "Contact only through so-and-so," or "Don't call too often, he's getting nervous."

Whenever a woman called Jane, she was asked who referred her. Any doctor who regularly sent women to Jane was contacted: "This is Jane. You've been referring women to me and I'd like to ask if there is some way you can help." Often the response was blunt, "Don't ever call me again." But others were willing to see women for follow-up exams and a very few agreed to be available for emergencies. The informal doctor network was constantly changing. A doctor might begin to worry what the hospital staff was thinking, or a counselor might get feedback from a woman that she had been treated insensitively.

Through their limited number of backup doctors they were able to fill in some of the gaps in their knowledge on a case-by-case basis.

*The Medical Committee for Human Rights (1964–1974), organized nationally by health care professionals, supported progressive issues, such as abortion rights, and provided medical services during urban riots and political protests.

For the time being they had to content themselves with building on what they knew in this piecemeal fashion. As infuriated as they were by the doctors who refused to help them, especially those who referred women to them, they were equally grateful to the few doctors, like Jenny's neighbor, who made themselves available. But the women in the group knew that depending on medical professionals would take them only so far.

CHAPTER 6

The women in Jane weren't the only people counseling and referring women for abortions. Women's liberation groups in many U.S. cities set up similar services. Others, who were not part of women's liberation, provided referrals. Pat Maginnis in California early in the 1960s passed handbills out on street corners listing the best Tijuana clinics, clinics she had personally checked out. In New York Lawrence Lader, a cofounder of NARAL, after writing a book about abortion in 1966, announced that he would provide referrals to women. He was quickly swamped with requests. In 1967 the first Clergy Consultation Service on Abortion began operating out of Judson Memorial Church in New York City under the leadership of its Baptist minister, Howard Moody.

A similar clergy service was organized by another Baptist minister, Harris Wilson, the dean of Rockefeller Chapel, the cathedral at the University of Chicago. In December 1969, having already referred about five hundred women, the Chicago clergy group went public in a lengthy article in the *Chicago Sun-Times*. Harris was known around the university community for his progressive positions and had cofounded Illinois Citizens for the Medical Control of Abortion (ICMCA). In the 1950s, as a university chaplain in Boston, he had actively worked to lift Massachusetts's ban on contraceptives.

Harris Wilson had been encouraged by Howard Moody to start

the Chicago group. They were both ministers in the American Baptist Convention (renamed the American Baptist Churches, USA in 1971); both were involved in civil rights and opposed the war. They had worked together on church policy and for a fairer national drug policy. Together they drafted a resolution, which was passed at the American Baptist Convention in June 1968, calling on ministers to counsel and assist women with family planning and abortion. At lunch one day early in 1968, Moody said to him, "You've really got to get involved in this abortion thing." He went on to explain that he and his assistant, Arlene Carmen, had organized a local network of clergy to counsel and refer women for abortions. The clergymen were also taking a vocal public position advocating legalized abortion. Harris's only response was "Oh." He had been lobbying for legislative change with ICMCA but hadn't given much thought to actually finding abortions for women. He was on the faculty of the School of Divinity, teaching a course on human sexuality in the School of Biological Sciences, ministering to his university congregation at Rockefeller Chapel and preaching. He wasn't looking for more work.

In the spring of 1968 a Baptist pastor at Indiana University in Bloomington called Harris with a request: "You live in the great big sin city. I've got a problem and I think you can help me. There's this young couple. They're both in graduate school and the wife is pregnant. If the pregnancy continues she'll have to quit work and he'll have to drop out of graduate school and it looks like a big mess because they're close to being done." The couple could not travel to Moody's network in New York, but Chicago was only a few hours away.

Harris Wilson answered, "Well, I don't have any idea where you procure an abortion in Chicago, but if they want to talk to me, send them up, and, in the meantime, I'll find something."

He contacted a woman he knew in the dean's office, thinking, if anyone knows, she'll know. She was a member of WRAP, the campus women's liberation group. She was also helping Claire with her abortion referral work. She gave him Claire's number. "I made the contact and the couple went and had the abortion," he recalls. "They came back to the chapel office, and told me they thought it was great that it could be done. Then they went back home and I never heard from them again."

Within a few months more people came to Harris looking for abortions. He was able to send all of them to Howard Moody's group in New York. He thought out-of-state referrals might shield him from prosecution and he felt more comfortable with the clergy network than with the contact he'd made in the dean's office.

As a member of the executive committee of his denomination Harris frequently went to New York for meetings. On one of these trips Howard Moody said to him, "Look, you've got to do this yourself out there. We just can't take all the referrals that are coming through from Illinois." This time Harris replied, "Okay, Howard, we'll start a Clergy Consultation Service in Chicago."

In March of 1969, a month after the NARAL organizing conference in Chicago that he attended, Harris called together forty-five clergymen from the Midwest. "Being out there on the front lines was not the kind of thing Baptists are noted for," he remembers, "but there was Howard Moody in New York and another Baptist minister in Bloomington, and a Presbyterian minister in Fort Wayne, Indiana, and a whole network of guys, ministers and rabbis." He brought in a gynecologist from Billings Hospital, part of the University of Chicago, to explain the medical aspects of abortion, and a lawyer who outlined their risks and liabilities. After the meeting about twenty clergymen decided to get involved.

Besides the actual referral work, their task was both political and educational. They would work overtly for legalized abortion and educate people about the issue. Their cloak of moral authority allowed them to take a public stand. But if they were going to go public and deliberately attract attention, they could not risk announcing that they were sending women for illegal abortions in Chicago.

The clergy group regularly referred women to Puerto Rico, Mexico City and England. "We were making a big deal of the fact that we were sending people all over the world for abortions," Harris recalls. "Well, we were, but that's not all we were doing." They sent some women to a doctor in Michigan and counseled women who could not leave Chicago. For those women they found a few local doctors, but that part of their work they kept secret. One was a surgeon who offered his services to his minister, a member of the clergy network. Every Wednesday night he performed up to four abortions in a hotel room. Harris also eventually developed a close relationship with the doctor on Sixty-third Street.

Jane decided that contact with Harris and the clergy would be mutually beneficial, since both groups shared the same mission. Miriam, whose husband worked for the university, approached him. Miriam found out from Harris that Jane was only reaching the tip of a huge iceberg. They were getting ten calls a week, but the clergy was getting ten calls a day. While Harris wanted to exchange information with Miriam, one of his concerns was to maintain a distance between his group and Miriam's. He thought it would be politically wise if they tried to avoid using the same local sources.

As clergymen they had a certain protection that Jane didn't have. It had to be the clergy who took the public role and announced what they were doing, since, unlike Jane, they were people with stature and no one thought of them as subversive. Each group continued to operate on two different levels and kept in touch through regular meetings between Miriam and Harris.

The clergy spoke with the moral force of religion. The American Baptist Convention's tradition encouraged individual freedoms in theology, church practice and morality. In an article on abortion that he wrote in 1967, Howard Moody stated: "It is a violation of every Protestant ethical stance to support with civil law any matter of personal morality. . . ." Harris believed in the inviolability of a person's conscience and right to self-determination that extended to abortion.

In a letter to a nun who questioned his position, Harris discussed the theological difference between actual and potential human life: "Certainly the Christian teaching of respect for human life has always been in connection with living human beings and never intended to be concerned with sperm, eggs, fertilized eggs, embryos or early nonviable fetuses . . . As a minister I must consider the human trauma of a live, breathing woman and her interests over against the interests, whatever they might be, of a fertilized ovum . . . There are millions for whom the theological affirmation that 'a fetus is a human being' is not something to which they can give assent. For these people, an abortion . . . is a matter of conscience to be protected by the society in which they live . . ."

The clergy's role was to underscore the moral positions that differed from the Roman Catholic position. "The morality of consequences is what I always pushed," Harris says. "If a position, however well intended, has consequences which are deleterious and destructive, that has to be taken into account. That's what the Catholic Church doesn't get. They have no sensitivity on the issue." The question he poses is: Are women to be regarded as responsible moral agents or not? He explains, "It's an issue of control and that's an issue of morality."

In January Nick, Jenny's contact with Dr. Kaufman, the Cicero doctor, called from California. He hinted darkly that he had had some trouble with the Mob and had to leave town in a hurry. Back in November, Miriam had been shaken when one of the other doctors called her looking for Dr. Kaufman. She thought: Oh no. They're all connected; they're all part of the Mob. When Nick called Jenny he apologized for disappearing with no word. He was interested in resuming their business relationship and could fly in on weekends, if she had work for his crew.

Meanwhile, there was a breakthrough for abortion referral services, including Jane. In 1968 Milan Vuitch, a Washington, D.C., physician who regularly performed abortions at his clinic, was arrested. In November 1969 a circuit court judge dismissed the case against Vuitch. The D.C. statute, under which Vuitch had been arrested, was actually more liberal than other states', since it allowed abortions "necessary for the preservation of the mother's life or health." But the judge struck it down as unconstitutionally vague, which left D.C. with no laws prohibiting abortions. The government announced its intention to appeal the decision, but Vuitch went back to providing abortions, even expanding his practice. By February he was performing a hundred abortions a week. Vuitch charged $300 for an abortion. With an additional several hundred dollars for round-trip airfare from Chicago, his abortions were not significantly more affordable than the ones Jane could arrange in Chicago. Through Jane's contacts in D.C., the group sent some women to Washington who had both the money and the ability to travel.

Calls for abortions from all over the Midwest continued to mount. Sometimes the requests came in the mail:

> Pine St.
> Ann Arbor, Michigan
>
> To Whom It May Concern:
>
> I have been informed by a friend of mine who is a friend of ________ a former member of your group, that you can give me information about obtaining an abortion. I am married and about 1½ months pregnant. My husband and I can *not* afford a baby (he has 2 years left on his degree). We have been married only a month and do not want a baby now.
>
> I would sincerely appreciate any information which you can give us.
>
> Thank you.
> Ann

(At the bottom, in Jenny's scrawl, is a Michigan phone number and a note: *After ten o'clock. 7 weeks.*)

That winter the group decided to hold a public forum on abortion. Like that of the clergy, Jane's work had an educational and political dimension. But the group had a different audience in mind than the one the clergy sought to influence. The tide of women's rising consciousness was everywhere in evidence. The members of Jane wanted to build on that momentum. They wanted people to be aware of not only the need for abortions but that they were available. Abortion had been marginalized by the silence surrounding it. A public event would provide an opportunity for women to talk about their personal experiences with abortion. The forum would make a very public statement that abortion was not a shameful secret that had to be whispered. The shameful part was what women were put through in trying to get an abortion.

Lorraine took on the lion's share of the work, but she could not do it alone. They needed help to put on a major event. They contacted the Chicago Women's Liberation Union, which was in touch with women's liberation projects and consciousness-raising groups throughout the city, and a few other women joined them. Jenny called on two women she knew in NOW who were media savvy to help with publicity. They reserved a Protestant church's community center, the Blue Gargoyle, on Fifty-seventh Street and University Avenue in Hyde Park, the University of Chicago's neighborhood, for the evening of February 26, 1970. As Lorraine remembers, "The churches were very busy in those days. Every group under the sun was meeting in a church basement somewhere. Even the Lutheran Church, which I grew up in (a very conservative church), even the Lutherans in Hyde Park were involved in a lot of political activity."

The ad hoc group planning the event called themselves the Chicago Women's Committee on Abortion. They found people through the women's liberation community willing to speak about their abortions. They named their event a Speak-Out on Abortion.* Lorraine designed the poster: "We used that psychologist's trick: a silhouette that's either two profiles or a vase, depending how you look at it. We printed up millions of copies." The text of the poster said: *Speak-Out on Abortion; For the Right to Control Our Own Bodies, Legalize Abortion.* The planning group announced the speak-out on local radio shows. The University of Chicago's newspaper, *The Maroon*, published an article: "Abortion Seminar to Be Held."

They researched the statistics, the numbers of women admitted to Cook County Hospital for septic abortions, the estimated deaths, and the history of abortion. It was then they discovered that throughout history abortions had been performed by women, midwives and healers—in fact, by everyone but doctors.

When the evening of the speak-out arrived, over five hundred people crammed into the Blue Gargoyle, a turnout the organizers had not expected. Lorraine was the moderator, representing the Chicago Women's Committee on Abortion. She outlined the history and politics of abortion, noting that it wasn't until the latter part of the nineteenth century that abortion had been banned, even by the Catholic Church. Lorraine's opening remarks were brief. This wasn't a lecture, but a chance for women to speak publicly about private personal experiences. Harris Wilson was on the panel. He explained the Clergy Consultation Service's work.

Five women on the podium described their illegal abortions. One, Claire's friend, a member of the Westside Group and the CWLU, had gone to Puerto Rico for hers. Shaking, she read a patronizing letter agonizing over abortion which her boyfriend, who had abandoned her, sent just before the operation. Jenny described her own struggle with the medical authorities to get a legal abortion to underscore the

*The previous year a radical feminist group in New York, Redstockings, had held the first Speak-Out on Abortion.

need for women, not physicians, to control the abortion decision. A few women in the audience offered, unsolicited, their stories of illegal abortions.

To protect themselves, Jane had decided not to announce what they were doing. Claire, who was not aware of that decision, got up and said, "You should know that there's a women's liberation group that can help you get an abortion. Their number is 643–3844." She suggested that people donate money to the group, and several hundred dollars was collected that night. On the platform, Jenny and Lorraine exchanged looks. Jenny thought, Uh-oh, there's probably cops here. But it was too late. Whether or not they planned on keeping the group secret, it wasn't a secret any more.

CHAPTER 7

After Claire announced the existence of Jane at the speak-out, some women who had been at the event were interested in joining. This presented Jane with a new problem. Since these potential new members didn't know anyone in the group, there was no one to vouch for them. The core group—Jenny, Miriam, Lorraine, Karen and Carol—wondered if they should make it a policy to screen all new volunteers. "We had women coming in who wanted to help women but didn't have the same political foundation, were perhaps not as politically conscious, perhaps not in a space where they wanted to do something quite so illegal," Carol recalls. "Then we were caught. What would we do?" Some women had probably not thought through the ramifications of being involved in abortion counseling, the legal liability, the personal liability and responsibility they had to accept. Maybe they assumed that the group sent women out of state or somehow arranged hospital abortions or only used reputable physicians. How would they react when they learned that Jane sent women to underground abortionists? The last thing the group needed to worry about was a member turning them in to the police.

The women who were likely to accept both breaking the law and dealing with underground practitioners were women who wanted to do something tangible with immediate results. That kind of commitment didn't depend upon subscribing to a particular radical political agenda. Certainly Lorraine never defined herself as a radical. The determining factor was a person's willingness to take responsibility and to act responsibly. As Karen notes, "Politics doesn't matter. What matters is action and service. That's how to build a movement."

Even without a political litmus test, integrating new members without jeopardizing the group's security required planning. Miriam suggested that, to protect themselves, they initially keep the details of who did what vague, train each new person as a counselor, and later, over time, as they got to know and trust her, fill her in. Information would be shared only on a need-to-know basis.

The first person to join the group after the speak-out whom no one in the group could vouch for was Cynthia. She was a member of NOW who had been alienated by the radical rhetoric that had permeated the CWLU retreat that fall. It was clear to her that NOW was viewed with disdain by the women's liberation movement.

NOW was part of the branch of the movement that was fighting for women's equality as a civil right. These women's rights advocates sought to achieve that goal through litigation and legislation. Since its main target was discrimination in employment and education, its first national campaign was directed at sex-segregated Help Wanted ads in newspapers, a pervasive practice that reinforced women's limited employment opportunities. NOW, organized by professional women, was structured hierarchically and used traditional civil rights tactics—letter-writing campaigns, lobbying and picketing. Women's rights proponents positioned themselves as the reasonable, credible alternative to the more strident and radical advocates of women's liberation.

Women who identified with women's liberation criticized the women's rights branch of the movement for its limited agenda, an agenda that was geared toward the educated and well-off. Their goal, women's freedom, was not going to be achieved through a civil rights agenda. No amount of litigation would eradicate sexism any more than the 1964 Civil Rights Act had ended racial discrimination or gaining the right to vote had altered women's status. Women had to struggle for their liberation and that required a radical approach, one that went to the root of the problem. The oppression of women was systemic, requiring a massive overhaul of society.

Composed of autonomous groups, the women's liberation movement shunned hierarchical structures as in themselves oppressive. Within the movement there were major disagreements over theory and tactics. But whether they argued that sexism was just one more expression of capitalism's evils, like racism and imperialism, or that the subjugation of women was fundamental, they advocated sweeping changes that could never be accomplished by tinkering with laws.

Acting on their convictions, women's liberation members disrupted the Governor's Commission on Abortion hearings in New York City in February of 1969. The all-male commission scheduled fourteen expert witnesses to testify. Only one was a woman, and she was a nun. As reported in *The New Yorker* magazine, when the first witness began to speak, one of the protesters called out, "Okay, folks. It's time to hear from the real experts." Another shouted, "Where are the women on your panel?" When a reform-minded senator berated the demonstrators, "There are people here who want to do something for you," one of the women responded, "We're tired of being done for! We want to do for a change!" Locked out of the hearing, the women described their illegal abortions to the reporters present. Afterward they decided it was imperative that women break their silence publicly and tell the truth about their illegal abortions. A month later, on March 21, they held the first speak-out on abortion in New York City, a year before Jane's speak-out.

New York Radical Women and Redstockings, two of the earliest women's liberation groups in New York, developed and promoted the concept of consciousness-raising as an organizing tool out of which a new feminist analysis would emerge. Rather than depending on the government, the women's liberation movement was committed to the creation of alternative institutions, such as women's centers, and alternative projects, like Jane, controlled and designed by women to meet women's needs.

But whatever the differences in philosophy and tactics, all the branches of the women's movement agreed that women had to have control of their reproduction in order to be full human beings. The right to an abortion was a fundamental step toward women's equality and working for that didn't require a particular political perspective.

When Cynthia heard about Jane at a NOW meeting, she was gratified that a feminist group was arranging abortions. It seemed exactly the right approach. She went to the speak-out hoping for a chance to sign up. Abortion was important to her, so she was willing to bridge the differences between NOW and women's liberation.

In 1960, when Cynthia was twenty, she had gotten pregnant. Motherhood was the last thing she wanted then, but she had no idea how to get an abortion. Marriage seemed her only option. In those days "nice" girls got married if they got pregnant.

She knew she was supposed to feel fulfilled as a wife and homemaker with a husband who provided for her, but instead she felt depressed and unsatisfied. It wasn't until she read *The Feminine Mystique* that she realized she wasn't unique. Describing the impact the book had on her, she says, "It was like when you found out that other people masturbated and you discovered it wasn't your own secret little strange thing: a matter of relief that I wasn't insane."

By 1968 she had three children and her marriage had become bitter. During the Democratic National Convention a friend invited her to a meeting to start a NOW chapter in Chicago. She was hesitant. She thought NOW was for career women, not for housewives like her, and, at the first meeting, she was the only housewife with small children. The committee she worked on, the Family and Cultural Committee, which was supposed to deal with day care and abortion, was all but inactive. The main thrust of Chicago's newly formed NOW chapter was confronting overt discrimination. NOW picketed

United Airlines headquarters in downtown Chicago to protest a commuter flight to New York that was for men only. They demanded service at exclusively men's sections of major restaurants. When Cynthia heard there was a feminist abortion group she was anxious to join, thinking that, at least in her purview, no other woman would have to bear a child she did not want.

After the speak-out she went to her first meeting of Jane. She was keenly aware that the group was uneasy with new members. They warned her that there were risks involved, both to her and to other women, and she had to act responsibly. She could go to jail for working with them. To Cynthia that seemed unlikely. There were people all over the country violating laws on moral grounds to protest the war or to support civil rights. She could hardly consider herself a criminal for helping someone get an abortion.

To train her as a counselor, Miriam had Cynthia sit in on a few counseling sessions. Then Cynthia was on her own. After counseling a woman, she called Miriam, who made the arrangements with the doctors. Cynthia learned from Miriam how to describe an abortion, but no one in the group told her the specifics, such as the identity of the doctors the group used. She accepted having only limited information. She understood the need for secrecy and trusted these women because they were part of the women's movement.

Nick, Jenny's contact with Dr. Kaufman, flew in from California every weekend. Jenny and Miriam wondered why he, the middleman, had to be in Chicago for the abortions. But, since Dr. Kaufman's abortions were competent and he was willing to negotiate, they did not press Nick. They kept looking for other doctors, following whatever leads they got. At any time Nick and Dr. Kaufman could disappear again as they had in November. Besides, the more options they had, the more leverage they had.

Dr. Kaufman performed abortions either in a woman's own home or in motel rooms. When he used motels women had to pay for the room in addition to the abortion. Jenny arranged the home abortions in a geographic progression from one end of the city to the other. She convinced Nick to schedule several abortions in a row at one motel room, so that the room cost could be shared. However, even when several women used one room, Dr. Kaufman's people tried to collect the full room charge from each of them.

The answering service the group used made them uneasy; sometimes the operators jumbled the messages. Jenny discussed the problem with Nick. If they had a more reliable way for women to contact them, she was sure their business would increase. On one of Nick's weekend flights to Chicago he brought them a telephone answering machine, having convinced his partners that it was a worthwhile investment. In 1970 answering machines were rare. Nobody owned one. The machine Nick brought was a reel-to-reel device, the size of two VCRs, with a beeper for picking up messages. Lorraine and Jenny marveled at it. "It was a pretty splendid thing," Lorraine recalls. "And I kept it in a room practically all by itself."

Answering machines were so unusual that some people who called did not understand that they were talking to a machine. They rambled on, mumbled incoherently and hung up, or left complicated messages about when to call, who to ask for, who not to talk to. In at least one instance, someone left the number of the public pay phone from which she happened to be calling.

The cost of the abortions was a constant problem, since few women, regardless of their economic status, could easily manage $500. Now that the number of abortions they arranged had increased, their loan fund couldn't keep up with the demand. For poor women even a reduced price was impossible, so Jane could help few of them. Sometimes the service had to turn women down for lack of money. Miriam and Jenny pleaded, cajoled, made deals and promises with their contacts: Take this one for less and we'll send you five at full price. At that point Jane was receiving enough requests for help that they could negotiate from a position of strength. Jenny came on strong: You're making more money now than ever before because of the volume we're sending your way. You can take a cut on this one. Miriam and Jenny, in conjunction with whoever was calling women back, most often Carol or Lorraine, decided which doctor to send each woman to. As they planned the week's work Jenny might say, "We sent Dr. X someone for less last week, so we better send him someone who can pay the full amount this week." They decided to ask every woman who could afford $500 for an additional $25 to help pay for women who didn't have the money.

At meetings, the group reviewed the week's activities: how many women had called, where they were referred, and what the feedback was. They talked over particular problems that had arisen during counseling sessions, like a hostile boyfriend or a woman who insisted she wanted an abortion but gave off signals that she was conflicted. One common problem was a mother who dominated her teenage daughter's session. With the mother monopolizing the conversation, it was difficult to find out if the girl wanted the abortion and understood the procedure. In these discussions, Miriam's social work background was invaluable. She could usually offer an approach to diffuse a difficult situation.

Whether the women contacting them were college students, suburban housewives, teenagers or working women, each one's situation was unique. Every week some new problem arose to which the group had to figure out a response. They knew that at any time an undercover cop, posing as someone needing an abortion, could contact them. When Lorraine returned a call to a woman who mentioned she worked for the police, Lorraine was concerned enough to bring it up at a meeting. They knew that even before Jane existed Claire had arranged abortions for family members of policemen. That a woman worked for the police was not enough of a reason to refuse to help her. Miriam checked with her doctor contacts and found one willing to perform an abortion on an employee of the Chicago police; Lorraine agreed to counsel her.

At the counseling session Lorraine warned her, "If you rat on us you'll be ratting on a sister. Then, someday you might need help and we won't be here anymore."

"I won't do that. I'm serious. I promise I won't cause you any problems," the woman pleaded.

Lorraine, still nervous that it might be a setup, drove her to the North side rendezvous with the doctor and home again after the abortion. There were no repercussions. In fact, for months afterward the woman called Lorraine to talk over her personal problems.

When Helen got pregnant in March of 1970 she was unemployed, broke and in an unhealthy relationship she knew she had to end. She had a master's degree in chemistry from the University of Chicago, and, after a stint teaching in Ghana, returned to Chicago to teach nursing students. She had just quit that job when she found out she was pregnant. A friend, a University of Chicago security guard, gave her Jane's number. Her counselor, Lorraine, lived a few blocks from Helen's Hyde Park apartment. When Lorraine began describing contraception options, Helen cut her off. She had an IUD which obviously had failed; she wasn't pregnant because she lacked information. She says, "I'm sure I came across as cold and businesslike because I was upset and depressed about the whole situation." Lorraine asked for an extra $25 to help toward other women's abortion. "If you can spare it, give it to me," she said. "If you give it to the doctor, he'll just pocket it. We'll let you know the date of the abortion. The doctor will call you and tell you where to meet his people."

Helen didn't have $500 but a friend sent her half of it. Someone had lent Helen's friend money for an abortion in Puerto Rico a few years before. Now she saw Helen's need as a chance to pay back one good deed with another. Helen's boyfriend gave her the rest.

Waiting for the counseling session, waiting for the abortion—Helen was consumed by the waiting. She could hardly think of anything else. She knew she might be risking her life, but she didn't feel she had any choice and Lorraine's honest and straightforward manner was reassuring.

Jenny arranged with Nick for Dr. Kaufman to perform Helen's abortion. On April 9, Dr. Kaufman's nurse called Helen: "Do you live alone?"

"Yes," Helen replied.

"Is your building safe? Can we do it in your apartment?"

An hour later the nurse, a hard-faced blond, arrived. She searched every room, opened the closets and even looked under the couch. Helen's dog sensed something strange and started barking.

The two women went into the bedroom. The nurse put a heavy plastic sheet on the bed, instructed Helen to remove her clothes from the waist down and adjusted the sleeping mask on Helen. Then she let the doctor into the apartment; the dog's barking increased. When the doctor came into the bedroom and shut the door, the dog started lunging at it.

The nurse sat next to Helen on the bed and held her hand while the doctor began the abortion. To help her relax, he recited "The Face on the Barroom Floor." Throughout the abortion Helen kept calling to her dog in a futile attempt to quiet her. The incessant barking added to the tension in the room.

The doctor explained that the scraping sound she could hear was the sound a curette makes on a clean uterine wall, an indication that he was almost finished. To Helen it seemed as if the whole room was filled with the hollow scraping sound. Then it was over. The doctor removed the instruments, washed them and left. The nurse took off the blindfold, helped Helen clean up and, then, as quickly as she had come, she was gone.

For the next few days Helen couldn't stop crying, which was disconcerting because what she honestly felt was overwhelming relief. Later she talked to a friend, a biochemical researcher, about her emotional crash. Her friend explained that recent studies indicated that the sudden change in hormonal levels after an abortion or a birth might trigger depression. Even though these biochemical effects were not widely known at the time, Jane had found out about them from their medical contacts and had included a sentence about postabortion "blues" and hormonal changes in their pamphlet. Because they used the pamphlet primarily for outreach, Helen had not seen it and, unfortunately, Lorraine had forgotten to mention it.

Nevertheless, Helen was so impressed with her contact with Jane that she joined the group. When she counseled women she drew on her own experience, preparing them for the emotional changes they might experience after the abortion.

The clergy and women's liberation referral services were challenging the legitimacy of the abortion laws by defying them. Meanwhile, those who were working to change the laws through the courts and state legislatures were having a series of successes. In the fall of 1969 the California Supreme Court exonerated a doctor charged with referring a woman for an abortion. The court found that the right to an abortion followed from the right to privacy in matters of sex, family and marriage. In reaching that judgment they drew upon the Supreme Court's 1965 contraception decision in *Griswold* v. *Connecticut*, in which a right to privacy in these matters had been established. It was a line of reasoning that had been promoted by legal scholars. In terms of legal precedent the decision was momentous. It laid the groundwork for other cases around the country. But, since the court was responding to a case generated before California's 1967 reforms, it did not overturn the new law, which established limited "therapeutic" categories under which an abortion was permissible. And, in practical terms, it had little impact on women in Chicago. California was too far away to be a useful resource for them.

Closer to home, in Wisconsin, Illinois's northern neighbor, a doctor indicted for performing abortions petitioned the federal district court to rule on the constitutionality of the Wisconsin abortion statute. In March of 1970 a panel of judges struck down the restrictive law, stating that, based on the Griswold decision, "a woman's right to refuse to carry an embryo during the early months of pregnancy [the first four months] may not be invaded by the state . . ." Wisconsin immediately appealed the decision and the state's attorney general warned doctors that they would be prosecuted if they performed abortions. The Wisconsin case pointed to the limits of a district court's decision. Based on the court's action abortions should have been readily available, but, because the attorney general announced that the state would not comply with the court's ruling, few doctors were willing to risk the possibility of the criminal prosecution that this statement conveyed. Jenny remembers following up leads on doctors in Wisconsin who were supposedly performing abortions in their offices, but none of them materialized. Eventually the group found one doctor in Wisconsin to whom they were able to send some women, but he was swamped with local patients. In fact, the Wisconsin doctors were not unreasonable in hesitating to act on the district court's finding: a year later the U.S. Supreme Court ruled on Wisconsin's appeal and overturned the district court's decision.

In February of 1970 Hawaii passed an abortion reform bill that legalized abortions performed in a hospital before fetal viability, generally interpreted as 24 weeks of gestation. The bill also included a ninety-day state residency requirement for women. Though an important state reform that helped build momentum nationally, Hawaii's statute had little impact on the lives of women in Chicago.

But in April New York passed a bill that, in less than a year, had an enormous impact. Since 1965, reform bills had been submitted unsuccessfully to the New York legislature. The 1970 bill fell short of outright repeal but was more liberal than any previously passed by a state legislature. It legalized abortions up to 24 weeks of pregnancy when performed by a licensed physician with the consent of the woman. The bill widened the rift between reformers who backed it, and those who argued that anything less than total repeal was a defeat. New Yorkers for Abortion Law Repeal, led by Lucinda Cisler, argued that only complete repeal validated a woman's right to control her body, a necessary step for her liberation. They passed out copies of their ideal abortion law—a blank sheet of paper—and warned that maintaining the government's power to legislate abortion, as the New York law did, would lead to an erosion of that right. As Cisler noted, "The most important thing feminists have done and must keep doing is to insist that the basic reason for repealing abortion laws and making abortions available is JUSTICE: women's right to abortion."

On the April day that the bill was voted on in the New York Assembly, it seemed destined to be defeated by one vote. At the last minute Assemblyman George Michaels, representing a heavily Catholic upstate district, rose and, in a shaking voice, citing his conscience and his family, switched his vote from no to yes, assuring passage of the bill and ending his own political career. Governor Rockefeller signed it into law, effective July 1, 1970.

While New York's new law seemed to be a victory for women, from a women's liberation perspective it was less than that. Any reform, no matter how liberal, was incompatible with repeal because it did not address the root of the problem: the right of women to full control of their destinies. On the other hand New York's law had an enormous psychological impact on women all over the country. If abortion was legal in one state, why should it be illegal in others? Women were coming to believe they had a right to an abortion that they were not going to apologize for demanding.

C H A P T E R 8

On an early spring day Dr. Kaufman and his nurse were performing an abortion that Jane had arranged in a motel in Hyde Park. As he was finishing the abortion, someone started pounding on the door and a man's voice yelled, "Come on out of there, baby killer!"

The woman whispered, alarm in her voice, "Oh no. That's my husband. He promised he'd stay away."

Within seconds the doctor finished the abortion. His nurse helped the woman dress. The pounding on the door grew louder, the man screaming that the people in the room were killing his wife.

For a moment the hallway was quiet. The nurse and the doctor prepared to make a getaway but, as soon as they opened the door, the man pushed his way in shouting, "I'm going to kill you, you baby killer."

The woman ran out the door and down the hall; her husband chased after her. The doctor and nurse took off in the opposite direction. As they walked into the crowded lobby trying to look nonchalant, the husband appeared: "There's the baby killer, I'm going to kill you."

The nurse headed one way, the doctor another, the husband in pursuit, yelling after him. He zigzagged through the parking lot and ran through alleys. When he was sure he had evaded his pursuer, he found a public phone and called Jenny.

Jenny raced out the door to rescue him. The shaking and exhausted man who hopped in her car was Nick, the man she had been negotiating with who called himself Dr. Kaufman's middleman. Before she could say anything, he told her the doctor had escaped separately. But Jenny knew now what she had only previously suspected: Nick and Dr. Kaufman were the same person. But if he insisted on pretending Dr. Kaufman was someone else, she would play along. "It was," she recalls, "a very shallow ruse."

He spent the rest of the day unwinding at Jenny's. She handed him a joint. He hadn't smoked pot in years but he took it. As he smoked he felt more relaxed than he had in a long time. "I was pretty shook up," he recalls, "and it was a relief to be with a pal and talk about it."

Since their first negotiating session almost a year before, Jenny had tried everything she could to build a friendship with him. She called him regularly, sometimes daily, discussing other doctors, problems that had come up, anything she could think of in a conscious attempt to ingratiate herself into his confidence. She even called to congratulate him the day his daughter was born. If she could make him a friend, gain his trust, and turn this business relationship into something more intimate, she might be able to win concessions from him that would be to the group's advantage, and especially to the advantage of the women they served.

As they sat and talked in Jenny's living room, she suggested it might be safer if they used her apartment or the apartments of people she trusted for the abortions. Given the past few hours it seemed worth trying. "And," Jenny offered, "why not stay at my house when you come into town."

It wasn't the last they heard from the irate husband. A week later he left a message for Jane. When Jenny returned his call he said his wife was in the hospital because of the abortion and he wanted his money back or he was going to the police. Contrary to what the husband said, his wife, who was in touch with her counselor, had fully recovered. Jenny arranged to meet the husband the next day on a street corner downtown. She offered him a $250 refund if he signed a statement saying the abortion was done with his full knowledge and consent. He refused. Jenny told him to send her the hospital bill and walked away. That night he called and threatened to come after Jane with a gun if she didn't pay him the full amount. Jenny told him that, if he called them again, she would report him to the state's attorney for extortion. He never bothered them again.

For an illegal group to threaten anyone with prosecution was sheer bravado. But it worked and it taught them an important lesson: Stick to principles and never give in to threats or intimidation.

The "shallow ruse" of the doctor's identity ended a few weeks later when Denise, Nick's nurse, asked Jenny to help with a woman who could not handle the blindfold. Jenny's job was to hold a pillow in front of her face so she couldn't see the doctor.

Jenny watched the abortion, fascinated. In a matter of minutes Nick said, "We're all done."

The woman asked incredulously, "You mean, it's over?"

What impressed Jenny more than the speed with which Nick worked was the atmosphere he created. He had struck up a light conversation with the woman, so that the time and discomfort of the abortion slipped by.

Jenny suggested that Nick let her attend every abortion. Nick recalls, "They wanted to move in right from the start, one of their crew members on the job, an inspector, so to speak, but I said, 'No way.'" But he no longer had a reason to exclude her. She knew who he was. She kept at him and he relented. It was what Jenny had hoped for from the beginning. If someone from Jane was present for every abortion, the group could make sure that women were well treated.

Now when Nick came in on weekends, he stayed with Jenny and her family. Jenny had Nick where she wanted him, under her roof if not quite yet under her thumb. After work he relaxed around Jenny's kitchen table with her husband, Glen, and any friends of Jenny's who happened to stop by, while Jenny paced, smoked cigarettes and chewed her fingernails. They played Ping-Pong and cards. The games were punctuated by Jenny's unending political diatribes. She badgered him about his high fee and berated him with the hard realities that women faced, using as examples the women on whom he performed abortions. He had never considered the consequences for a woman or for an unwanted child. He thought abortions were like mink coats: lots of women wanted them, but not everyone could afford one. For him it was a business, nothing more.

There were unexpected consequences from using apartments for the abortions. Sometimes five women waited together in the living room. When the first woman came out of the bedroom, relieved and no longer pregnant, the tension in the room lessened. If she survived, then, most likely, each of them was going to survive. Whether they were teenagers or older married women, rich or poor, whatever their race, an instant camaraderie developed among them. What they shared was so fundamentally female that, for the time they were together, they transcended their differences and reached out to each other across barriers that normally divided them. Women shared stories of failed birth control and difficult relationships. Older women put their arms around young, scared girls, comforting them.

Jenny did not immediately inform the other members of Nick's identity or that she was sitting in on the abortions. Only Miriam, as the other doctor contact, knew every detail. Jenny never came to a meeting and said, "I'm thinking of doing x, y or z." Instead, she seized the opportunities that circumstance presented. Any changes, whether finding a new doctor, dropping a doctor, or working out of apartments, she and Miriam presented to the group at large as *faits accomplis*. The division of tasks, which they had instituted from the beginning to protect themselves, led to a division of knowledge. That sense of privileged information was further entrenched by their decision to inform new members on a need-to-know basis. There were no complaints. The others were pleased with the changes and the progress the group was making.

By mid-spring 1970 the counseling service was arranging about two dozen abortions a week. As the number of calls they received grew, the administrative position, which they called *Jane*, became more complex. Carol had been handling it almost exclusively since the winter. She took the messages from the answering machine, called women back, assigned counselors, checked back to find out who had been counseled and how much each one could pay. Then, in consultation with Jenny and Miriam, she scheduled women for either the two days Nick worked or for one of the other doctors they used.

The *Jane* duties had become full-time work, work that couldn't be put off until Carol could squeeze it in. If she didn't get it done, women suffered. Unlike many of the other women in the group, Carol didn't have a husband to support her. She was in school and needed to make money, but with Jane's administrative work there was no time. She had to get paid for what she did for the counseling service or she had to quit and find a job. Even though Carol was morally conflicted about taking money from the group, she asked for a salary for *Jane*. She remembers, "Here we were talking about fighting the exploitation of women and then we create this organization that has a wonderful moral thing about everybody giving. The same old shit, a double message. The work was worth something and to expect anybody to do it and not pay them, that was an insult." The group agreed to pay Carol $50 a week, and soon raised it to $100.

As their work expanded, so did the number of women who wanted to join. It was no longer feasible to bring in new members individually at regular meetings. Instead, they decided to hold one large orientation session with both current members and prospective members in attendance. At meetings, on top of the review of the week's events, they figured out what they wanted new members to know. They hoped that the orientation session would weed out those who, on second thought, might not be able to accept what the group did. For women who decided to stick it out, counselor training would continue as before: each new person assigned an established counselor as a Big Sister to train her.

Late in the spring about twenty women, half current members and half new members, attended an evening orientation session. Lorraine handled most of the presentation, describing the necessity for their work and giving a brief history of the group. Lorraine explained how she'd gotten involved and what she had done as the first phone Jane. She explained the group's role with the doctors and with the women. Counseling, the basis of their work, prepared women for the abortion and educated them about their bodies, reproduction and contraception. It also had a political dimension. Counseling for an abortion was a time of crisis in a woman's life, when she was more open to new perspectives. They could use that opportunity as an educable moment to show her how her personal problems connected to a broader social picture and to orient her mind in a different and possibly radical direction. If she questioned society's attitudes about abortion, she might begin to question much more.

Lorraine warned the new women that what they were going to do was illegal and they could go to jail. There was no one outside the group to turn to. They depended on each other and had to trust each other. Lorraine said, "The minute you're involved, you're involved, so if you rat on us you'll be ratting on yourself." The service worked because of the trust they built with women who needed them. If they had one cardinal rule, it was never lie to the women you counsel.

Out of the first new counselor orientation, only a few women decided to get involved. One was Elizabeth, an attractive sandy-haired suburban public high school teacher who had attended the speak-out in February. What had impressed her was that women were actually helping other women get abortions that were safe, even if they weren't officially sanctioned. She was dissatisfied with the women's meetings she had attended: "I didn't want to go to NOW meetings and talk about changing attitudes and policies. I needed to do something to help women where I would get immediate rewards and gratification."

As a practicing Catholic, she was brought up to believe that abortion was murder, but she knew that pregnancy sometimes wrecked people's lives. In high school she read about the suffragettes and later researched the church's position on abortion. She discovered that in 1869 the church's position on abortion had changed.* Before that, the church held that up to the time of quickening, when a pregnant woman felt fetal movement (determined as forty days for a male fetus, eighty days for a female fetus), when the soul entered the body, abortion was not murder but a sin akin to adultery. For eighteen hundred years abortion was no big deal for the Catholic Church, so, Elizabeth thought, don't bother me now.

The fact that what she was going to do was illegal was almost beside the point: "I didn't want to get arrested, but if I thought about that all the time I wouldn't do it, so I didn't think about it."

She arranged to meet the first woman she was counseling on her own at a bench in front of Sears in a suburban shopping center. They had picked neutral turf because Elizabeth lived in an all-white suburb where anyone black attracted attention. She did not want this black woman to feel more uncomfortable than she already did. As Elizabeth was about to leave for the meeting, her son put his arm through the storm door. There was blood everywhere. Her first instinct was to cancel her counseling session and rush him to the hospital. But she had made a commitment, not only to the group but to this woman whose welfare depended on it. Elizabeth convinced her husband to take the boy and she kept her appointment. It was the first time she had not taken total responsibility for her child and the first time she realized she could expect her husband to do his part. Rather than feeling racked with guilt she felt elated.

---

*For an explanation of this change, see Jane Hurst, "Abortion in Good Faith: The History of Abortion in the Catholic Church," *Conscience*, March/April 1991.

Julia, a friend of Cynthia's from the neighborhood, whose children played with Cynthia's, came to the same orientation session. At twenty-nine she was a housewife and mother of four. As soon as she graduated from college at the University of Chicago, she married Herb, who was almost twenty years older than she. Being a housewife and a mother was exactly what she wanted to do.

Julia did not consider herself an activist, although she attended civil rights and antiwar demonstrations, SNCC (Student Nonviolent Coordinating Committee) meetings on campus and political lectures when she could. With four small children, the youngest a baby, she had little free time.

When Cynthia told her about Jane, Julia was immediately interested. She was looking for something useful to do with the two free hours she had each week, and she cared about abortion. A number of her college friends had had abortions. This group sounded like an extension of the kind of support her friends had given each other and she felt that "it seemed to be an issue one could deal with by dint of one's personal energy."

From what Cynthia told her, Julia could counsel one or two women a week at home in the evenings when her husband was at work. She wouldn't need a sitter. It was an issue she cared about, a problem that had a solution. It was not going to interfere with her family life.

On July 1, 1970, New York's new law went into effect. New York City and state health commissioners had proposed guidelines that, if adopted, would restrict abortions to hospitals. As in other states that had reformed abortion laws, hospitals were reluctant to perform them. Howard Moody, founder of the New York Clergy Consultation Service, noted, "A woman can spend days and weeks shoved from hospital to hospital before she finds one willing and able to assist her." Almost no hospital offered abortions past the first trimester, even though the law legalized abortions up to 24 weeks of pregnancy. It took months of arduous work on the part of activists before a variety of freestanding clinics opened in New York City, which brought down the cost for early abortions from several hundred dollars to a little over one hundred. But on the day the law went into effect, some physicians in New York state began performing abortions in their offices. Through their contacts with the clergy and elsewhere, Jane got the names of a few of these.

When a student at the University of Chicago contacted Jane she was referred to one of these doctors. She had suspected she was pregnant but every pregnancy test came back negative, until the last one. By then she was four months pregnant. She knew about the change in New York's law and wanted a legal abortion. Her counselor gave her two options: either travel to England for an induced miscarriage, which required a three-day hospital stay, or try a doctor who had recently opened a practice in Buffalo, New York, and performed late D & Cs. She chose Buffalo.

When she arrived at the doctor's office, his nurse demanded the money in advance and immediately counted it, which gave the whole situation a sleazy, illegitimate feel. The operation was long and tiring, but professional, until the end. Then the doctor held up a bloody plastic bag filled with the fetal pieces for her to see, and said, "Look what you've done."

Back in Chicago the student wrote a letter to Jane about the doctor's insensitivity and suggested that, before they sent anyone else, someone confront him about his attitude. Her experience reiterated something the women in Jane knew: a good abortion, even if legal and performed by a licensed physician, was about more than medical competence.

As Jenny had discovered, Nick's care for the women he was treating was in marked contrast to these stories of medical insensitivity. Jenny brought in Miriam, her counterpart, to work with Nick as well. Although the larger group didn't know it yet, Jenny and Miriam now sat through the abortions that Nick performed, held the women's hands and assisted with other small tasks, such as changing sheets and scrubbing instruments.

On an early summer Saturday a woman from the suburbs was about to leave for Hyde Park for her abortion with Nick when two police officers grabbed her as she got in her car, the address she was going to in her hand. A coworker she had confided in had tipped them off. They told her they knew what she was planning to do, and they were going with her.

Trying not to panic but to think of some way to warn Jane, she said, "I have to check on my son before we leave. He's at my neighbor's. I'll be right back." She ran to her neighbor with her counselor's phone number, "You have to call this woman right now. Tell her that the police are with me."

Her counselor frantically called around until she found someone who knew where Nick was working. She drove over to the address and alerted the workers. Madly they cleaned the apartment, and everyone but the counselor was out the back door in what seemed like seconds. She sat down to wait.

The doorbell rang. It was the woman she had counseled and a man. The man asked about the abortion. She played dumb: "I don't know what you're talking about. You must have the wrong address. There's no abortions happening here." He waved money in her face, demanding the abortion "his wife" was supposed to get that day. She kept repeating that she had no idea what he was talking about when an army of police officers charged up the stairs and in the door. For a few minutes it was chaotic as the police tore the place apart searching for evidence. Finding no sign of what they were looking for, the officers had no choice but to leave empty-handed.

Only two women's quick thinking saved them from certain arrest. If something similar happened again they might not be so lucky. They had to come up with some way to guard against that eventuality.

At a meeting the whole group was filled in on what had happened. They decided to set up a formal gathering place, separate from the apartment they used for the abortions, to act as a buffer. Should the situation be repeated, they might, at least, buy themselves a little time. They called the gathering place the Front and the apartment they used for abortions, the Place.

From then on counselors called women the night before their abortions with the address of the Front and encouraged them to bring someone along for support. Women brought their parents, husbands, boyfriends, friends, and, when child care was a problem, their children. *Jane* called the OOTs, the out-of-towners, directing them to the Front for counseling just prior to their abortions.

At least one, and usually two, counselors spent the day at the Front checking off women's names as they arrived, providing information, offering reassurances and reviewing aftercare instructions. During the day a few women at a time were driven from the Front to the Place and back again after their abortions.

Now for each of the two days a week that Nick worked, Jenny had to find two apartments, a Front and a Place. Few people she trusted were willing to turn their apartments over to an illegal operation even for a day. They also needed people to work at the Front and to drive women back and forth. Any group member could staff the Front, but the driver had contact with the Place and Nick was nervous about being seen. He insisted that it had to be someone of whom he approved. Jenny, in her attempt to gain Nick's trust, was caught between Nick's demands and her loyalty to the group.

Jenny turned to a couple of close friends, Val and Ricky, who had both met Nick while he was staying at Jenny's. He knew them; he approved of them. When Jenny asked Val for the use of her apartment, Val was ambivalent. She thought abortions should be legal, but she had never considered taking matters into her own hands. Raised in a conservative midwestern town, Val's image of illegal abortions was of unsavory people butchering women in dark dirty alleys. Being involved, however tangentially, in what she considered a dangerous medical procedure, frightened her.

Under pressure from her good friend Jenny, Val reluctantly agreed to let the service use her apartment as a Front. Soon Jenny convinced her to drive women from the Front to the Place. Val recalls that "all through my involvement I had to be dragged kicking and screaming by Jenny—to use my house, to drive, all the steps, because of the need." Driving gave her intimate if only brief contact with women whose lives were going to be changed that day. The intensity was unlike anything Val had experienced.

Jenny's other good friend, Ricky, considered herself a Marxist revolutionary and sported, over her close-cropped Afro, a blue Mao cap with a red star. She had close ties to the radical factions of the New Left, specifically the Weathermen. The FBI was investigating her and the Red Squad,* the special police surveillance unit that monitored and harassed anyone suspected of being subversive, was watching her. She was one of the few women of color involved with the Chicago Women's Liberation Union. Most white women she dismissed as liberals, but she recognized abortion as the core right through which all other rights flowed. Abortion dovetailed with her advocacy work for prisoners through the women's prison project, which, like Jane, was part of the CWLU: "I didn't see any difference between working for the rights of women in prison and working for our rights on the outside when we're in this kind of prison."

Nick was socializing with Val and Ricky when he stayed at Jenny's, but they didn't know who he was or what he did. He liked them; Jenny trusted them, so he let Jenny tell them who he was. When Ricky found out that Nick was the doctor, she was a little disconcerted that he was the same person she played cards with and got high with at Jenny's in the evenings.

When Jenny asked to use her apartment, Ricky thought it was an odd request because the Red Squad was watching her Hyde Park apartment house. "There wasn't a tenant in the building the Red

*Kirkpatrick Sales notes that every major city had a Red Squad. By 1969 the Chicago Red Squad had five hundred acknowledged operatives.

Squad didn't have a file on," she recalls, "including one woman with a thousand cats who was a little eccentric and therefore a candidate for the Red Squad."

Jenny was desperate for places, so she took the risk and used Ricky's apartment for the actual abortions. Now that she knew who Nick was, Ricky stayed and helped. She made sure there was orange juice for women after their abortions, changed the sheets and cleaned the instruments. She brought Nick's money to the bank and exchanged the small bills for large ones, so that Nick could fly home with a less obvious wad. She sat with women during their abortions, held their hands, offered head rubs, told them stories, anything she could think of to help them through it.

Out of Nick's insistence on hiding his identity, Jenny had created a secret group, composed of women who were trusted personal friends, women Nick knew and of whom he individually approved. None of them were members of the Abortion Counseling Service. Ricky thought counseling was beneath her. She wanted to be where the action was. Val's ambivalence kept her from joining. Jane's members, who counseled women, made the phone calls and worked at Fronts, did not even know that a secret group existed.

CHAPTER 9

Through the spring and summer of 1970 so many new members had joined that when Karen, one of the original members, returned after her baby was born, she felt she was coming back to a different group and she no longer saw a role for herself. Even before her daughter's birth she was drifting away. The illegality made her nervous and she was never comfortable as a counselor. "I'm a much better organizer than a doer," she notes. She didn't like taking calls during dinner or in the middle of the night from women she counseled. Her husband resented the intrusion on their private life. By the fall she was no longer an active member, but she continued to keep Jane's loan fund money in her safe-deposit box, wheeling her stroller into the bank on a regular basis.

In September Carol, who had, since the winter, diligently handled *Jane*, the administrative work—calling women back, assigning counselors and scheduling their abortions—took a job with the House Democratic staff in Springfield, Illinois's capital. She planned to use her position to get abortion reform passed.

Carol commuted to Chicago on weekends to work with Jane. The service was the first opportunity she had had to use her intellect effectively and she didn't want to give that up. She continued counseling women, but she had to relinquish her administrative duties. By the time she left for Springfield her work had mushroomed. Not only was the group receiving more calls than ever, but now *Jane* had to make sure everyone scheduled for an abortion had the address of the Front. Most often, they didn't know whose place they were using until the night before, so *Jane* had to make at least a dozen calls that evening. Even for full-time work, it was too much.

The obvious solution was to divide the work and have two salaried positions. The new position, *Call-Back Jane,* called the people who had left messages on the answering machine. She passed on their basic information to the administrator, now referred to as *Big Jane,* who assigned counselors, scheduled the abortions, and was the group members' central source for information.

As some of the more experienced and trusted women left the group, new members were finding that working with Jane was having a profound effect on them. Being involved in abortion counseling had become their educable moment. Elizabeth, the Catholic suburban schoolteacher who had joined in July, had always worked in hierarchies, like the high school in which she taught. She took her problems to higher-ups and never considered that the people on her level, the other teachers, should solve them. She had been wary of women, assuming they each had a private agenda. But in the service women were reaching out to other women, working cooperatively to achieve a common goal. She was learning to respect women and trust them.

Jane was completely separate from the rest of her life. No one except her husband knew what she was doing. Nothing had prepared her for it, not her education or her career. She says, "It was outside my ken. I learned I could move outside of all that and function well, and that built self-confidence, self-esteem and a feeling of strength. If I could do that, I could do other things."

Julia, the mother of four, was changing, too. She had never felt like a secondary person, never felt oppressed as a woman. She was too strong and competent for that. She did not personally need women's liberation. During training she had tuned out the discussion about the political underpinnings of the group's work. Her job was to help other women solve this one problem—abortion.

But, when she volunteered her spacious house in Hyde Park as a Front, she began interacting with sometimes twenty people a week. The Front and counseling brought her into contact with women who were overwhelmed by the obstacles in their lives. They had problems no abortion was going to fix. One woman confided, "I have three kids, my husband beats me and I can't even tell him I need an abortion." Without a context for their problems, Julia felt that counseling was a depressing exercise. She thought, There must be a way to understand what's going on in their lives and help them get a handle on it. The more she thought about it, the more she realized that what was wrong with their lives was that they were women. It was her intimate contact with women's experiences, so different from hers, that brought her to feminism: "It wasn't my lack that led me into women's liberation, but other people's lives and how it would press on me. I couldn't do much for them except get them an abortion until I got it hooked into a philosophy." Then she could offer women a feminist perspective which they could use as a tool to understand and improve their lives.

As Julia applied her newfound analysis to the experiences of the women she met through Jane, she began speaking out more at meetings, a voice of reason that cut through extraneous layers of discussion. She was solid and unshakable, qualities that balanced Jenny's intensity and Miriam's soothing indirectness. She was a big dark-haired woman who wore wire-rimmed glasses over her close-set eyes and she laughed easily. The other women in the group relied on her judgment. Miriam and Jenny took note. There were other conscientious members, but they were looking for someone who could take a leadership role. Julia was exactly that kind of person. Miriam started spending free time with Julia. Their children were about the same age, so the kids occupied each other while their mothers talked.

Miriam asked Julia to drive women from the Front to the Place. At the Place Julia met Jenny's friend Ricky. She thought, Why is she never at meetings? It dawned on Julia that there were probably other people intimately involved in the process who never came to meetings. She remembers that "the sense of a secret group on the other side of what was going on was quite strong." Since those women were taking risks that she wasn't, she accepted being kept in the dark.

At meetings she was beginning to understand the group's structure. She had initially thought Lorraine, because she led the orientation, had a central role, but Julia could now see that Lorraine, who had limited herself to counseling women, had little power. Of the twenty women in Jane, everyone seemed more or less on the same level except for Miriam and Jenny, the only people who had direct contact with the doctors. Their special knowledge gave them greater control. An egalitarian group existed, but the real decision makers, Jenny and Miriam, were on another level. These were the women who ran the group.

Julia was one of those women who got pregnant no matter what contraceptives she used, so she was more dismayed than shocked when she realized she was pregnant that fall. She went to her gynecologist to confirm it and said, "I think I'm going to have an abortion. Maybe I'll go to New York."

He responded, "You don't have to go to New York. We've got people in Chicago who will do it. If you're interested, my receptionist will give you the name."

Of course she was interested. When the receptionist gave her Jane's name and number, Julia smiled to herself. She didn't say, "Oh, I work with those people," but she stored that useful bit of information away. If he was sending women to them, he might be willing to provide medical backup.

She was the first counselor in the group to have an abortion through Jane. On a regular work day, while she was blindfolded like any other woman, Nick performed her abortion.

By the fall of 1970 a few freestanding clinics were operating in New York City, providing abortions to women whose pregnancies were

10 weeks lmp or under. Howard Moody of the New York Clergy Consultation Service on Abortion was instrumental in organizing one of these and the Chicago clergy group was sending women there. For about $300, airfare included, women in Chicago could fly to New York, have an abortion and return the same day.

Within a year, as more low-cost clinics opened, the availability of legal abortions in New York would have a dramatic effect on the kinds of women who needed Jane. Already the change in New York's law gave Jenny ammunition in her never-ending argument with Nick over how much he charged. If he continued to demand $500 per abortion, when going to New York only cost $300, he was going to price himself right out of the market. Once women started going to New York, who would be left in Chicago? Poor women, teenagers, women in such difficult straits that they could not leave town even for a day. How was that going to affect his income?

Over games of Ping-Pong and cards the battle raged. She and Nick were friends and he was dependent on Jane. Jenny's group provided him with more business than he had imagined and therefore more money. Jenny harped on him, "Just how many pairs of shoes does your wife need anyway."

"There's the criminal element who disregards the law and the straight people who always regard it," Nick recalls. "But these people were something else. They were radicals." That anyone would commit a crime to get an idea across was a concept he found both shocking and dangerous. Get involved with radicals and the FBI starts chasing you and the next thing you know, you're in jail.

He thought their attitude toward money was even more shocking: "Even in the Bible it says, 'A man is worthy of his labor,' so it was inconceivable to me that anybody'd want to do something for free." Also, he didn't trust anyone. He suspected that, if he lowered his price, they would keep charging the higher amount and pocket the difference. What was to stop them from ripping him off?

Jenny never let up. She was attempting, through the force of her will and the persuasiveness of her arguments, to turn him and bend him to the needs of women. It wasn't his style to argue. He would have preferred to walk away, but with Jenny there was no walking away. It reminded him "of this story about a Polish cardinal under house arrest in a castle and this commissar is brought in from Russia and they talked for ten years. At the end both parties were changed."

His automatic response when she made a demand was, "Fuck that shit."

"You want to go tell the rest of the group what your answer is," she'd answer, her eyes flashing.

"I'm not talking to them. I'm talking to you."

"No, you're not. Twenty other women want to know why you're saying no. What am I supposed to tell them? You think they're all wrong and you're right?"

"I don't care what you tell them. I'm not telling them anything. I'm telling you."

One argument was about money. Jenny had finessed one discount abortion after another and more free abortions than he had bargained for. The first time he agreed to perform an abortion for $25 he knew he had lost the money battle. Late in the fall he lowered his price to $350 per abortion. With $25 added on for Jane's loan fund, the total price was $375. It was still more than what it cost to fly to New York, but it was an improvement over $500.

Jenny and Miriam fought an even fiercer battle with Nick about control or, more precisely, who could be present for the abortions. Jenny and Miriam wanted to bring in women from the group he had never met, but he said, "No way, you're stuck with the job. Nobody else gets to be there." It was a matter of self-protection. He knew what happened: when the heat came down, people talked. He wanted as few people as possible to be able to identify him.

"Who the fuck do you think you are?" Jenny was furious. "There are all these people working together and they are just as entitled and if they want to come . . . . Maybe they have questions to ask you . . ."

He put his foot down: "No way am I going to get involved in that." He had never been part of any group and he wasn't about to start now.

To Jenny and Miriam he said: "It's either these girls or it's not going to happen."

Miriam played good cop to Jenny's bad cop. She massaged Nick's ego. She understood his position. But he had to see their side, too. He was the one putting pressure on them, not the other way around. Jenny had ongoing medical treatments for the Hodgkin's disease that continued to plague her, two small children and other commitments, like her seat on the Chicago Civil Liberties Union board. Miriam and her husband had just adopted a baby. Her family needed her. Ricky was employed now and had only limited time for the service. Val, still ambivalent, was busy, too. It was Nick's demands that were causing unnecessary hardships. They had worked together for over a year. He liked everyone he had met so far. Miriam promised that whoever they proposed would be as responsible and trustworthy as they were. To his arguments, Jenny always raised the specter of the group, the twenty other women backing her. What could he say to that? On his side, there was nobody but him.

He couldn't deny that working with the group was a definite improvement. Jane members handled the administrative details; women came for their abortions prepared. All he had to do was the surgical procedure. He was even taking lunch breaks. Whoever was driving from the Front to the Place picked up sandwiches or Chinese food.

But by far the biggest change in the working environment was having Miriam, Jenny and Jenny's friends sitting with women through their abortions. He understood the fear he saw in women's eyes and it pained him: "Being frightened myself when I go to the dentist I know exactly what they felt—absolute terror." Whoever sat on the bed, he remembers, "talked to them just like family, held their hands, told them stories, and really, just carried them through the whole thing. It made my work easier." As the women having abortions relaxed, their muscles relaxed, and the surgical procedure was easier to perform.

Nick was impressed by the personal touches, birth control information, help with cab fare or child care, and the careful follow-up attention. Teenagers, for whom the abortion may have been their first gynecological experience, were treated with extra tenderness. "It was changing into a much more mellow affair," he recalls. "It was homey with mom there. Miriam was a good mom."

If Nick was feeling positive about the changes, his nurse Denise was not. Too many people knew who he was. It put them at risk. She resented Jenny's growing influence over Nick and worried that the other women were usurping her position and might threaten her financial interests. But Denise went along with the changes. With ten or more abortions a day, she needed the help.

The pressure from Jenny and Miriam wasn't the only pressure Nick was feeling. His wife, in California, was fed up with her husband's weekends in Chicago. What was going on between him and those women? The two of them had other business in California. There were rumors that the money he earned from abortions was a fraction of what he and his wife brought in from their S/M publishing business. He was changing and she didn't like the changes she was seeing. Late in the fall of 1970 they separated; Nick moved back to Chicago.

By then some of the women assisting Nick were doing more than holding women's hands. He taught them how to give an intramuscular shot of Ergotrate, the first step in the abortion. Jenny and Miriam finally convinced Nick to let them bring in a few women from the group to help. The first two were both women Nick had met informally while staying at Jenny's. Since Jenny and Miriam were so adamant about bringing in new women, he agreed to those two because he already knew them and liked them. He would bend a little, but he insisted on control.

CHAPTER 10

Once Jenny and Miriam convinced Nick to let selected Jane members assist him with the abortions, the process began to open. As long as the work area in the apartments they used was shielded from the view of women arriving or leaving, any group member could drive women from the Front to the Place. Jenny and Miriam were inching Nick and the group in the direction they envisioned for their service: full participation and control by Jane members. Even if few women were aware that a secret group existed, members now knew that Jenny and Miriam attended the abortions. At meetings they reported anything unusual they witnessed, like a hemorrhage Nick had managed, in order to expand the entire group's knowledge. No one in the group objected to Miriam and Jenny's new role. In fact, everyone was pleased that someone from Jane was around during the abortions.

Almost every month there were orientations for new members. Out of each session only a few women decided to join. Some established members left the group because they were too busy with other things, or they had lost interest, or they were moving away from Chicago. Since every month one or two new members joined and an equal number left, the size of the group remained fairly constant—twenty to twenty-five members.

When Deborah joined in the fall of 1970 she was in the process of a personal transformation that had begun a few years earlier while she was teaching English in a high school in the northern suburbs. She was the kind of teacher who drew students to her. After school her students came to the apartment she shared with her husband to bake cookies and talk about books. By late 1968 they were talking about more than books. They wanted to discuss the war, racism and the student movement. She wasn't ignorant of these things, but rather, she says, without conscience, it was as if they were happening in some distant place and did not affect her. Her students made her feel the immediacy of the social turmoil around her. They played the counterculture's music for her and they even introduced her to drugs. They opened her eyes to the world outside her comfortable suburban existence.

Her students questioned the grading system in high school and the need for compulsory attendance. They challenged the dominance of the teacher with the big desk in front of the class, deciding what is true and what is false. Once she faced their questions, she began to change. She no longer thought of herself as the authority who had all the answers and her students as the empty vessels she filled with knowledge. Instead, she began to recognize that she and her students were partners in the educational process. She was learning as much from them as they were from her. She no longer wanted total control. By 1970 she and a couple of other similarly minded teachers found themselves under fire. She says, "We could see how that kind of thing develops—letters in your file, complaints, parents on the phone to the principal, other teachers refusing to eat with us in the cafeteria. I began to think about the institution of high school as the students perceive it. I could never be the same kind of teacher again and because of that I was fired."

By the end of the spring of 1970 she was unemployed and had separated from her husband. That summer she experimented with psychedelic drugs. In an altered state she started to think about herself as a woman and about women in general.

She was considering joining the women's movement when, at the end of the summer, she thought she was pregnant. She called a medical student she knew and asked him where to get an abortion. He said, "All the interns at Cook County Hospital say call this number and ask for Jane. She'll take care of you."

Miriam returned her call and the two women spent almost an hour talking on the phone. When Deborah found out she wasn't pregnant she called back to let Jane know she wanted to join the group. "I didn't say to myself, 'Abortion is an issue I can get behind.' I didn't know how to identify something as 'an issue.' I wasn't thinking in those terms then," Deborah recalls. "But I realized, perhaps not consciously, that joining this group would be a way to come to womanness—being a woman and doing for women. I wanted to do something that would make a difference in the world which I had just learned, at the age of twenty-seven, wasn't so good."

The orientation session Deborah attended was held at a church in Deborah's Northside neighborhood of Lincoln Park. The service had not only expanded its operation but had expanded its membership past Hyde Park's borders. Initially Jane had been a neighborhood organization. The first few members lived so close to each other that, Lorraine recalls, "we could almost open the windows and shout at each other across the street." But, over the past six months, a change had been occurring. Women, like Deborah, were joining from all over the metropolitan area.

At the orientation, Miriam, who was leading the session, warned the prospective members, "What we do is not only illegal but dangerous. Someone's uterus could be punctured; someone could hemorrhage from one of the abortions we arrange and we have to deal with the complications ourselves. If you can't handle the responsibility for people's lives you shouldn't be here."

New members sat in on counseling sessions with an experienced counselor to learn those skills. Lorraine explained to each new member she trained that they never asked a woman why she wanted an abortion. That was nobody's business but hers; only she could make that decision. If a woman wanted to talk about it, and some women did, the counselor's job was to listen without judging.

Lorraine began each session by explaining what the counseling service was and what the group's motives were. She asked the woman if she was sure she wanted an abortion. Then she asked, "Can you go to New York?" If the woman couldn't go to New York, Lorraine said, "Maybe we can work something out here in Chicago," and then she described the group's procedures.

The next phase was an explanation of an abortion: "Have you ever had a gynecological exam? This is what your cervix looks like." She drew a picture of a doughnutlike cervix attached to the neck of a pear-shaped uterus. After describing a D & C, Lorraine reviewed the aftercare instructions, including how to take the medications—Ergotrate for bleeding and tetracycline to ward off infection. She ended with a discussion of contraceptive methods and gave each woman a copy of *The Birth Control Handbook*. Lorraine embedded her political message in the information she gave and in her responses to the woman's questions.

At the first regular meeting that Deborah attended, Jenny's den was filled with women passing around pots of coffee and tea. The thrust of the discussion was to rotate responsibilities. Some women had been handling certain jobs for too long and they wanted someone else to do them. One of these was the weekly task of finding group members to work at the Fronts and to drive.

Someone turned to Deborah and said, "What about you?"

Deborah said, "Look, I just got here. I've got to be here awhile before I take anything on."

Miriam stared at Deborah as if to say, "Take it." Deborah picked up what Miriam wanted her to do as clearly as if she'd said it. Deborah thought, Miriam wants me to do it, so she said, "Oh, all right, I'll take it." After the meeting she told her husband, with whom she had reconciled, what had happened. She was stunned that she was being entrusted with so much responsibility so soon.

Since Deborah's new job required calling all the counselors until she filled each week's slots, she talked to everyone in the group regularly. Fairly quickly she knew on whom she could depend. She saw those same people singled out by Miriam and Jenny for more responsibility, just as she had been. She says, "I saw who was good and I saw what happened to people who were good."

Not only did she notice who was selected and who did the selecting, but also who ran the group. At meetings Jenny, in a constant wired state, hung out in the doorway, unable to sit still for more than a few minutes. She chewed the yellow off the end of one pencil after another. Miriam managed the meetings. She and Jenny were in constant eye contact. Deborah could almost see the messages passing silently between them.

Finding members to work at the Front required begging and pleading. Hardly anyone was anxious to spend an exhausting day with a living room full of strangers. With whomever women brought along for company and support, thirty or forty people might be in and out of whatever apartment or house was being used as a Front. Everyone was anxious; everyone was fearful and worried. The person who worked at the Front had to set a tone of reassuring calm while answering the same questions over and over. She counseled women from out of town and took responsibility for their follow-up. Some women returned to the Front after their abortions, cramping severely or sick to their stomachs and needed extra attention. When the person at the Front had a free moment, she packed the post-abortion medications, Ergotrate and tetracycline, into little white boxes. She handed out the donation cards for the loan fund. A day at the Front was never relaxing. Deborah describes the work as "being a stewardess with a radical feminist consciousness."

They hoped the Front would be different from a doctor's waiting room where people felt isolated from each other. They wanted people at the Front to understand that they were active participants, not passive receivers of a service. The loan fund cards explicitly stated that a donation "implicates me along with all others in the Abortion Counseling Service." Sometimes the person working at the Front asked people waiting to pack the boxes of aftercare medications. It was another subtle message that this was a joint venture: We're not doing something to you, but with you.

The language they used underscored that message. Women coming for abortions came "through" the service, not to it—a process, not a place. They were never referred to as patients or clients. If they were called anything it was counselees. Jenny thought that "patient" was a medical term implying subject and object: "We didn't think of the women coming through the service as objects we were going to work on. We always thought of them as partners in a political activity—partners in crime, to be exact."

The people who came to Fronts were a diverse group. There were kids of fifteen and women in their forties. Well-heeled suburbanites mixed with poor and working-class women. It was as if a demographer had taken a cross-section of Chicago-area women and thrown them together in a room.

It wasn't easy dealing with the people who stayed at the Front while their loved one went off with strangers. It was clear from their faces that they feared they might never see that person again. No matter how upset and worried they were, the counselor had to remain calm yet sympathetic. She had to maintain an air of competence, no matter how frazzled she felt.

Inevitably, at least once a day, when the driver returned to the Front with four women who had had their abortions, someone would ask in a panicky voice, "Where's my wife/friend/daughter? She left with this group but she didn't come back with them." As reassuringly as possible, the driver answered, "Don't worry. Nothing's wrong. She was just getting started when I left. I'll pick her up with the next bunch."

The driver ran errands. She picked up lunch or went to the drugstore for more sanitary pads or other last-minute items. She took bags full of small bills to the bank to exchange them for hundreds. Changing money made some women nervous. They thought they had "guilty of something" written all over them but, to their amazement, the tellers never reacted.

Whatever worries they had about someone new blowing the group's cover had so far proved unfounded. As Miriam suspected, potential members simply bowed out if they didn't want to take the risks and the responsibility. The group was unprepared for the one act they felt was a betrayal. In November a journalist, who had briefly been a member, wrote an article for a local alternative newspaper based on her experiences in Jane. The article sent a chill through the group. The author had counseled women and worked at Fronts; she knew how important their work was, yet she had exposed the group for the sake of a good story.

Miriam and Julia, the mother of four who had been singled out by Miriam and Jenny as a potential leader, spent more of their free time together, drinking coffee around Julia's kitchen table. One afternoon Miriam casually mentioned that Nick, their doctor, was not a licensed physician. Julia was not surprised or shocked. It had been her experience in college that the people who performed abortions were not physicians, no matter what they called themselves, so she had assumed the same was true of the men Jane used.

Jenny and Miriam were in the habit of bouncing ideas off a few trusted members before raising them at a meeting. It was a way they could gauge what the group's reaction might be, but it also built support for an issue they were concerned about mentioning. If some people knew before it was raised publicly at a meeting, then they had allies who had already thought it through and could help temper the group's response.

Miriam and Jenny knew about Nick. Other members either knew or suspected. A few of the women who had met him thought he was too slick, too much of an operator, to be an M.D., but most of the members assumed that if they called him a doctor, he must be one.

Nick had learned his trade from a doctor to whom his brother had apprenticed him. After Nick had been assisting the doctor with abortions for a while, Nick's brother paid the doctor to teach Nick this skill. Since then Nick had been the technician in a profit-making venture composed of his brother and his brother's girlfriend, Denise, who posed as the nurse. Nick only got a cut of the money which Denise collected and turned over to Nick's brother.

Even though they still occasionally referred women to other abortionists, Jane relied on Nick to perform the majority of the abortions they arranged. With no one else did they have such a close relationship. Jenny and Miriam decided the group had to be told that Nick wasn't a doctor. It was crucial information everyone needed. They knew some people might be upset and angry, but they believed their positive experiences with Nick over the past year and a half would amply balance the negative reaction.

When Miriam told Nick she was going to tell the group, he said, "Look, if you do that, I'm leaving and never coming back." He did not want twenty or thirty women knowing that much about him. There was a mystique he had as "the doctor" that strengthened his credibility and kept him at a distance. What leverage would he have as some ordinary man with a skill they needed?

Jenny countered, "These women are committing a crime, working their asses off and risking their freedom. How can you keep them in the dark? They have a right."

Miriam could not be dissuaded: "The group has to know and I'm telling them."

"If you do that, I'm gone."

They did not yell and scream at him, but they deluged him with logical, well-thought-out arguments that wore down his resistance. Through his work with Jane he was extricating himself from his brother's control and he relished his growing independence. Over the past year he had developed a satisfying and even pleasant working relationship with Jane. He had something to gain by staying, so Jenny and Miriam were able to convince him not to leave.

At a meeting in December Jenny announced that Nick was not a doctor. The room exploded. One of the suburban schoolteachers, with tears in her eyes, accused Jenny and Miriam of months of deliberate lying. Because of them she had broken their golden rule: Never lie to women. How could they put her in that position? Where was the trust on which their work was based? Miriam did her best to explain the battle they had had with Nick.

Another woman said, "This discredits everything we've done. We're deceiving people. We've got to disband the service."

Jenny sat through the uproar, increasingly annoyed with every comment. The last one pushed her over the edge, "How naive can you be? Did you think any doctor would work with us this closely? A disservice to women? Women are getting better abortions through us than they get anywhere in the city."

There was no disagreement about their satisfaction with Nick's work. He was both competent and caring. Obviously someone who was performing between ten and twenty abortions a day was more skilled than a doctor who performed only a few abortions a year. The feedback from the doctors that the women went to for post-abortion checkups was always positive. All the indicators told them that he knew what he was doing and probably knew more about abortion than most physicians.

They scheduled another meeting to give everyone a chance to absorb this news. At that meeting they would take up a bigger question: what to tell the women they counseled.

In the midst of the commotion, Deborah commented, "Well, if he can do it and he's not a doctor, then we can do it, too."

She noticed a small smile on Jenny's face. Neither she nor anyone else in the room except Miriam knew that Jenny had taken that step. Nick was teaching her to perform abortions.

CHAPTER 11

At the next meeting the turnout was smaller. The women who did not show up never returned to the group. No one remembers exactly how many women left: Jenny estimates it was a handful, while Deborah thinks it was almost half the group. But, based on the comments made at the previous meeting, the remaining members assumed that those women had decided they could not work with Jane if the abortionists the group used were not doctors. Other members responded like Cynthia: "I felt uncomfortable with it and I had to do some regrouping, but he was obviously competent. We'd had glowing reports from doctors' post-abortion checkups." For some members it was no problem. Even if they hadn't known for sure that Nick was not a doctor, it was what they had suspected or assumed and, since he was competent, they didn't care whether or not he had a medical degree. Regardless of how each member came to terms with the news, those who decided to stay were faced with another problem: what to tell the women they counseled.

A few women wanted to keep referring to the person who performed the abortions as "the doctor" when they counseled women. They thought women seeking abortions would feel safer believing he was a physician. That position provoked a heated response. To assume that the women they counseled had to be protected from the truth was disrespectful. They had a right to know: their lives were at stake. Besides, their service was built on trust and lying definitely violated that trust. Finally one counselor said, "I'm telling. That's it. What are you going to do about it?"

Miriam proposed a compromise. Counselors did not have to volunteer the information. If a woman asked, "Is he a doctor?" the answer always had to be "No," but, if the question wasn't asked, counselors weren't obligated to bring it up. It was a way to sidestep a truth that made some of them uncomfortable. There were a few women who could accept that Nick was not a doctor but could not accept that group members were going to tell women that; they decided to sever their ties with Jane.

The idea that someone other than a doctor could capably perform abortions had been suggested much earlier at a meeting in 1969, the first year that Jane existed. During one more discussion of the high cost of abortions and the frustration of dealing with the doctors, one of the members, a biochemist, said, "We should just learn to do them ourselves." Jenny and everyone else at the meeting was shocked. At that stage, they all believed that an abortion was a complicated medical procedure. But the next year, as Jenny sat with women and watched their abortions, that suggestion didn't seem so preposterous. She thought, This doesn't look so difficult. We could learn to do them and charge a whole lot less. But, at that point, that thought was nothing more than an abstract idea.

Then, on a day when Nick was working at an apartment near Jenny's, a woman who needed help came to Jenny's door. She was in the process of a miscarriage that had been induced by one of the group's doctors and was now in the late stages of labor. Jenny took her to Nick. He said, "We can help this one along."

The woman was in hard labor as Jenny helped position her on the bed. Nick reached into her uterus with small sponge forceps and began to pull. He turned to Jenny and said, "Here, you hold on to the forceps."

Jenny resisted, "No, I don't want to touch anything."

"Just try and see how much strength it takes," Nick insisted.

"No, I don't want to be a technician." She didn't want that kind of responsibility. She hadn't planned on being that involved.

But Nick kept insisting and Jenny relented. She put her hands over Nick's on the forceps and together they pulled until the woman miscarried. It took more strength than Jenny had imagined.

For Jenny that experience broke the taboo surrounding the instruments. She realized she could handle these smooth steel surgical tools. What had been a vague idea became persistent: We can learn to do this and we can charge a whole lot less.

Nick was willing to teach Jenny what he knew. The more she did, the less he had to do. She became Nick's apprentice. How Nick justified this to Denise, Jenny never knew. Jenny watched him intently and listened carefully to his explanations, following his instructions. Whenever she handled the instruments, he hovered next to her, ready to step in if she had a problem. Nick explained to the women whose abortions he performed that he was training Jenny. He was so skilled at establishing rapport with them that they were comfortable with Jenny learning.

Jenny learned to give an intramuscular shot of Ergotrate to prevent excessive bleeding, the first step in the abortion. Next, she inserted a speculum in the vagina to expose the cervix, the muscle at the neck of the uterus. Then she swabbed the vagina and cervix with Betadine, an antiseptic. Around the cervix she injected an anesthetic, Xylocaine, with a long needle that had a short bent point. Before any instruments could be introduced into the uterus, the cervical opening had to be stretched with a dilator.

Occasionally at meetings, over the next six months, as the group railed against the doctors they were using, Jenny would interject, "We should just learn to do them ourselves. Then we wouldn't be dependent on anyone else and we wouldn't have to charge so damn much."

No one took her seriously. Lorraine, or some other practical-minded member, would turn to her and say, "Are you kidding? We can barely do the piece we're already doing."

In the evenings, as her closest friends sat around Jenny's kitchen table, Jenny paced, a cigarette in her hand, words tumbling out of her. It was about control, women controlling abortions. That was the root of the problem. To be truly independent, women had to get the knowledge and skill to do abortions. If they had that, then they'd transform this service into the ultimate feminist project. Her friends listened to Jenny's ravings and thought the whole idea was wild.

Jenny was an arrow following her own trajectory. She had a kind of recklessness that was, at least partially, a reaction to her ongoing battle with Hodgkin's disease. For Jenny time was finite: she didn't know how much of it she had left. Leaning against the door frame to her den after a meeting, Jenny confided in Deborah that she was worried she would die or go crazy before she accomplished what she had to.

Before the group could accept that she and, by extension, they, could capably perform abortions, they had to accept that Nick, a man they knew was competent, was not a physician. When, after Jenny revealed Nick's status to the group, Deborah spontaneously made the connection and said, "If he can do it and he's not a doctor, then we can do it, too," Jenny's irritation with the other women's comments faded and she allowed herself a small triumphant smile. For Jenny it was the group's critical moment, the turning point.

Along with the surgical procedure, Nick was sharing other practical skills with Jenny. She accompanied him when he bought equipment at selected medical supply companies. He taught her the correct language to use when purchasing the curettes, forceps and dilators. The medications originally came from a doctor friend of his but, with the number of abortions he performed for the group increasing to thirty or more a week, his current source could not supply the quantities of tetracycline and Ergotrate they needed.

Jenny circumspectly approached a pharmacist she had heard might be sympathetic and explained what she needed. He agreed to supply the drugs on condition that she soak the labels off the bottles so they could not be traced back to him. Jenny bought boxes of syringes, huge bottles of tetracycline capsules, Ergotrate in both pill and liquid form, and the anesthetic Xylocaine.

By the end of January 1971 Nick no longer brought his "nurse" Denise with him. He decided it was just as easy to pay Denise for not coming, but he told Jenny that Denise had left town.

Nick still performed abortions on his own, independent of the group, and, instead of Denise, he took Jenny on these "house calls." His private cases were mostly married couples, Polish immigrants, referred to him by a Polish doctor friend.

Jenny remembers those families as hardworking, practical people who didn't want the church or their relatives to know what they were doing. When she and Nick arrived at their neat little bungalows, Jenny went in first. She checked the lace-covered dresser for an envelope with the money in it and looked around to make sure they weren't walking into a trap.

Whether Nick's willingness to train Jenny stemmed from his pride in his skill and his pride in his teaching abilities, or was a result of his growing affection for her, once she realized she could learn what he knew, she became insistent. Her behavior toward Nick altered. During the summer, even while fighting with him about money, Jenny had been flirtatious and deferential. By the winter she was taking control. "Why should you have all the knowledge? Teach us," she demanded.

By 1970 abortion reform had been debated by more than half the state legislatures, with twelve states enacting modest, therapeutic reforms. In 1970 Hawaii, New York, Alaska and Washington legalized abortion, with various restrictions. In New York City by 1971 there were freestanding low-cost clinics that served women from all over the country in the early stages of pregnancy. In Chicago the *Call-Back Janes,* who returned Jane's messages, referred any woman who could travel to those clinics. Then, on January 29, 1971, the U.S. District Court for Northern Illinois overturned Illinois's restrictive statute on the grounds that it was unconstitutionally vague, and issued an injunction against enforcing the state's law. Jane members weren't sure how to react to the ruling. It might mean the end of their service. Jenny felt that the judicial and medical communities in Illinois were too conservative and would resist implementing the decision. The group decided to keep operating, act as if nothing had happened, and see what the future brought. The Cook County state's attorney immediately appealed the injunction to the Supreme Court and, on February 10, Justice Thurgood Marshall issued a stay. For less than two weeks abortions had been legal in Illinois.

In 1969 and 1970 many national organizations, including the American Public Health Association, Planned Parenthood and the board of trustees of the American Medical Association, as well as religious organizations, such as the board of managers of Church Women United, all supported repeal. All over the country women, clergymen and physicians were speaking out in favor of legalizing abortion. Women's liberation groups organized forums and demonstrations, and provided information and referrals to women needing abortions. The message of the women's movement resonated with a growing number of women who joined consciousness-raising groups and action-oriented projects. Speakers on women's liberation topics were in demand by student and community groups. In Chicago, the Women's Liberation Union organized a speakers bureau. The CWLU usually contacted Jane to provide speakers on abortion.

Jenny was one of the few women in the group with public speaking experience, but her vocal cords had been damaged by radiation treatments. Using her voice for extended periods of time was painful. She encouraged other members to make the presentations or, if they were reluctant, to share the speaking duties with her. Including women who were inexperienced offered another kind of apprenticeship and expanded the pool of competent speakers. Carol remembers being on a few radio talk shows: "Jenny would sort of drag me along.

That's how people develop confidence. If someone drags them along they start thinking, Oh, I can do this; in fact, I might have skill in this area."

Jenny and Miriam were always on the lookout for promising women to whom they could pass on more responsibility. They were both feeling burdened by their leadership roles. They viewed Deborah and Julia as the most promising candidates to share their leadership and succeed them. Miriam noted Deborah's competence and liked her style; Julia's leadership abilities were evident at every meeting. While Julia and Miriam spent more free time together, Jenny befriended Deborah. After a meeting she asked Deborah to socialize with her and with her friends Val and Ricky, who were part of the secret group that assisted Nick. She casually mentioned to Deborah that they helped during the abortions. It was only then that Deborah discovered that women she didn't know were directly involved in the abortions.

Julia and Deborah had noticed each other early on at meetings and had begun a friendship. They talked about the secrecy in the group, the unacknowledged leadership and the skewed power they were both beginning to recognize. Deborah was particularly sensitive to issues of power. She and two other teachers were in the middle of eight months of reinstatement hearings in her former school district from which they had been fired for their unorthodox teaching methods. The hearings' weekly sessions drew hundreds of parents and students. As the sessions dragged on, the three teachers realized that their chances of being rehired were slim, since the same people who had fired them were presiding over the hearings. It was a lesson in the politics of power. While the hearings unfolded, Deborah was confronting the politics of power in a very different setting. Instead of the school board and administration in control, it was Miriam and Jenny.

In January, Jenny went on a much needed vacation. When she returned it seemed to her that Nick had been backsliding. Out of his own paranoia, he had limited involvement in the abortions to a few people he was close to and trusted. That was not the direction Jenny intended.

Jenny and Miriam discussed what to do. They were in the habit of planning strategy together. Their personalities were opposites. Jenny, blunt and straightforward, had no tolerance for emotional or interpersonal dynamics. Miriam never said anything directly. She paid attention to the ways that people related and often found herself in the caretaker role, explaining Jenny to the rest of the group. Because their styles and personalities differed, they influenced different members. Before meetings they discussed who should raise what issues in order to achieve consensus, to keep the level of dissension to a minimum. They were certain the work would suffer or the group could be torn apart if divisions emerged or meetings degenerated into political arguments.

Miriam and Jenny decided that only women who were members of Jane, that is, women who counseled and attended meetings, could assist on work days. A few women who worked with Nick were already members. Ricky was not interested in counseling, but Val ended her wavering and joined the counseling service. Jenny and Miriam pressured Nick to accept more women from the group. With each new person they had to overcome Nick's resistance.

At the end of a day when Julia was driving women from the Front to the Place, she was invited into the kitchen to meet Nick. Whether Nick was going to check her out and give his approval or whether Jenny and Miriam had said, "We're bringing her in, so you might as well meet her," Julia never knew, but after that she was asked to assist with the abortions. "I wasn't anxious to do it," she remembers. "I kind of was resistant to take the time away from my family. All I know is that someone thought I was trustworthy enough to bring in. It wasn't because I pushed."

At first she only held women's hands during their abortions. She learned what to do by watching Miriam, whose task was to be as reassuring as possible as she explained each step in the procedure.

Through every abortion Nick engaged the woman in lighthearted banter, asking about her family, work or school, using his charm to put her at ease. Julia felt that her interactions with women were secondary to his.

Even the lowered price of $350 for an abortion was a problem for many women who called Jane. Julia counseled a woman early in her pregnancy who had only $100. They spent part of the counseling session talking about where she could get the rest. Julia said, "You have lots of time. Why don't we postpone your appointment and that will give you a chance to borrow the money from your sister-in-law." The following week the woman called Julia to say she had another $100 and explained that she had been turning tricks to get it. Julia was appalled. At the next meeting she said, "If people have to turn to prostitution to get an abortion something is wrong here."

On the other hand there were women who claimed they could afford only $50 but came to counseling sessions in fur coats. When confronted with someone like that, counselors felt, Why should we say yes to her when she's wearing her money on her back. Other women have to go without. They've tapped every source they could, used their rent money, or, like Julia's counselee, prostituted themselves to pay for their abortions.

As long as the group had to depend on abortionists, money would be a major issue. Nick might be willing to loosen his control. Control wasn't as important to him as money, and he wasn't giving that up. Jenny had made her bargain with him, but she never stopped pressuring him for more financial concessions—one at reduced charge, another for free.

The calls to Jane for help continued to increase, indicating that their phone number was becoming known throughout the city. To meet the demand Jenny and whoever was *Big Jane* scheduled more abortions per day. In a year the number of abortions Nick was expected to perform on each of the Fridays and Saturdays he worked with the group grew from a handful to twenty. He complained that it was too much work, but Jenny knew that, with his speed and skill, he could handle it. An uncomplicated abortion performed in the first ten weeks of gestation took him under fifteen minutes. She organized the workplace to maximize efficiency without affecting quality or support. Using apartments with at least two bedrooms, he could perform an abortion in one while, in the other, trained women from the group were beginning another. All he had to do was complete one and go to the next. He says, "Everything worked smooth. There was a big cast behind me. You can't have it that smooth with just a few people. This person did this job and that person did that job. And at the end of the day, it was satisfying." He was part of a team working together toward the same goal. He had come to see that "it's a lot easier to work with twenty people on a project than to do it all yourself."

It hadn't been his habit to explain the procedure to women during their abortions. That was something that Jenny and the others added. From personal experience they knew that a woman's comfort level was directly related to the control she felt she had. That sense of control came from understanding what was happening, so they explained in detail each step as the abortion progressed. It was obvious to Nick that the women whose abortions he performed were less frightened now than they had been when he was working on his own. He watched as the process changed and evolved.

Jenny constantly questioned him about why he did certain things the way he did. He always answered, "I don't know why. That's how it's always been."

She'd say, "Well, can't we change it?"

His natural reaction to change was resistance. He'd begin to think about Jenny's suggestion and, before he had a chance to say anything, Jenny instituted the changes. He had to admit that whatever Jenny proposed always proved to be for the best.

Over the past year the group's function had changed. They were no longer just counseling women and referring them to competent practitioners. They were directly involved. They arranged the places for abortions, were present for them, and, increasingly, handled more of the medical work. They were responsible for these abortions. The separation between the group and the abortionist faded. They had evolved from a counseling organization to an abortion service. To the outside world they were still known as Jane, but, reflecting that change, internally they referred to themselves as, simply, the service.

Sometime late in the winter of 1971, the group rented an apartment in Hyde Park to use for abortions. Finding apartments to borrow was always difficult. Not only were few people willing to lend the group their homes for an illegal activity that could land them in serious trouble, but, even for those who were willing, the results could be disconcerting. Coming home after the service had used their apartment, the residents might find towels and clothing missing. A shirt had been pulled out of a closet for a woman who had blood on hers. As for the towels, the women working had every intention of cleaning and returning them, but intention did not always translate into action.

Jenny asked her friend Val to rent the apartment under an assumed name. Val had never done anything like that before and she found it personally radicalizing: "I was basically a law-abiding citizen with a fairly strong belief in the rule of law. It gave me a new image of myself, not only doing something that was against the law, but, more important, being part of a group of people taking matters into their own hands because the law was not meeting their needs." Using the name Gwen Bartman, Val rented an apartment at 5120 Hyde Park Boulevard.

Even with their own apartment, for security reasons, they used private homes when they could find them. The more they moved around, the less likely it was for some nosy neighbor to notice the constant traffic in and out. Having their own apartment assured that, in a pinch, they always had a place empty and available.

CHAPTER 12

Through the winter of 1970–71, one or two new members joined from each monthly orientation session. Some of these women had had abortions through the group, some were friends of service members. Others initially contacted Jane for someone else.

When Kris joined Jane that winter she and her husband, Bill, were teaching at an alternative Catholic high school for girls on Chicago's West Side. Its mission was to give kids living in poverty a chance at a better life. Her students' academic careers were continually on the verge of being overwhelmed by unstable home lives, abuse and teen marriages. Many of their problems were so complex that there wasn't much Kris could do about them. When one of her students confided in her that she needed an abortion, Kris thought, this is a problem I can handle. She called around and eventually found Jane's phone number. "I was terrified to make the call," she remembers. "My palms were sweating because I thought I was getting involved in the underworld. And then this very normal person with the most pleasant voice called me back and said, 'Yes, we do this, but your friend will have to call us herself.' "

After her abortion, the student called Kris with a temperature of 102. Kris thought, Oh shit, she's going to tell and the school will go down the tubes. Kris got in touch with Jane, who sent antibiotics that cured the infection. By then Kris had had a series of phone calls with the mysterious Jane. During one of them Jane said, "We're looking for counselors. Are you interested?"

Kris thought for a moment and said, "Sure." Her contact with Jane had been reassuring. The woman she had talked to seemed decent and this was a service her students needed. "She wasn't the only student that had gotten pregnant in the course of the few months I'd been there," Kris recalls, "so I wanted to know more about it, if I had to do it again. These students had fewer choices than anybody and, if they got saddled with kids real early, it seemed like their lives were over. It felt to me that by doing this one little thing you could change a woman's life. You didn't have to change her values or walk her through any kind of experience. All you had to do was give her a choice."

Kris had grown up in a small town in Indiana where girls either got married and had babies or went to college. With her long blond hair she had been the perfect cheerleader and prom queen. "I had no intellectual tradition and certainly no moral tradition that I was aware of," she says.

In 1966 she entered college at the University of Indiana in Bloomington and fell in love with Bill, an engineering student. She was not involved in student politics until her junior year when her activist roommate took her to a demonstration that shut down the university. Suddenly Kris was protesting all the time: "We sat in on Dow Chemical* and people got beaten up by the police."

By 1968, as Kris planned her wedding, the protests on campus had escalated to bombings. When she graduated, she and Bill moved to Chicago. She saw teaching as a way to channel her newfound anger at injustice in a positive direction.

Kris had never attended a political meeting that wasn't dominated by men, so her first Jane counselor training session was disorienting.

*When Dow recruited on campuses, it was a target for student protest because Dow manufactured napalm, which was used extensively in Vietnam. Napalm, a flammable jelly that clings to skin and vegetation, was dropped from airplanes, burning everything in its path.

"One thing," she recalls, "that was weird about it was that there weren't any men around. Nobody asked about them. Nobody said, 'Do you live with somebody,' or, 'What's he like.' It was so odd to be in a group of women where men were not an issue at all. That absence, it was like silence after a lot of noise and that really intrigued me."

Her biggest concern was that counseling women for abortions would affect the school adversely. She worried that if she got arrested for working with the service the diocese would stop supporting the school, forcing it to close.

Soon after she joined, a woman she knew in Bloomington came to Chicago for an abortion. She told Kris that one of the radical student leaders had gotten her pregnant and abandoned her, saying, "I don't care if it is my baby. It's just not my responsibility." For the first time, Kris felt a tremendous anger at the privilege that men had to do what they wanted and just walk away.

Kris didn't consider herself a feminist; the women in the service were the first feminists she had met. "I am a situation ethics person. I don't think ideologically," she says. "At that point I was not passionately attached to the women in the group, but I was passionately attached to the feeling of doing something on my own."

The women in the service furnished the apartment they had rented with an assortment of odds and ends purchased from secondhand stores or donated by members and friends. Posters, designed and produced by the Women's Graphics Collective, another work group of the Chicago Women's Liberation Union, decorated the walls. In one, an abstract flower design surrounded the message: "Sisterhood Is Blooming. Springtime Will Never Be the Same." A tacky bamboo bar stood in the corner of the living room. Each of the two bedrooms had a mattress on a box spring on the floor, covered with an India print bedspread. Their one extravagance was the brightly patterned sheet sets they bought at Marshall Field's basement.

On work days, Fridays and Saturdays, the crew met at the apartment early. They boiled the instruments, filled syringes, made the beds with fresh linen and covered them with heavy plastic sheets before the first group of women arrived from the Front.

Through the winter and spring Nick taught Jenny the practice of abortion. Sometimes Nick had no interest in, nor patience for, teaching, but at other times he seemed almost driven and Jenny had to seize those moments. During an abortion he would hand her a curette and say, "Here, you scrape around and check if it's clean." At first Jenny handled the instruments gingerly, afraid she would injure someone or cause pain, but Nick ordered, "Harder, pull toward you. You can't be afraid to use your muscles; you can't be so afraid to cause pain that you don't do the job right." If a woman was bleeding abnormally but not dangerously, Nick handed Jenny the forceps: "There must be a piece of placenta still in there. Get it out, will you?" He watched while Jenny proceeded, making it clear he was not going to step in until she had at least tried.

Bit by bit, Jenny learned to perform an abortion. Nick never left her side, directing her, ready to take over if she had problems. She was both thrilled and terrified, torn with conflicting emotions. Relying on Nick to perform the abortions was comfortable. He took the direct risks; she and the other women felt shielded by their roles as counselors and assistants. But she knew that if Jane was ever going to be independent, she and the others had to learn and they could learn only by doing.

Giving an intramuscular shot and inserting a speculum were hardly invasive procedures, but dilating (the D of a D & C) the tight muscle of the cervix was. Jenny injected the anesthetic Xylocaine around the cervix to dull the cramping sensation dilation produced. After assessing the cervical canal's direction with a sound, a soft metal rod that she balanced delicately between two fingers as if holding a drumstick, she placed the dilator into the cervical opening, the os, and slowly stretched it so that instruments could be inserted into the uterus. It required attentiveness and caution.

After dilation she reached into the uterus with small sponge forceps and removed the fetus and placenta piece by piece. She could not see what she was doing. She had to do it by feel, from her hand through the instruments inside the woman, her other hand on the woman's abdomen. She had to visualize what she was feeling. She had to be sure nothing was left in the uterus that could later cause bleeding or an infection. When she had removed everything she could, she used a hollow, spoon-shaped curette (the C of D & C) to scrape clean the ridged walls of the uterus. Using forceps and curettes, she repeated the process. When the uterine wall was clean and the abortion completed, the curette scraping on the wall made the same sound as a thumb scraped along the roof of the mouth.

With his years of experience Nick completed an abortion much quicker than Jenny. The faster the abortion was done, the sooner instruments were removed from the uterus, the less chance of problems during or afterward. With practice, Jenny's speed increased. As they worked together their respect for each other deepened. They shared something that set them apart, something society deemed unacceptable for either of them to do. They were outlaws together.

Following behind Jenny in the training process were Pam and Julia. It was Jenny who had asked Pam to join the group early in 1970. They had met when Pam was a graduate student working on the conspiracy trial of the Chicago 8. She was a shorter, blond version of Jenny. She was single and her time was her own. Pam and Julia were trained by both Jenny and Nick. Nick's ambivalence about teaching was apparent. On the one hand he wanted to be relieved of the responsibility and the workload. He often warned Jenny that he wasn't going to be around forever. On the other hand, he was protective of his skill and resented the group's encroachment on his authority. Julia had to prod him: "Here, give me that instrument." She felt he had too much ego invested; his pride got in the way of teaching. Jenny had none of that. It was always her intention to learn in order to teach others. And Jenny was someone Julia knew personally, her peer. "She was doing it every bit as well as he and that meant for sure I could do it," Julia recalls. "There was no magic attached to her—none to him either, but there was a distance."

The workers explained to each woman having an abortion that the group trained people the way anyone learns, by practice. Before an apprentice learned something new, she asked the women having the abortion for permission. The trainer was always right there, directing, ready to step in. Including the woman having the abortion in the actual process added to the political dimension of their work. Not only were they demystifying medical practice for themselves but for every woman who came to them. With women aware of their training method, Jenny gave directions out loud: "Pull the curette toward you all the way around, never push. Now scrape harder until you hear the rasping sound." She asked the woman having the abortion, "Can you hear that sound? Does it feel any different?"

Each of the women learning to perform abortions had to come to terms with causing another woman pain. No one wanted to do that, but they never considered using systemic painkillers or narcotics, which might complicate the medical situation. A drug reaction could put a woman in unnecessary danger. They only used drugs that were absolutely necessary: Ergotrate to prevent bleeding, and Xylocaine as a local anesthetic to ease the cramping associated with dilation. The only other point in an abortion that was painful was at the end when a nearly empty uterus contracted down on the instruments. Instead of using drugs, they learned that the discomfort of an abortion could be safely and effectively managed through counseling, respectful treatment and support. Every woman was awake during her abortion. Each one was reminded that, no matter how strange the sensations that she was feeling were, she could handle them. She was going to be in control. She could ask them to stop for a few minutes. She could do anything she wanted except scream or move around. If she screamed a neighbor might hear and call the police; if she moved she could be injured by the instruments.

For most women, depending upon her pain threshold, her level of comfort, and the length of her pregnancy, the abortion felt no worse than menstrual cramps. But for some it took all their will to get through it. They bit on washcloths or squeezed the assistant's hand so tightly that her circulation was cut off. Sometimes the person doing the abortion took a break to give a woman a chance to relax and stretch her shaky legs.

Each woman interacted with the people who performed her abortion. The conversation helped her relax and what she was feeling helped guide the abortionist, who asked, "Are you feeling cramps now?" Scraping a clean uterine wall with a curette produced cramping, while scraping one covered with soft tissue usually produced no sensation. Service members believe that their successful medical record was a function of the preparation and participation of the women having abortions and directly related to their limited dependence on drugs.

Learning each new step in the process terrified Julia, but with repetition her confidence grew. Jenny might say, "You set up this person for me and I'll watch you do her. She looks pretty together." As a teacher Jenny was both conscientious and direct; she didn't coddle anyone. "There was something about the way Jenny functioned," Julia recalls, "that I trusted out of hand, so when she said, 'This is what you do,' I said, 'Okay,' and didn't question it. I felt she would not push me to do something I couldn't."

Early in the spring Deborah met Nick as a precursor to assisting. She was driving women from the Front to the Place when Jenny invited her to the back of the apartment to watch an abortion, saying, "Nick said it was okay." "She said it deliberately," Deborah remembers, "in a way that would make me feel chosen." Jenny introduced her to Nick and the woman on the bed and asked her if Deborah could observe.

The woman, in the process of having an abortion, was in her late twenties or early thirties. At the foot of the bed, Nick worked quickly with forceps and curettes. Deborah felt a shot of adrenaline course through her. She was struck by the power of what she was seeing: "It was about mastery, not of the woman, but mastery of our lives, like one of those signs in Times Square with the words going around: *This is it. This is the real thing here. This is what's supposed to be happening.*"

Deborah was fascinated: "I was blown away by the blood. I'd never seen such a thing before. There was blood on the woman's thighs, blood on Nick's wrists, on the bed. It was dealt with in a certain normal everyday way, like you were cleaning up the kitchen, matter-of-fact. He could have been a bricklayer. He could have been doing any other seriously learned craft that was messy. It was the workerlike quality of the action which impressed me. I mean, this business of the hands and the blood and mucus and the Kleenex stuffed under her butt to absorb it, and seeing this very businesslike relationship between the abortionist and the woman having the abortion. Here was this half-naked woman, talking, laughing, occasionally asking questions, definitely relating to the person who was working on her body (and he dealt with her body with complete respect)." Instantly Deborah understood that the drapes, the uniforms, the barriers that the medical profession erected between patient and practitioner, were not a function of either the woman's needs or the needs of the situation, but were about appearances and status, like a general's gold braid. It reminded her of the scene in the *Wizard of Oz* when the wizard is revealed: *Pay no attention to that man behind the curtain.*

There was nothing magical about an abortion. The techniques were very straightforward, just like counseling was. They were skills that, with practice and care, Deborah could learn and any of them could learn. That realization translated to medicine in general. Doctors weren't the All Powerful Oz, demanding unquestioned obedience. Doctors were craftsmen, their skill appreciated and respected. Once the women in the service had stripped away the medical profession's mystique and taboo, they could relate to the technical skills they were learning as not only useful but infinitely interesting.

By the early spring of 1971 Nick and his wife had reconciled. He returned to California but continued to fly to Chicago on weekends to perform abortions for Jane on Fridays and Saturdays, much to his wife's dismay. If anything, his reconciliation pushed him to train Jenny even more aggressively, so he could sever his ties to Jane and take some of the pressure off his marriage. Once Jenny was fully trained, that would be the end of his constant arguments with her and Miriam about control.

Now that service members were handling more of the work, Jenny convinced Nick to accept a fee per day instead of per abortion. Because Jenny had finagled so many free and discount abortions, she calculated that Nick wasn't going to notice much change in the amount of money he took home. Jane would pay the rent, buy supplies and equipment, and finance the phone system. In exchange Nick received a flat fee per day no matter how many abortions they scheduled. Without noticing it, he became Jane's employee. He says, "At first they had no power and then they had it all. I didn't care about the power, I cared about the money and I didn't give that up."

Once Nick agreed to a per diem, the group lowered its price for an abortion to $300. As long as they brought in enough money to cover expenses, they could be flexible about what women paid. Each counselor asked for $300 but no one ever again was turned down for lack of funds; no woman was forced to prostitute herself or use her children's food money to pay for an abortion. The driver collected the money in the car so that none of the workers at the Place knew how much each woman had paid. There were days when most women paid so little that they didn't bring in enough money to cover even Nick's daily fee. Furious, he would blow up at Jenny. Then the next service meeting had to be devoted to figuring out ways to encourage women to come up with more money. Everyone in the service agreed that each woman should pay something. It cost money to perform abortions. Paying was one way women owned what they were doing and participated in it, and participation, they had discovered, was as much a key to a successful abortion as anything they did medically. Abortion wasn't a charity for helpless women: it was an act of responsibility.

. . .

That same spring of 1971 the group had another issue with which to grapple. In the winter, within weeks of each other, both Lorraine and Deborah got pregnant. Lorraine had been in a fertility workup for several years. Deborah's pregnancy brought her closer to the women she calls "the mothers of the service," Miriam, Jenny and Julia, who all had children under the age of eight. By the spring both women's pregnancies were obvious, which initiated a discussion at a service meeting about whether women coming to them for abortions should be exposed to pregnant counselors and assistants. Some members thought it might be unfair to the women. They wondered whether, as Deborah remembers, "it would make woman feel like we could have babies but they couldn't. Would we be perceived as oppressors if we were going to take their babies away, but we were allowed to have our babies?"

Other members argued that to shield women needing abortions from pregnant counselors did a disservice to women and reinforced society's negative attitudes about abortion. Abortion was part of the continuum of women's lives, not separate. A woman who decided to get one was making a responsible decision. Any woman who needed an abortion today might have had a baby the previous year or would choose to the next year. In any case, during counseling sessions, women were in their counselors' homes, around their families. They weren't hiding their children.

Several years earlier in 1968, before the group existed, Claire, who had been counseling and referring women on her own and subsequently organized Jane, had faced the same problem. When she was pregnant she decided not to counsel women, wanting to protect their feelings. Now, three years later, the women in Jane unanimously came to the opposite conclusion. Lorraine's and Deborah's pregnancies would not be hidden from women. The group's political understanding of abortion and its relationship to women's lives had evolved. The women they counseled didn't need to be protected.

Lorraine talked about her pregnancy with the women she counseled. Since she had had an abortion years earlier, she could draw on that experience as well. She was an example of a person who had made one decision at one time in her life and a different decision at another.

Only two women commented on Deborah's pregnancy, both of whom she met at the Place. The first was an older woman who asked, "They let you be pregnant here?"

Deborah said, "Yes, we talked about it and decided that it was okay. There's another woman who's pregnant, too. We believe women should have babies when they want them and abortions when they need them."

The other was a high school student who had had a difficult time during her abortion. Afterward, as Deborah sat with her on the couch in the living room, she collapsed in Deborah's arms, sobbing, "I killed my baby, but you'll be a very good mother because you are taking care of me."

Deborah was horrified. The counseling session was the place to address these feelings. Hadn't her counselor talked with her about this? Deborah asked, "If you felt that way, why did you do it?"

"My mother said if I have this baby she'd see to it that the welfare people take it away from me, so what's the point." She hugged Deborah's belly, "I killed my baby and here's your baby. I'm glad you helped me, but I wish I could have a baby like you."

Each woman and girl who contacted Jane came through the service bearing the weight of her own personal circumstances. Whatever those were, the women in the service tried to create an environment, both in counseling sessions and during the abortions, that was more than comforting and consoling. If a woman was forced into an abortion, like that high school student, nothing could ease the emotional pain. But, if, as in the overwhelming majority of the people the service dealt with, the abortion was her choice, even if that choice was circumscribed by medical, social and economic factors, an abortion with Jane was a surprisingly positive experience, as many women expressed at the time, or in follow-up calls, or later in letters.

When Molly called Jane in the spring of 1971 she knew more about abortion than she ever wanted to know. A year earlier, at the end of her second year in college, a student she hardly knew, who lived in her dorm, brought Molly to her room. She had just had an abortion and she needed help. When Molly walked into her room there was blood everywhere. Molly called the doctor who had performed the abortion. He told her to put ice on the girl's abdomen and elevate her feet. The ice stopped the bleeding. The next day Molly went to a bookstore looking for information on abortion but could find nothing.

Molly, a tall, sandy-haired young woman with broad features, came from a large Irish Catholic family on the East Coast. In high school she had been a baton-twirler, a class officer, and was voted Most Popular. She arrived at Elmhurst College outside of Chicago a week after the demonstrations at the Democratic National Convention and thought, Hey, the times they are a-changing and I'm ready to do something.

On campus she joined Revolutionary Youth Movement II, a radical faction of SDS, but she had as little interest in ideological dogma as she had in school. In 1970, after two years of college, she dropped out and moved with her boyfriend to a tiny apartment in Lincoln Park on Chicago's North Side. She took whatever minimum-wage jobs she could find. In the fall she was pregnant.

As a Catholic she was ambivalent about birth control. According to the church, if she took birth control pills she would be committing a mortal sin every day. Somehow, she didn't believe she was going to get pregnant. When she did, she made an appointment with the same doctor the woman in her dorm had seen. He confirmed her pregnancy but refused to help. "Go to New York," he said. "It's legal there."

Molly contacted the Clergy Consultation Service on Abortion, who could send her to a New York clinic for $300 including airfare. On her subsistence-level salary she didn't have $300 and she had only a limited amount of time before it would be too late for a clinic abortion. She was rescued by a friend who borrowed the money. "I don't know what possessed her," Molly remembers. "Every paycheck I paid her back. I was religious about it. She saved my life."

With only a novel for company, she flew to New York and had the abortion. She had no second thoughts: "I was twenty, in a relationship with a guy I shouldn't have been with. It was wonderful not to be pregnant. I felt like I had a new lease on life."

Unfortunately, she couldn't shake her Catholic ambivalence about birth control, so she was not as consistent using it as she should have been. Six months later, in the spring of 1971, she was pregnant again. She couldn't tell anyone because, since she needed a second abortion, she assumed she'd be judged. And she could not face going to New York again.

She found Jane's phone number in an underground newspaper, *The Seed*. When *Jane* told her their charge was $300, Molly said, "I've only got a hundred dollars." *Jane* said, "Fine, you can work something out with your counselor." For the next few days Molly stayed by the telephone, anxiously waiting for her counselor to call.

Her counselor, Charlotte, lived in her neighborhood. Charlotte was unconcerned about the money. She said, "Pay us when you can." She told Molly that she had joined Jane after her own abortion with the group a few months earlier. Molly noticed that "Charlotte's kids were crawling all over the place and I thought that was real nice—a woman who had two kids and did that. It made it seem more part of everything, not real bizarre."

The day of her abortion, Molly took the El alone to the South Side, a part of the city with which she was unfamiliar. The Front, which was packed, was in a dorm room at the University of Chicago. She sat in a corner reading *Sometimes a Great Notion* and waited her turn.

Deborah was driving. Molly was touched that a pregnant woman was taking risks for her.

At the Place she met Julia, who prepped her for the abortion, explaining each step and checking to make sure Molly was comfortable. Then Julia said, "Now we're going to blindfold you because the person who does the abortion is going to come in. Is that okay?" Nick came in and began a lighthearted banter with her. Julia held her hand. Molly found herself laughing and talking. The New York abortion had been fine, but this one was much better. "People were right there for me," she says. "I didn't feel like I was having an illegal anything. I didn't feel like I was having anything done to me. It was like I was part of the scene."

By the time her abortion was completed it was late afternoon and Molly had not eaten since early that morning. She was light-headed and shaky. Julia took her into the kitchen and gave her a hard-boiled egg and a cup of tea. On the way home Molly kept thinking, I just had an illegal abortion and it was the best medical experience I've ever had. She tried to explain to her boyfriend, Dean, how positive and affirming her abortion had been.

CHAPTER 13

Everything they were learning about abortion and women's bodies was fascinating to the members of Jane. Not only was the information essential for them to do their work, but they realized that all women needed it to take control of their lives. In researching abortion, service members had discovered that they couldn't rely on a medical profession that stigmatized all abortion practitioners as quacks and butchers, no matter how competent they were. While some doctors performed abortions themselves and others worked closely with illegal practitioners they trusted, the profession's public position was that abortions were complex and dangerous.

In the late 1800s the AMA had spearheaded the campaign to prohibit abortion. Their public reason for banning abortions was to protect women's lives from unsafe practices, but, in fact, their motivation had much more to do with control. In the period leading up to that prohibition, the regular physicians, represented by the AMA, were attempting to discredit other medical practitioners, such as midwives, who practiced abortion, in order to assure their dominance over medical care. These regular physicians also positioned themselves as the moral guardians of "women's purity," promoting "the cult of motherhood." In that context women's sexuality, divorced from procreation, was viewed as unnatural and abhorrent. During the mid-eighteenth century the birth rates of middle-class native Protestant women, the patients of physicians, declined, while those for poor and immigrant women, many of whom were Catholic, climbed, so the anti-abortion campaign played into nativist and class fears, as well. Since then medicine's official spokesmen had maintained their vocal anti-abortion position. That stance had biased the few articles on abortion the group found. The doctors they knew who were willing to share their knowledge had little to impart, since they rarely performed abortions. The women in Jane had to learn by watching Nick and doing them themselves. They learned to manage each possible complication as it arose. It was the only way they were going to learn. Anything unusual witnessed by the women who assisted at abortions, such as a woman whose excessive bleeding was brought under control by a bag of ice applied directly to her abdomen, they reported at meetings to further the total group's education. Jenny brought the instruments to meetings so that all counselors would have a clearer idea of the process and, therefore, be able to explain it better.

Most of the women who came to them knew little about their bodies. Hardly anyone they counseled understood the process of conception or knew what her cervix was or where it was. Few women thought they had a right to such basic information, as if their bodies did not belong to them. Those who wanted the information had no idea where to look; those who looked, like Molly, couldn't find anything.

Without access to information women were vulnerable to misconceptions and myths passed through the grapevine and dependent on what their doctors deigned to tell them. Many women had all kinds of erroneous ideas about conception. They thought they couldn't get pregnant the first time they had sex, or while they were menstruating, or if they didn't have an orgasm.

If Jane members shared what they had learned with the women who came to them, the service would be more than a Band-Aid. Otherwise, all they were doing was responding to one crisis after another. No matter how good they were at that, it was not going to change women's powerlessness. They didn't want any woman to have to turn to Jane a second time and they wanted women to grow from their contact with the service. Women educated about their bodies could ask intelligent questions, demand answers and refuse treatment. They were less likely to be mistreated by the medical profession. Women had to know how their bodies worked; to not know was to risk their lives.

Miriam found a copy of a new book, *Women and Their Bodies* (later retitled *Our Bodies, Ourselves*),* printed on newsprint, written by a group called the Boston Women's Health Collective, when she spoke about abortion in Michigan in the spring of 1971. The women of the Collective, in their introduction, stated that they intended that the book be used as a guide for discussion courses, so that women could learn as much or more from each other as they could from the text. Miriam read each chapter with growing enthusiasm: "It was spectacular. The attitude presented in the book, like *The Birth Control Handbook,* was what we wanted people to hear. It talked about the fact that people had the right to information and that it was useful to know how your body worked, nothing magical or mysterious. It was cheap, too, only thirty-five cents. It's kind of fun when you find something written that agrees with the way you think about things. It doesn't happen too often."

Miriam brought a copy back to Jane. Written in plain language, the book covered everything from anatomy and physiology to sexuality, birth control, pregnancy, abortion and childbirth, ending with a chapter entitled "Women, Medicine and Capitalism." It discussed how difficult it was for women to get the information to educate themselves. In the introduction, describing their process to the reader, the Collective members state: "It was exciting to learn new

*Since 1973 *Our Bodies, Ourselves* has been published by Simon & Schuster and is available in bookstores.

facts about our bodies, but it was even more exciting to talk about ourselves, how we could become more autonomous human beings, how we could act together on our collective knowledge to change the health care system for women and for all people. We hope this will be true for you, too."

The service ordered boxes of the book from the Boston Women's Health Collective's printer, New England Free Press; every counselor had a stack. In addition to *The Birth Control Handbook,* women who came to Jane for an abortion got a free copy and took extras for a sister or a friend. The counselors read it, too, and, even though they considered themselves well educated, they learned more about their bodies from the book than they had previously known.

Knowledge was changing Jane's members. They were growing more confident, learning to trust themselves and their own judgment. Even the newest members, like Donna, were affected.

In 1966 Donna, a shy redhead, entered college at the University of Chicago. Two years later, after being teargassed at the demonstrations at the Democratic National Convention, she dropped out. She never felt comfortable in the university's highly intellectualized atmosphere, and, although she had radical views, she did not feel at ease with campus political groups: "I ran into a kind of romanticizing of the working class which I found intolerable, coming from the working class and knowing how boring those people's lives were and how racist they were. I didn't have to grow up to work in a factory. I worked in a factory to pay for college."

After she dropped out of college, she and her boyfriend moved to San Francisco. Within months she was pregnant. "I had no intention of having a baby at that time," she recalls. "I was just a fucked-up kid. I didn't know what I was doing; I could barely take care of myself." California allowed abortions to protect a woman's physical or mental health. Planned Parenthood referred her to two psychiatrists from whom she needed validating letters before an abortion could be granted. She had to convince both psychiatrists that she was suicidal. She was admitted to a hospital for her abortion, kept for two nights on the psychiatric ward and given a general anesthetic; to compound her humiliation, they shaved her pubic hair.

Back in Chicago, working as a secretary at the university, she attended a talk on abortion at which Jane's number was announced. Her own abortion had been isolating and difficult. She thought, I should help other women because this is something I know about. She called Jane.

Donna lacked self-confidence, but being in Jane had an immediate effect on her. She devoured her copies of *The Birth Control Handbook* and *Our Bodies, Ourselves.* "Knowledge is strength," she says. "If you don't know things you can't ask questions, you can't refuse. You're just taken advantage of or mistreated."

Shortly after she joined the service, she went to a family planning clinic for an IUD. There had been a discussion at a Jane meeting about problems associated with the Dalkon Shield. She told the doctor at the clinic that she didn't want that kind of IUD: "So I'm lying on this table in the stirrups with this thing, this drape, over me and some man I'd never seen before sitting between my legs. I said, 'I'd like to see this IUD before you put it in me.' He showed it to me and I said, 'But that's a Dalkon Shield. I thought they were being taken off the market.' So I'm lying there having an argument with this man, with my legs spread open, with no clothes on. He had all his clothes on; it didn't seem fair." She left the clinic without an IUD. "Learning a little about birth control made me able to argue with this guy," she says. "Getting the knowledge enabled me to speak for myself."

One of the counselors' tasks was to help each woman turn her depression about having to get an illegal abortion into anger at a society that forced her to break the law. Choosing an abortion might represent the loss of a possibility, but that experience could be used to discover new possibilities. Jane wasn't doing favors. Jane was helping each woman take stock of her life and make an adult decision. When, after an abortion, a woman hugged Jenny, thanking her, Jenny would say, "Don't thank me. Just go do something with your life and share what you've learned." She would leave Jane not only with information she needed, but, perhaps, with a clearer sense of herself. From her contact with the service she could take something positive and useful besides the negative—not being pregnant. Miriam felt that "it was a stronger decision that each woman made coming and having an abortion with us because we reinforced it, talked about it, as a decision. Maybe this is romanticizing it, but I think that for that moment she had made a stand in her life."

One of the opportunities they had to influence people was at the Front. Since people arrived and left throughout the day, Fronts had a chaotic quality, like a bus station, but with heightened tension.

Some members felt that by allowing Fronts to be merely waiting rooms where people milled about or sat in terrified silence, they were ignoring a precious opportunity. They had a captive audience. If they were, as they professed to be, a radical organization whose goal was to raise women's consciousness, rather than do-gooder social service types, they should make the most of this fortuitous situation. Political discussions about the war or feminism should be initiated to make Fronts part of the educable moment.

Other members disagreed. They felt that to use Fronts for political education was taking advantage of women. No matter what they, the members of the service, believed about the war, capitalism or feminism, the women who came to them were desperate and vulnerable. To do anything but help them relax was exploiting their situation. Counseling and the abortion were politicizing experiences; as for the rest, leave it alone. The group never resolved the disagreement. Each worker handled Fronts in her own way, whether she turned the TV on to soap operas or attempted to get people talking.

However much the women in Jane wanted to maximize the educable moment for the women who came through the service, their primary responsibility was to help each woman do what she really wanted to do. The counseling session was the best opportunity for that. Nan, a graduate student in anthropology, counseled a college student who came with her parents. The young woman was trembling, staring at the floor. It was obvious to Nan that she didn't want an abortion, but couldn't say so in front of her parents. Nan said, "I need to talk to your daughter alone."

Nan took her into another room and said, "I'm going to tell them that we can't do you."

The girl looked aghast and asked, "Why?"

Nan said, "It's obvious you don't want one."

"Yes, but you can't tell them because they'll blame me."

"I'll try to think of an excuse," Nan said.

Nan racked her brain but all she could come up with was the truth, so she said to the girl's parents, "Look, she hasn't told me she doesn't want an abortion because she doesn't want to betray you or offend you. She loves you very dearly. She's trying to do what you want, but she can't hide how she feels."

Her father blew up; her mother looked annoyed. Nan made tea for everyone and kept them talking until they calmed down. The girl sat there, terrified. As they were leaving, the mother turned to Nan and said, "I really hadn't thought about it like that. It will be all right. He'll calm down."

Many young women were too frightened of their parents' reaction to even tell them they were pregnant. They were certain they would be beaten and thrown out of the house. Others refused to tell, not because they were afraid of their parents' response, but because they did not want to disappoint them. "They would go to a butcher before they'd tell," Nan says. "It made me realize that as much as I believe parents should know what their kids are doing, realistically laws to that effect only drive kids to butchers." Every counselor spoke with teenagers who refused to tell because they wanted to protect their parents; they did not want to cause them pain.

Being able to get an abortion often had a positive effect on teenagers. Kris, teaching at an alternative high school, saw the difference that access to abortion made on her students: "The students I knew who had abortions really did change their way of thinking about themselves. These women, by doing it, took control of their lives. By making a very heavy choice they realized they could make heavy choices. Instead of the negative choices they made before, like whether to kick the guy out of the house, or to move from one burned-out building to another, they started thinking about things like: Do I want to go to college? What kind of job do I want?"

Some of her students, who had been floundering, turned their lives around after their abortions. One girl from a Polish family, Kris recalls, "didn't have any aspirations for herself. The abortion was hard for her to do, but, after that, she picked herself up, her grades improved and she ended up going to college, which was a choice I don't think she would have ever made before." These students were at a crossroads. The decision they made could determine their futures.

Some young women, like Celia, came to Jane conflicted but resigned. Their abortions were often difficult and painful. In Celia's case, contact with Jane led to personal growth.

"I was so overwhelmed with emotional pain after the abortion," Celia says, "that I broke up with my boyfriend. It was like he let me down because he didn't stand by me. He always said, 'We're going to get married.' And then, when I got pregnant, he said, 'Well, we can't get married.' I said, 'Fine. We don't have to get married. I'm going to have this baby.' And he said, 'What will my family say? What will your family say?'"

Celia was a sophomore at a Catholic college and a product of a strict Latino Catholic upbringing. When she found out she was pregnant she couldn't believe it. Her boyfriend, Eddie, hadn't ejaculated inside her nor had he fully penetrated her. When she told Eddie she was pregnant she hoped he'd say, "It'll be okay. We'll have this baby and just move up our marriage date." But he never did. She gave him all kinds of reasons why they should have the baby; he countered every one of them.

She and Eddie had been putting aside money for their marriage, working during the school year and in the summer, but they hadn't managed to save much. When a friend at school gave her Jane's number, Celia didn't think she could afford an abortion. Her friend reassured her, "That's not important. That's not what they're in it for. You can give thirty dollars or three hundred. If you have more money they ask for more so it can make up for the ones that can't pay as much." Celia liked the fact that profit wasn't the group's motive.

Eddie went with her to the counseling session at Julia's. "Julia had told me to come after seven so she could get her kids to bed," Celia remembers. "One of her kids came downstairs, a little boy in Doctor Dentons, looking for a book. I didn't know people who lived like that: a family, in this big house, with all these books all over the place." Julia served them tea. The phone rang constantly; a couple of other people wandered in. It made the whole experience seem normal.

Julia asked, "Are you sure you want to do this? There have been times when women backed out at the last minute, which is just fine, too." Celia kept thinking, I wish Eddie would say something.

Except for her friend at school and Eddie, she hadn't told anyone. Since her mother was a practicing Catholic, Celia felt she could not turn to her or to anyone else in her family. But Julia understood. Celia felt that "the church was going to be pissed; my parents were going to be pissed. Everyone was going to be pissed, but here was this woman who wasn't upset, who was very supportive." She left Julia's house relieved that she understood what was going to happen to her, but, still, she was terrified.

The day of her abortion, as she and Eddie drove to the Front, she turned to him and said, "It's not too late. We can still change our minds." Eddie said nothing. They drove to Hyde Park in silence, listening to the radio. The Front was crowded. Except for a few whispered conversations, everyone was quiet.

In the car going to the Place, the women were silent, but once they arrived they started talking: "Are you nervous?"

"Yes."

"I'm really scared, too."

"Is this your first time?"

One or two women had had abortions before and were reassuring: "You'll be in and out in no time."

When it was Celia's turn she went into a bedroom where Julia was waiting. When Julia put the blindfold on her she began to shake, so, instead, Julia held a pillow in front of her face. The abortion took longer and was more painful than she expected partly because she had underestimated the length of her pregnancy by almost a month. To keep from screaming she bit the pillow and squeezed Julia's hand as hard as she could. Julia kept talking, offering encouragement: "You're doing great. It's almost over."

Afterward Celia went to her parents', feigned the flu, and curled up on the couch with cramps. She felt as if she'd "been ripped apart, like something had been taken away from me." When the semester ended, Celia dropped out of college, moved into the city and got a job.

She read the copies of *Our Bodies, Ourselves* and *The Birth Control Handbook* Julia had given her. Six months after her abortion, she asked Julia and Miriam to lead a discussion group in her home based on the books. Later, in a neighborhood community center, she and Julia offered the same course to other women. One class led to another. Eventually Celia got a job at a local hospital as a patient representative. There she taught classes for other Latinas on birth control, child care and nutrition.

"Women should have a choice," Celia says. "I believed it back then; I continue to believe it. However, for myself, I don't think I could ever do it again. There's a part of me that regrets having done it. I don't regret the abortion, but I do regret not having had the courage to do what I really wanted to do, and that was not have it. There's a difference." But through that experience she met Miriam and Julia, two women who became her role models. They visited her, bringing cheese and bread (Celia supplied the wine) and spent hours talking and listening to music together. As difficult as it was for Celia, the abortion was a catalyst: "I never saw myself going out and teaching other women what I had learned until I had gone through that experience. It helped me branch out in a direction that was foreign to me."

She gave Jane's phone number to women she knew who needed abortions. Then and now Celia is pro-choice: "I feel it's important to separate my own personal feelings from what needs to be a woman's right to decide for herself."

CHAPTER 14

For most women, finding a competent abortionist was a matter of luck, money and knowing the right people. It could take weeks or even months of surreptitious asking around. Sometimes, by the time a woman found one she thought wasn't going to kill her, her pregnancy had advanced past the point where a D & C could be performed. Nan, one of Jane's members, a graduate student in anthropology at the University of Chicago, had been in exactly that position. Even though her boyfriend was a medical student and asked every doctor he knew, it took so long to find someone competent that Nan had to be induced to miscarry. As soon as Jane began, the service had been contacted by women in that same situation. At first, the only options available to the group required travel out of the country or cost $1,000. Most of the women who called them needing that type of abortion did not have the money to do either. Group members who took those calls listened to the desperation in women's voices and felt helpless. They knew that women that desperate and frantic would try anything, no matter how dangerous, to do what they felt they had to do.

When "Nathan Detroit" had called Jane late in 1969 and spoken to Lorraine, he'd offered them something other than the D & C procedure he arranged in Detroit. He had access to a compound called Leunbach paste which, when inserted into the uterus of a pregnant woman, induced labor within forty-eight hours. He rattled off a list of the ingredients and explained that the paste worked by separating the placenta from the uterine wall. With the paste he could perform an abortion up to six months of pregnancy. He agreed to come to Chicago to demonstrate this method if Jane had a few willing women.

At the next meeting Lorraine relayed Nathan's proposal. The group responded positively. It was worth pursuing. They might be able to help women they had previously turned away. It sounded almost magical, a paste that induced a miscarriage. Compared with the $500 that women had to pay for a D & C abortion, Nathan was asking only $100 for each of these.

Miriam had heard about Leunbach paste from one of her early doctor contacts. Over the next few weeks the group looked into it. They found references to the use of the paste in Europe with indications that sloppy preparation or application could be dangerous. Jenny asked Nick; long before his contact with Jane he had used it successfully, but his source had disappeared. Jenny's doctor friends didn't know and couldn't find out anything about it. Since it was neither legal nor approved, regular pharmacological sources didn't mention it. Whenever the group tried to research abortion, they were frustrated by how little they could find.

Meanwhile, Lorraine collected the names of women who were willing to try the paste. A counselor explained to each woman that they didn't know much about it and hadn't used it before. All they knew was what Nathan had told them: a paste was inserted and afterward they would go through a normal miscarriage.

When Lorraine had four women who wanted to try the paste, she called Nathan. She met him at the airport and drove him to each of the women's homes. After injecting the paste through the cervical opening, Nathan advised each woman to wait until her contractions were five minutes apart, then go to a hospital feigning premature labor. He suggested they act dumb, say they didn't know what was happening. No one, he assured them, would be able to detect that anything had been done. He explained that labor in a miscarriage was often harder than a full-term delivery because the fetus was so small. They could expect hours of painful labor. Nathan was in and out of each apartment in minutes. Counselors kept in touch with the women and all four women miscarried without incident.

At the next meeting Lorraine gave a positive report on the paste. It seemed simple and uncomplicated and, other than the tube of paste and applicator, no special instruments were needed. And it worked quickly. Lorraine's one difficulty with the procedure was spending an evening with Nathan. Although he treated the women decently, in the car, between their homes, he was condescending and arrogant: "These dumb girls get themselves knocked up and I have to save their lives." The less she had to do with him, the happier she would be. The next time Nathan came in with the paste he went to one counselor's apartment where a few women needing induced miscarriages were waiting for him. Again, the women went to hospitals to miscarry.

Going to a hospital to miscarry posed problems. It was well known that hospital personnel might contact the police if they suspected that a woman had had an abortion. Since abortion had been prohibited in the late 1800s, medical institutions were required to report instances when women sought medical care for complications. Women were pressured to tell who had done it, sometimes before they were treated. When a woman was gravely ill, police or doctors elicited dying declarations, submitted as evidence against whomever had performed the abortion. Without a private admitting physician who could smooth over suspicions in the emergency room, women whose miscarriages were suspect might be questioned by police and threatened with criminal action. And then there were the financial considerations. Women without medical insurance couldn't afford emergency room care. For a woman trying to keep what she was doing from her family, a hospital stay was a real problem. If the group managed the miscarriages themselves, women could avoid both the hassle and the cost of emergency treatment altogether.

The next time Nathan brought the paste they borrowed an apartment to use for the miscarriages. For the next three days Lorraine and two other counselors took turns staying with the women Nathan induced while they labored and miscarried.

One of the women whose miscarriage Nathan induced with the paste was in her mid-forties and had grown children. The others waiting to miscarry were all teenagers. None of the counselors in attendance had had a child. The only one there who had given birth was the middle-aged woman.

The place they had borrowed was a less than spotless student apartment. While they waited, the women cleaned it and washed piles of dirty dishes together. Over several days a camaraderie developed. Lorraine remembers that "mostly we talked a lot. We had a little consciousness-raising going on, talking about how you get pregnant, and why you got pregnant, and whether you're ever going to get pregnant again. Of course, at that point, nobody is ever going to get pregnant again."

Lorraine helped the young women miscarry. The older woman was the last to go into labor. She began bleeding heavily and it was obvious, even with the little practical knowledge they had, that she was not having a normal miscarriage. They rushed her to the emergency room at Cook County Hospital. Through a source at the hospital, Lorraine found out that the woman had had a previous cesarean section that may well have affected her miscarriage. It was important information that she had kept from them.

She wasn't the only one who neglected to tell her counselor something the group needed to know or who gave them misinformation. Others also withheld critical medical information, putting themselves and the group in jeopardy. They were more terrified of being turned down for an abortion than of risking their lives.

Since Jane was operating on the margins of medical practice, there were limits to the medical knowledge available to them. When a new technique or an idea presented itself their response was: Let's see what we can find out about it. Let's be cautious, but let's try it and see what happens. If they had confined themselves to only what was acceptable for them to do, they would have severely restricted women's options. They had to learn by doing, discard what didn't work, build on what did. Each abortion could present new problems. The only way to proceed, if they hoped to become more proficient, was to deal with problems as they arose. "We were just learning how to respond to emergencies," Lorraine recalls. "Sometimes we didn't react very well. We took it one step at a time."

At the next meeting after the miscarriages, Lorraine reported to the group. They discussed how the situation might have been handled differently, what added medical information they needed, and what they could do to improve this service. They had a way to help women whose pregnancies had advanced past the point where a D & C could be done; whether or not they should use it was moot. Women needed abortions just as much at four months as they did at eight weeks.

The number of women for whom they induced miscarriages was a small fraction of the total number of women calling them for help. Of that fraction, anyone with money, insurance or Medicaid was encouraged to go to a hospital to miscarry. Some women miscarried on their own with their mother's help or a friend's. The group's assistance was available for women who chose it and, most often, these were either young women or women with no one to help and no resources.

Only a few counselors were willing to assist women with miscarriages. Nan, whose induced miscarriage had motivated her to join Jane, helped several times but never felt comfortable with it. Since she had had one herself, she argued that this was a service they must provide. But every time she sat with women during their labors she couldn't shake the memory of her own, which had resulted in an infection that had put her on the hospital's critical list for three days.

She felt "constantly worried about the woman. I was a little too leery to be doing it myself, so I just backed away."

Whether or not counselors were unwilling to participate in miscarriages due to personal ambivalence or discomfort, they couched their reluctance in terms of the added responsibility and time commitment required. Counselors who worked with these women, referred to as long-terms, shorthand for long-term pregnancies, had to be with them throughout the process. Once labor began, if a problem arose, the counselor had to deal with it on her own. "You couldn't leave a woman alone; you had to be with her all the time," Nan remembers. "These things could drag on and maybe you'd have to turn her over to someone else, that is, if you could find someone else." It was difficult for women with children to take that kind of time away from their families. A few counselors accepted the responsibility for these women, not always because they wanted to do it, but because no one else would.

Pam was one of those who agreed to help with long-term abortions. She was motivated by personal experiences. As an infant, before she was adopted, Pam, the child of a teenager, was physically abused by her maternal grandmother. Pam believed that "an unwanted child lives in hell." She had worked at a boys' training school, a reform school, where the parents rarely visited. There she noticed "so many sad faces, the faces of unwanted children."

Women in the group who had given birth taught Pam what they knew about labor. One provided training in Lamaze breathing techniques. Other than that, Pam was on her own. She learned what to do by trial and error. If there were problems she called Jenny, who contacted one of the physicians she knew. A friendly pharmacist gave Pam emergency medications and information. Occasionally one of Nick's associates delivered ampules of Pitocin, a drug that stimulates uterine contractions, which she used to control excessive postpartum bleeding.

Pam traveled around the city to assist those who needed help. Sometimes she found herself at a front door, arguing with a parent or husband who tried to prevent her from getting to the woman inside who needed her. She spent one evening in an apartment in the West Side ghetto with a young woman who was miscarrying while she and the woman's mother chased rats across the kitchen floor with brooms. Once she attended a miscarriage in a motel near Great Lakes Naval Base and had to contend with two belligerent drunken sailors in the room.

In a crisis, the counselor in attendance took the woman to the nearest emergency room but, as a matter of self-protection, usually did not go inside with her. If the counselor went in, the hospital staff's suspicions might be aroused, especially if the women were of different races. Occasionally a counselor did accompany a woman, passing as her friend. Nan went with one woman whom she later saw lying on a gurney, visibly upset. She had been told that the hospital wouldn't help her unless she gave them the name of the person who had done it. Nan reassured her that, since they had admitted her, they were legally bound to treat her. The woman relaxed and said, "Oh yeah, they have admitted me. It would be kind of funny if they wouldn't treat me now." Within minutes she was wheeled away for care.

Years before she joined Jane, Carol had helped a friend miscarry; now she attended some of the miscarriages. It was not something she actively chose either, but she agreed to do it when no one else was available. What Carol remembers most is the waiting, strangers in an apartment waiting together: "We talked. I had a real sense of sharing a precious intimate experience that, in a funny way, felt life-affirming."

Carol noticed a distance between the members who assisted with miscarriages and the rest of the group: "The people who did them were kind of the stepchildren in the group, treated like the family secret. There was a relationship between that faction of Jane and Jane, like there was between Jane and the medical establishment: We're glad you're here, but we don't quite acknowledge that you're here."

There was no denying the need. Anyone who handled *Call-Back Jane* talked to tearful women over three months pregnant who were begging for help. Women confided in their counselors that they'd tried to abort with nail files and crochet hooks and mysterious pills that someone had given them. The thought of what desperate women might do if they were turned away made it almost impossible to say no. Beyond that, philosophically and morally Jane was committed to each woman's right to an abortion at any stage of pregnancy. But few members wanted to be directly involved in miscarriages. At meetings, the tension between what they believed in and what each of them would take on could easily have led to an attack: "If you feel so strongly about this, then where the fuck are you?" A counselor who thought something ought to be done should be willing to do it. Every time the question arose, a member stepped in, "If no one else will do it, then I will." But, if no one had volunteered, they might have had to accept that there were limits to what they could do. Were they responsible for every pregnant woman who wanted an abortion? They wished every miscarriage they handled was the last one.

The situation was extremely painful for teenagers,* who, because of their youth, often denied they were pregnant until it was physically obvious. Each night they prayed it would go away, but it didn't. Because of the time it took to miscarry, the higher incidence of complications, and the support needed to get through it, counselors encouraged teenagers terrified of telling their parents to talk to them: "You need their help. You might be surprised by the support they give you." In any case, if a sixteen-year-old had to be admitted to a hospital, her parents were going to be notified. It was better if she told them first.

Inducing miscarriages forced them to confront an issue that they

*While the service set no age limit and did not require parental approval, most young teens came with their parents, whereas most older teens, not surprisingly, came alone.

had previously considered only in the abstract. Were they going to induce a miscarriage for a woman at any stage, no matter how late in pregnancy? At some point, a miscarriage might result in a premature baby. Did they want to be responsible for a disabled child? The pregnant woman had to take some responsibility for her situation. The group had to set a limit beyond which no miscarriage was induced.

But even if they agreed to set a limit, they had no accurate method for determining length of gestation other than externally estimating the size of the uterus. Basically they had to rely on what women told them, and that was not always accurate. Women who menstruated for the first few months of pregnancy misjudged their conception dates. Even physicians' estimates were sometimes off by a month. Some women lied, terrified that the group would turn them away.

And, even if they could judge precisely the length of each pregnancy, they believed that the decision to have an abortion at any stage of pregnancy rested solely with the woman. It was a moral decision only she could make. The group acted as instruments of her will. Nan, having had a miscarriage herself, felt that "if it's the mother's decision, it's her decision. You should tell the mother that she might want to rethink it because there's a chance the child might survive and be damaged. Did she want a damaged child? But ultimately it's her decision." They were haunted by the lengths a woman would go to if they refused to help her. Nan knew from her own personal experience that "women will opt for butchers and die if they feel that desperate." But, by agreeing to perform an abortion they were more than instruments, they were actors, participants, just like the woman herself. Did they have a right and a responsibility to set limits? When the demands of women's immediate needs conflicted with the group's responsibility, a friction was created that they never thoroughly resolved. The discussion surfaced intermittently. As long as abortions were illegal and women were forced to search through the underground, the group was going to face some very troubling situations.

Miriam agreed to counsel the women they suspected of having advanced pregnancies. Even though she believed that a woman had a right to an abortion at any stage, she tried to talk these women out of one. She had a child who was born seriously retarded and, though the disability was not a result of a premature delivery, she used her daughter as an example of what might happen if they were determined to have an abortion. Miriam, a powerful persuader, was usually successful.

Nathan came to Chicago only a few times to administer the paste. For the next few months he supplied it to the group and Nick inserted it. Jenny wondered why it wasn't used more widely and why she couldn't find out more about it. By the winter of 1970, they stopped using it. Nick had an alternate method to induce miscarriages. With small forceps he tore the amniotic sac, and, by pressing externally on a woman's abdomen, expelled the amniotic fluid. Labor could start anywhere from a day to two weeks later, which made it more difficult to monitor these women. Rupturing the amniotic sac increased the possibility of an infection. Women had to be carefully cautioned not to take baths, have intercourse, or put anything in their vaginas.

Nick wasn't comfortable with miscarriages. Because of the time factor and the possible complications, he felt more vulnerable to prosecution. But, if the group managed the miscarriages, he would induce them. Counselors had to maintain daily contact with women to make sure they took their temperature and to remind them of what to avoid that could cause an infection. Women who miscarried anywhere other than in a hospital had a cleanup D & C with Nick as soon as possible after they miscarried to prevent problems from retained tissue. Pam remembers that "virtually everybody showed up for their cleanup D & C. Infection, infection, we really emphasized the dangers of postpartum infection in counseling."

By the spring of 1971 Jenny felt competent to handle on her own the technically simplest abortions, inducing miscarriages. She set up another work day, Thursday, to do these abortions. On Thursdays there was no Nick or any other hired outside abortionist. They would not have to worry about collecting enough money to pay someone. No egos had to be stroked, no one's identity had to be protected. They didn't have to use the blindfolds that Nick demanded. On Thursdays they had total control.

As training, Deborah assisted Jenny with miscarriages on Thursdays. Jenny reached into each woman's uterus with forceps and tore the amniotic sac. Once the sac was broken, she expelled the fluid by pressing on the woman's abdomen. Looking over her shoulder at Deborah, she explained as she pressed, "Down and in, down and out." To the woman she said, "You push, too. You press from the top of the uterus." All three of them pushed together to expel as much fluid as possible.

Later that spring, on a Thursday, their work day without Nick, Jenny was inducing miscarriages. The last person that day was a nineteen-year-old woman who was about fourteen weeks pregnant. With forceps Jenny reached into her uterus and broke the amniotic sac, but, when she removed the forceps they held a very small, translucent limb. She stared at it while her mind raced. She knew that an exposed bone could puncture the uterus during labor. She thought, I've got to finish this abortion, right now.

There was a hurried conversation among the women working. "I don't see how we can send her on her way when we've got a fucking bone here. I've got to do a D & C," Jenny said.

The other women asked, "Do you think you can do it?"

"Well, yes. We don't have any choice," Jenny answered.

The young woman on the bed asked, "Is something wrong?" When they told her what they were going to do, she was pleased that the abortion was going to be completed that day. One of the counselors assisting began explaining a D & C to her.

This was Jenny's first solo D & C abortion, without Nick standing by, and it was not going to be a simple one. As a pregnancy advances, the muscular wall of the uterus gradually thins as it stretches, and that increases the possibility of excessive bleeding or puncture during an abortion. Nick regularly performed D & Cs at this stage without problem. Jenny knew she had to be extra careful. As she proceeded, she coached herself silently: *Okay, be cool. Reach in with the forceps, explore the uterine wall for material, gently twist to make sure it's loose, now pull the forceps through the cervix.* When she was about three-quarters through there was a small gush of blood. She picked up the curette: *Now scrape the placenta down off the wall so the bleeding stops.* When the bleeding subsided, Jenny switched back to the forceps and then returned to the curette to make sure the wall was clean. She could feel the woman's uterus contract and become firm. When she removed the speculum and said, "There, all done," the room exploded in excitement.

There was a gleam in Jenny's eye while she was concentrating on the abortion. If she could handle a complicated one on her own, she could handle any abortion. Very soon they were not going to be dependent on anyone but themselves. But her elation had a somber edge. Independence meant that they would not be shielded from the consequences of performing abortions. But, now that she had the skill, she was going to use it. From that day on, without mentioning to Nick what she was doing, she performed a few D & C abortions each Thursday along with induced miscarriages. The service was rapidly moving toward a time when it would fulfill her original dream: to work on a project that was strictly for women, by women, and at the will of women.

Only a few months earlier the group had had to come to terms with the news that Nick, the man they called "doctor," was not, in fact, a doctor. Now the group had to accept that not only weren't doctors performing Jane's abortions but that women in the group were.

Lorraine, one of Jane's original members, was apprehensive when Jenny announced at a service meeting that women were learning to do abortions. She didn't think that working with Nick was enough training and she said so. But a half-dozen other members who were, unlike Lorraine, assisting or training as abortionists, argued that this was exactly the right direction. The only difference between them and Nick was that he was a man and they were women. Lorraine was overwhelmed by their reaction. Jenny had presented this news to the group as a *fait accompli*. Once something had not only been decided, but acted on, Lorraine and the other members found it almost impossible to argue with or undo it.

For a few members this latest revelation was more than they could handle and they left the group. At each stage of their evolution women dropped out if they could not accept the direction the service was taking. Jane members had been counselors, assistants and nurses, in women's traditional and acceptable roles as helpers. Now Jenny's skill was forcing them to look at themselves in a dramatically new light and, Deborah recalls, "That's why the shit hit the fan. One group left when they weren't doctors; they weren't the right men to follow. When, whoever *they* were, we were going to do it, another bunch left because it was just not acceptable for women to take the power into their own hands."

CHAPTER 15

Two years earlier, in 1969, even though the handful of women who organized the group had divided the work, the members worked together as equals. Since they were in the process of building something out of nothing, every decision was discussed. But that was no longer the case. The service called itself a "leaderless democracy" but, in fact, their structure, although no one overtly stated it, was a series of concentric circles. On the outer edge were women whose involvement was limited to counseling; in the center was the inner circle composed of Miriam and Jenny. They made the decisions about Jane's practice, without input from the full group. By late winter 1971 the inner circle included Deborah, Julia and a few others. They met before service meetings or over cups of coffee in the afternoons around Julia's kitchen table.

At one of these informal meetings the inner circle decided not to refer any more women to outside abortionists. From then on, either an abortionist worked for them, like Nick did, or they weren't going to use him.

Other discussions revolved around their practice: How much Ergotrate are we giving each woman and is it enough? Or they focused on group members: Is so-and-so doing a good job? Jenny, on the lookout for members to move into more trusted positions, might ask, "What about that one?" The discussion continued until eventually

Jenny or Miriam made a pronouncement. Miriam usually had the final say about people; Jenny had the definitive word on procedure.

While the inner circle met in the afternoons, the full membership got together once a week at night. At those meetings *Big Jane* passed around three-by-five-inch index cards, each listing information on a woman who had called them, so that members could select women to counsel. While women volunteered to work at Fronts or drive, the stack of cards passed around the room. Every week the stack grew larger. Since at least six members attended abortions, counselors asked, "Who sat with Marcia Adams and how did it go?" But that exchange was a background buzz to the formal discussion, not part of the agenda.

Because of the ongoing hearings regarding her teaching position, Deborah was particularly sensitive to issues of power. Julia instinctively reacted against exclusivity. During meetings of the inner circle the two of them started pushing Miriam and Jenny to open up the process: "What's going on in these little meetings should be going on in the big meeting."

"Well, is it really good to discuss all these things with everyone?" Miriam might respond. "It could be dangerous for them and they probably don't want to know this stuff. They probably want to be able to do what they're doing and not be burdened with the details."

"People have a right to know what's going on and, anyway, I'm going to tell them," Deborah answered.

At service meetings, Deborah and Julia began mentioning what the inner circle had discussed, forcing Miriam and Jenny to acknowledge it. But their effectiveness at undermining the autocracy was limited. Since they had privileged positions within it, they were invested in it. "We were not knights in shining armor ourselves," Deborah notes. "We accepted the role of princesses to their queens, so we were successful at reform but not at revolution. That's how it always works when you try to use power you're given that way."

Women who only counseled had few complaints about how the

group functioned. They were on the periphery of the concentric circles of responsibility, knowledge and power and were only interested in a limited role. But those on a middle level, such as Cynthia, grumbled. She watched as others were moved into positions of trust, assisting Nick. Most of those women had joined after she had and she resented it. For a group that talked egalitarian politics, it was a contradiction. Clearly, there were the ins and the outs, and Cynthia was out. She was irritated that critical information and decisions were kept from her: "I never bought into doling information out on a need-to-know basis. It made me very angry. If a decision affects you, directly or indirectly, and may end up meaning your life is on the line, you damn well better have a say in it."

Membership in the inner circle was fluid. It was based on friendship, on personalities, on availability during the day. Anyone could attend, that is if she knew that people were getting together. Geography played a part in who talked to whom. For the Hyde Park women, like Miriam and Jenny, it required little effort to stop by Julia's for a cup of coffee. Counselors who lived on the North Side shared the thirty-minute ride to Hyde Park for meetings or work days and, therefore, talked regularly to each other. The schoolteachers who lived in the far south suburbs felt separated by not only their suburban lifestyles, their physical distance and their full-time employment, they felt there was a political distance. Along with Cynthia they were members of NOW. In Cynthia's view, the leaders looked down on NOW and tended to favor women who came to Jane from the Chicago Women's Liberation Union. But that didn't account for Julia and Deborah's rise. Neither of them were CWLU members or adhered to any ideology, yet they were both being groomed for leadership. A common though subtler dynamic was at work: the women in Jane gravitated toward people who were similar, people they liked. Cynthia's exclusion had more to do with her personality, which many members found grating, than with her politics.

Kris, who taught at the alternative Catholic high school, had been attending inner circle meetings at Julia's invitation. She deflected the complaints about the existence of an in-group by saying to other members, "These people are just willing to take more responsibility than you. If you feel that they're not behaving appropriately, you can take action." But Kris's justification failed to recognize that the people excluded did not have the information they needed to act independently.

Some of the group's secrecy was inherited from Nick. Jenny often found herself in the position of having to balance his needs against the group's. Pam was committed to keeping a lid on the information flow. Since she had ties to radical groups, she was more attuned to the dangers they faced. She chastised the others for speaking too freely: "You're living in dreamland. There are informers, phone taps, people are being followed. We can all go to jail."

Did everyone need to know where the drugs came from or how equipment was purchased? As they gained control, how much of their inherited paranoia could they shed, given that every day they were committing multiple felonies? What struck Julia was that "it was very unclear how much needed to be secret and how much was kept that way out of a kind of spookiness that happens with secret organizations. Because of that, a lot of things just weren't discussed at all, which was kind of odd when you consider that the purpose of the group was to disseminate information."

For the most part, women questioned the process—how decisions were made and who made them—not what those decisions were. The response from the leaders was always the same: "Look, we don't have time for that. We have hundreds of women waiting for abortions. Their lives are at stake," which implied: If you raise this, you're the problem. Jenny had a charismatic quality that placed her above criticism. Her knowledge, her skill, her willingness to take responsibility were respected by everyone. She could be intimidating in her clarity and directness. The only thing she cared about was getting the work, which multiplied weekly, accomplished efficiently and effectively. Miriam was just as adamant in her control even though her style was more conciliatory. She and Jenny were a formidable pair.

Jenny, still battling Hodgkin's disease, felt her health deteriorating. The whole weight of the group seemed to rest on her and the responsibility was crushing. As the only fully trained abortionist she felt she couldn't quit. To protect herself she limited her interactions with the larger group. Her attendance at Jane meetings waned; she stopped counseling. It made it even harder to confront her, which added to Deborah's frustration: "Jenny hardly came to meetings and Miriam wouldn't deal."

The power inequities within the group were difficult to address, partially because those in power refused to acknowledge them. Most members accepted the status quo. Others chose not to confront the leaders because if they did they would have to accept more responsibility. On the other hand, Julia notes, "some of us are so controlling that it would never occur to us that we are not the responsible person."

If the group at large was not privy to the inner circle's workings, no one knew what individual counselors were saying to women in their private sessions. Aside from initially sitting in with an experienced counselor as training, counselors were not monitored by each other. The only clue as to what went on in a session was how a women responded during her abortion. It became apparent to the members who assisted that some women hadn't been sufficiently prepared. A woman who did not receive adequate information was likely to have serious difficulty coping with the procedure. After her abortion she might say, "That was nothing like I was told it was going to be."

They decided to address this problem by including a mock counseling session as part of their training. At the second orientation meeting for new members, the trainer went through the entire counseling process as if she were actually counseling a woman. The trainer described the process—"From the Front you'll go in a car with other women to another apartment or house . . . When it's your turn you'll go into a bedroom . . . "—included a description of the abortion, and ended with aftercare and birth control information. Adding this detail to their training assured that at least new counselors started with the same information.

Still, some counselors were not doing an adequate job. A few women let their own emotional issues overwhelm their counseling sessions. The group hadn't set up a mechanism for addressing those problems openly. In most cases women who were not up to it realized it on their own and left. When that did not happen another counselor eventually had to suggest, "Maybe you shouldn't be doing this."

The absence of any stated power structure allowed for individual initiative or a lack of it. Some people turned to the inner circle to solve a problem. In contrast, when Cynthia was *Big Jane,* she fired a *Call-Back Jane* for not doing her work in a timely fashion. When Cynthia told her she was out, the other woman responded, "You can't do that."

Cynthia countered, "You want to bet?"

Without clear lines of authority, Cynthia could do what she thought was right. She felt, Somebody has to do it and, since I'm scheduling abortions and directly affected, I have to.

With no acknowledged structure, there was a constant tug-of-war between the demands of efficiency and the need to maximize group participation. That tension was compounded by their fears of prosecution. There were no clear boundaries around how much information needed to be kept secret to protect the group. No one doubted that, if they had to face legal consequences, everyone was culpable, even if she was not making the decisions.

It was a group dynamic full of contradictions. Beyond providing abortions, Jane's mission was to give each woman some power and control over her life, and, yet, the group itself was tightly controlled by a handful of women. In the service power came from responsibility, but a few decided who would be given more responsibility. Philosophically they believed the means were the ends, but their ends sometimes subverted the means. Each desperate woman who called was treated with the utmost respect, but within the group the backbiting and gossip were endless. Without a way to honestly confront one another, much that needed to be openly addressed festered, waiting to explode destructively.

For the members of Jane, their primary allegiance was to the group. Their loyalty to Jane was similar to the loyalty that combat troops feel toward their unit. They relied on each other. If a member did not do her part responsibly, the entire group might face medical and legal troubles; their work would suffer. And the work took precedence over their internal dynamics. Hundreds of women's lives hung in the balance. In desperation they had turned to Jane. For the women in the service it was a heady responsibility. Their personal satisfaction was enormous because the results were tangible. A woman came to them with a problem—a pregnancy she did not want—and Jane solved that problem. Jane's members took pleasure in their own competence, in acting responsibly and in their certainty that what they were doing had to be done. Their loyalty to the group mitigated the tension, but it never erased it.

Miriam and Jenny continued to pressure Nick to let them bring new women to work days. But, now that they worked one day a week, Thursday, when Nick was not involved, they could begin to train anyone they wanted as an assistant. Assisting was a prerequisite for doing abortions, but not every assistant was trained to perform abortions. At a meeting late in the spring, Jenny asked who wanted to learn to assist. Lydia, who had joined a few months earlier, raised her hand.

Lydia had been adopted by a Swedish immigrant steelworker's

family and raised in a blue-collar neighborhood in Chicago. In college she took birth control pills that were supposed to be foolproof but, even on pills, she got pregnant. When no local doctor would give her an abortion, she went to the library. There she found references to abortions induced by taking quinine tablets.* She took quinine, too desperate to heed the warning that large doses of it could be fatal. "I was bleeding all over the house," she remembers, "and my ears were ringing." She miscarried, the bleeding stopped, but her ears kept ringing for two years.

Lydia was living with her husband and two children when she joined the service early in 1971. Driving for Jane she noticed that, on the return trip to the Front, after their abortions, "Many women felt empowered because it was the first adult decision that they had made. With Jane they didn't have to lie down and leave their power outside the room. I remember how happy they were, surprised they were so happy and doubting whether they should be happy."

When Jenny asked, Who wants to assist? Lydia shot her hand up. A few weeks later, while she was driving, she was invited to watch an abortion. At home that night she cried because, even though she had had two children, she had never seen her own cervix.

Lydia lived through her mind and not her body: "I always thought of myself as a head on a platter, like John the Baptist." Attending abortions helped her come to terms with her own physicality. At first she was uncomfortable touching other women's bodies, but soon it felt normal: "Before long I found myself stroking women's thighs, like you would a hand, not sexualized."

Jane members were used to talking with strangers about the intimate details of women's bodies, abortion and sexuality. As counselors helped with the abortions, they, like Lydia, grew comfortable with

*Injesting large doses of quinine acts as a dangerous, even fatal, systemic poison whose side effect may be a miscarriage.

the physical contact. Although they never touched women with sexual overtones, they were aware of women's sexuality. After all, their pregnancies were a result of it. Women's sexuality had been controlled by a morality in which they were either Madonnas or whores, and by laws that prohibited contraception and abortion. "She had her fun, now let her pay for it," treated pregnancy as a punishment for sexual activity. The women in Jane, along with other feminists, understood that women had a right to sexual pleasure. It was essential for their liberation.

CHAPTER 16

When Miriam's husband, David, bumped into a woman he knew who had recently dropped out of the service, he asked why she had left. "It was too intense for me," she said. "I'm amazed at the women who do it."

He shook his head, "I think they're all obsessed."

David supported Miriam's work, but even an understanding partner had limits. The telephone rang constantly; the service intruded on farnily time. Jane had become more of a commitment than any of the women in the group had expected. Most of the members' husbands and boyfriends, like David, helped in any way they could, but a few were actively hostile. One husband barged in during a meeting in his living room, drunk and obstreperous.

The men drove women to the bus terminal or the train station. They delivered emergency medications and socialized when they were home for Fronts. It might not be their own project, but they could play a part, however tangential. But the amount of time and emotional energy going someplace other than their relationship was fertile ground for resentment. David and Herb, Julia's husband, over beers in Jimmy's Woodlawn Tap, muttered half-jokingly to each other, "We're sick of this women's lib crap."

Kris's husband, Bill, who taught at the same alternative Catholic high school as Kris, thought that "Jane never felt thrilling, just a lot of work. On the face of it, it's not a rational decision to risk yourself for somebody else, a stranger who you never saw before and you'll never see again. That's the engineer in me adding up the equation."

One night while she was frosting a cake, Bill came up to her: "Would you rather help women or be with me?"

She looked up at him, annoyed, "You know, I think this is the wrong relationship for you because this is not a choice for me. I have to do it and you're just going to have to accept it. Why do you see the service as competition?"

She put down the spatula and left the apartment with their dog. As she walked down the street, the dog racing ahead, Bill caught up with her. He took her arm and pleaded, "Don't leave. I'll deal with it."

For Julia's husband, Herb, the service felt "definitely romantic. I would often think, who else in the whole city or the country is involved in something as exotic as this, as important as this?" Herb loved being around women: "I'd come home and see all these women and just be happy."

There was such an assumption of heterosexuality in the service that no one considered that some members' partners might be women. A few, when they suspected that another counselor was a lesbian, reacted out of fear and ignorance. After a work day, when the assistants were sitting around unwinding, one of them commented, "If Roseanne is a lesbian, maybe she shouldn't be an assistant." Of course, no one questioned Nick's heterosexuality or whether it was appropriate for him to be performing abortions. Roseanne once confided in Julia that as a lesbian she felt invisible, but she did not feel that the service was a safe place to come out.

Over the following year-and-a-half attitudes in the women's liberation movement and in Jane evolved to such an extent that when Grace, an out lesbian, joined in 1972 she was a welcomed addition to the group. Grace's personal growth in 1971 and 1972 was similar to what many other women were experiencing through their contact with the women's movement.

In 1971 Grace was living with her husband, a graduate student at the University of Chicago, and their two small children: "I had these little babies and I didn't even know how to drive. I was carting them and the groceries and the laundry all over the place." That year she and another young mother who lived next door attended a series of talks on women's issues sponsored by a local community organization. At the end of the eight sessions, Grace and a few other women decided to follow the course organizers' suggestion to form a consciousness-raising rap group. Grace, with her New England reserve, had never talked openly about anything personal, least of all sex, and she found the rap group "really explosive. We started talking dirty real fast. We were talking about things we never talked about before and never thought we'd be able to, and that's an incredibly intense experience."

Since pregnancy tests were available only through clinics and doctors, the Women's Liberation Union asked Grace's rap group to set up a pregnancy testing service in Hyde Park. Several times a week, in a nearby Lutheran church, they offered the tests. Grace was amazed by how busy they were: "Women came from the suburbs, from all over, for a lousy pregnancy test they can buy in a drugstore now. People were nervous and upset. We'd let them watch while we did the test."

Meanwhile Grace's marriage was deteriorating. Arguments, which had begun when she attended the classes, increased. They fought about housework, about child care and, once Grace realized how depressed and lonely she had been, they fought about everything. Finally her husband moved out.

After Grace's marriage ended, she came out as a lesbian. For the first time in years she did not feel isolated. In the women's community she found "the support that I absolutely had to have to make such a drastic change in my life." When Grace joined the service she did not hide her sexuality. In the movement lesbians were confronting heterosexual women, forcing them to examine their assumptions and prejudices. Grace never felt stigmatized in the service.

Her work with Jane was another way she was taking charge of her life: "I felt so powerful and I had been so powerless."

Through the winter and spring of 1971 many middle-class women in the Chicago area flew to New York for abortions. These were women who not only had the time and resources to fly but who also felt comfortable getting on a plane and traveling to a strange city. Some women could not leave Chicago because they had to keep the abortion secret from their families or because their husbands tightly controlled their money. Others were teenagers and young adults; many were older working-class women. As spring turned to summer, the women who turned to Jane were increasingly women of color, women like Betty.

Betty had always wanted a big family. By the time she was thirty she and her husband had five children. When her youngest child was killed by a car late in 1970, Betty stopped taking birth control pills. But, once she got pregnant she thought, This doesn't make sense. I'm trying to replace something that God took away and, if He wanted to, He could take away all of my kids.

She had heard that quinine tablets caused abortions, so she took them, but did not miscarry. Then she worried that the quinine had damaged the fetus and that, she felt, would be devastating. Getting pregnant had been a mistake; quinine had only compounded it.

A friend told Betty that she had managed to get a legal abortion by telling her doctor that she would kill herself if she did not get one. She suggested that Betty try the same ploy, so Betty made an appointment with her own doctor, a black physician in her neighborhood whom she trusted. When she mentioned her friend's advice, he responded, "Why would you want to say something like that? It will follow you the rest of your life." He was not opposed to abortion. He gave her a few referrals, including Jane of whom he spoke so highly that Betty suspected he performed Jane's abortions. What she did not know was that he was one of Jenny's physician friends who provided backup for the service.

Her counselor explained everything, including possible problems she might have afterward and how to deal with them. "I didn't know exactly who was behind it," Betty recalls, "but I knew it was women's lib. All these people willing to help me made me feel like someone special."

When the abortion was scheduled Betty's husband left town, saying, "You know, I'd rather not be here because it's not my choice."

At the Front she talked with other women waiting for abortions: a teenager accompanied by her aunt, an executive secretary. One woman was about to separate from her husband; another couldn't afford one more child.

While Nick was performing her abortion, Betty talked about her son's death but, "They didn't let me dwell on that too much," she says. "I remember laughing. He was joking with me about having all boys."

That night she lay in bed with severe cramps and a fever. She prayed: Please don't let me die with my kids here and my husband out of town. In the morning her counselor, suspecting she had retained tissue, arranged for a second D & C with Jane, which cured the problem. Betty guessed what might have happened: "My counselor had said that he has to listen and if it sounds rough it means everything's been taken out. I believe, with all our talking during the abortion, that's why he didn't catch the sound."

Betty's doctor had given her Jane's pamphlet. She kept it and gave the phone number to every woman she knew who needed an abortion.

By the summer of 1971 Nick was performing fewer than half of Jane's abortions. Jenny was fully trained; Pam and Julia were well advanced in the process. Although Nick still flew in from California to work for

Jane on Fridays and Saturdays, their dependence on him was waning. On one of the three days a week that they worked Nick wasn't even in town. Jenny convinced him to lower his per diem. When he did, the group dropped its price to $100 per abortion, but women only had to pay what they could afford, which averaged about $50 per abortion. Some women paid nothing; others mailed their counselors regular installments until the $100 was paid in full. If a woman could afford only $7 for her abortion, that was what she paid.

The drop in price accelerated a change in demographics that had gradually been taking place through the past year. By the summer Jane's number had spread through the poor black communities on the South Side and West Side of the city. Since money was not an obstacle, Jane rapidly became a service for the poor. No one in the group had initially planned to serve a largely poor population, but that, as it turned out, was who needed them most. These women had few options and minimal health care. For many poor women of color in Chicago, Jane was the only part of the women's liberation movement that directly affected their lives.

Of the twenty-five to thirty members of Jane, the overwhelming majority were white. Since 1970 some women of color had joined the group, but there were never more than a few at any time. As the numbers of women of color, especially black women, coming through Jane increased, the group repeatedly discussed the need to find black women to work with them. They did not know how to go about recruiting those women. Few women of color were involved in the women's movement and, at the time, there was no black women's movement. Turning to radical organizations was not an option. Since the killings of Fred Hampton and Mark Clark in a police raid on Black Panther headquarters late in 1969, part of a national campaign to destroy the Panthers, black radicals in Chicago were under siege. They viewed women's liberation as an attempt to undermine black solidarity, and abortion as a potential weapon against their community.

To find counselors of color Jane had to turn to women they knew and to the women they counseled. But, whether these women were having enough trouble keeping their lives afloat, or whether a white group had no appeal to the majority of women who came through the service, the group never managed to attract more than a few women of color. As white women performing abortions for poor black women, they were vulnerable to accusations of genocide and racism. But it wasn't only a question of race differences but of class. Most Jane members were college educated and middle class. Could they begin to understand the problems of a woman trying to support a family on a minimum-wage income or a meager welfare check? But it was exactly their privilege that gave them the freedom to do what they were doing. Every few months at meetings they discussed the need to broaden their membership, but the composition of the group remained basically the same.

Nick was aware of the change in the kinds of women who turned to Jane. He usually didn't suggest improvements, but after a work day, as the workers relaxed, he said to Jenny, "Most of these ladies aren't getting any kind of medical care." He suggested that they start taking Pap (Papanicolaou) smears, the test for cervical cancer, for which his wife had recently been treated. On one of his weekend trips to Chicago he brought a teaching microscope, assuming that women in the group could learn to read Pap smears. He felt that "getting the microscope was the right thing to do. After all, I'd done okay and Pap smears more legitimized the whole business." He taught the assistants to take the smears; from then on, every woman who came to Jane had a Pap free of charge.

A cytologist who had once been in Jane agreed to teach Cynthia and another member to read the smears. They stained the slides but didn't have the expertise to recognize differences in cell structure, so the cytologist analyzed them. Later, one of Jenny's doctor friends sent them in with his and eventually the service established its own link with a lab. The total cost to the group for each Pap smear, including materials and lab charges, was under $4. Providing this test was a way that Jane could expand their service and give women some basic gynecological care, care no one else was giving them.

Through the summer of 1971 Jane performed abortions three days a week without interference from the police. Sometimes patrol cars cruised by the Place every few minutes or parked near the door. Now and then a panicky phone call to the Front or the Place, from a counselor who suspected the police had been tipped off, forced the work crew to leave by a back door and relocate to continue their work. Drivers watched for cars that might be following them. Waves of paranoia rippled through the group whenever odd clicks on their telephones indicated tapping. A few times Jenny answered her doorbell to find officers, acting on a complaint from a hospital, waiting to question her. One of her neighbors, with official connections, warned her husband that their house was being watched. Pam, while attending antiwar demonstrations, had had police officers call out to her, "Hi, Jane." The group knew that, at any time, the police could send a woman through the service or that one of their members might be an informer. Why the police didn't arrest them was a mystery. Did they recognize that Jane was a service to the community that acted as a safety valve? Although group members knew that they could be arrested at any time, there were months when the police ignored them and, during those periods, the fear of arrest faded into a dull background hum.

They were more vulnerable to prosecution when they had to send a woman to a hospital. Still, they weren't going to take any risks with women's lives. Whenever a woman had to go to the hospital, her counselor prepared her. She needed to know that she had a right to treatment, to refuse treatment and to be fully informed. If she was threatened by hospital personnel or the police questioned her, she did not have to say anything. Because medical authorities presumed the woman's ignorance the best strategy at the emergency room was to act dumb. It was one way to use the medical profession's prejudices to the benefit of women.

Over the past two years they had had disturbing reports from women who had had to go to a hospital. It seemed that poor women without insurance or on Medicaid might wind up with unnecessary hysterectomies when they went to an emergency room with complications from an illegal abortion, especially if they were women of color. Jenny knew that even if a uterus had been punctured a hysterectomy was not always necessary. A respected gynecologist had confided in her that he knew of at least nine uteruses he had punctured in the operating room and each one had healed by itself. Jane members began warning every woman who had to go to the hospital to fight for her uterus.

By late summer the group was performing twenty to thirty abortions on each of the three days a week they worked. The workload was a drain on the membership. Every day required two abortionists, two to four assistants, a driver and two counselors at the Front. Of the twenty-five to thirty members, fewer than half were willing to be directly involved in the abortions. Others might have been interested, but they had jobs that limited the time they could give to the service.

With Jenny, Pam and Julia trained, the group was no longer dependent on Nick. He flew in occasionally, but they did not really need him. Now and then they hired another abortionist, a black chiropractor, to work for them like Nick did, on a per diem basis. He introduced them to a different type of dilator, another kind of cold sterilizer and a tenaculum, a clamp to hold the cervix in place.

Even with a sliding scale and a maximum charge of $100 per abortion, for the first time the service had money. Along with *Big Jane* and *Call-Back Jane,* they could pay other women, which would relieve the pressure on those who could afford to work without a salary and increase the number of women being trained. They had always believed that their work was valuable and should be recompensed. But the possibility of paying more women brought up all kinds of issues.

Every counselor, whether she was trained to use curettes or not, considered herself an abortionist, especially when it came to the risks they were taking. To blur the distinction between abortionist and assistant, they referred to themselves as paramedics, in a conscious rejection of a hierarchy based on skill. Now they worried they might create another hierarchy based on salary. In the larger society a person's worth was measured by how much money she made. They did not want to replicate that system. All work for the service was equally important, except for counseling, which was valued above all else.

Even if all their work was equal, they considered whether some people should be paid more because they needed to support families. They believed that Jane was a model for a social and medical revolution and, if what they were doing was "after the revolution," it had to be right.

Finally the group reached a unanimous decision. Paramedics, whether abortionists or assistants, *Call-Backs* and *Big Janes* would be paid equivalent salaries. Those jobs required consistent attention. To maintain the voluntary nature of their organization, counseling, driving and working at the Front remained unpaid jobs that every member was expected to do.

Cash on hand was held by members around the city. One counselor kept it in a pickle jar under her bed. Miriam used her nightstand drawer until a burglar broke in and stole over a thousand dollars of Nick's money. After that, most counselors kept it in their freezers—cold cash, a service joke. No one kept track of it; no one had any idea exactly how much money they had. It was available on an honor system for salaries, supplies, phone bills and transportation expenses. It was also used to stock the Fronts with food. What had begun as coffee and tea had evolved into a smorgasbord of cheeses, crackers, fruits, juices, milk and cookies. They hoped contact with the service would be a politicizing experience, but they also wanted a day with Jane to be as pleasant as possible and feeding people well was one way to do that. For most of the members, good food was central. They brought pastries to work; they ate during service meetings, when the inner circle met, whenever Jane members got together. They used food to express the pleasure they took in life, as if eating well were the best revenge.

CHAPTER 17

When Jane was organized in 1969, the group was determined to make sure no one was injured by a Jane abortion. If they were going to violate a medical taboo and break the law, they had to be perfect. But, over the past two years they had learned that, no matter how conscientious and careful they were, they could not always avoid serious medical problems. There had been a few instances when nothing they did brought a woman's bleeding under control and they had to rush her to a hospital. A doctor's first responsibility was to do no harm, but, even for the best doctors in the best hospitals, things sometimes went terribly wrong. The women in Jane knew their knowledge was limited and their circumstances less than optimal. Abortion's illegality put them in that tenuous position. To compound the medical uncertainty of any surgery, the desperate women who turned to them sometimes lied about or neglected to mention existing medical conditions, the length of their pregnancies, anything that might prevent them from getting an abortion. The possibility that someone could die weighed on them. In orientation sessions they asked prospective members to consider how they would react if that happened. On work days, when an emergency arose, the people working wondered: What if? What would we do? But nothing prepared them for the reality.

On a routine work day in the summer, the workers had just completed an abortion. While they cleaned up the room, the woman got dressed and went into the living room to wait for a ride to the Front. When the assistant brought the next young woman into the bedroom for her abortion, they realized that she was already severely infected. They asked her what she had done, where she had gone, before turning to them. She said she had tried other things, but she didn't give them any details. The people who were working that day told her: "You're very sick. There's nothing we can do. You must go to a hospital immediately." They tried to reach her afterward to make sure she had sought medical care, but there was no answer. Several days later a counselor got through to a relative who responded to her query, "Delores? She passed." She had gone to a hospital and she had died there. Someone who had come to them for help had died.

A small group of service members, including Jenny, Miriam, Julia, Deborah and Cynthia, held an emergency meeting in Lincoln Park. They were somber as they sat in a circle, talking quietly, trying to piece together what had happened. They knew that it was likely that the police had questioned her to elicit a "dying declaration" naming the abortionist. "But we weren't nearly as concerned with fear as with the horrible tragedy of it," Jenny recalls. They knew Delores had tried other methods to abort: she had admitted it that day. They knew they hadn't caused her death, but they felt responsible. They had to find out what had happened.

One of their doctor contacts worked at the hospital where Delores had died. Deborah called him for any information that could shed some light on what had happened. In a hallway at the hospital he handed her a copy of the autopsy report, which indicated that Delores had waited more than a day before coming to the hospital. He had another critical piece of information: the word around the hospital was that the infection had predated her appointment with Jane by at least a week. And, he said, the police had questioned her.

A special meeting of the full group was called to share the information they had gathered. As the details of the story were recounted, a numbness spread through the room. They had founded the service to save women from dying and now the very thing they were trying to prevent had happened.

Each counselor reacted to the news based on her own individual experiences and attitudes. A few had dealt with women who had had major complications, such as hemorrhage or infection. But most of the counselors had never handled a serious problem. Whatever had been said in training sessions about the risks was theoretical; this was real. Kris, whose apartment had been the Front the day Delores had come, remembered that, "some women were really pissed off. They'd come into the service thinking it was a heads-up sort of organization and now somebody had died, so we're just like all the other back-alley abortionists." They said, She passed through our hands; we are responsible. There were other counselors who did not blame the group but, nevertheless, now that the worst had happened, they argued that Jane had to fold. They said, "We've overstepped ourselves. We are going to get caught. We've got to stop."

But the central core of the group, Jenny, Miriam, Julia, and Deborah, was determined and fought for Jane's continued existence. Kris was impressed that "the center always held in the service. The center was always focused on exactly what had to be done." The core group spoke forcefully: The women who come to us are desperate. They don't have any other options. This kind of thing will only happen to many more women if we stop. No matter what, we have to keep going. These women's lives are at stake. Now there's even more reason to go on. With her mouth drawn tight Julia said, "It's all going to be okay. We'll all be fine," as if willing it would make it so. But running underneath their discussion was anger. The law was wrong; it drove women to risk their lives. If abortion were legal, this would not have happened. Delores would still be alive.

Because the Front had been at Kris's that day, she knew she was implicated in whatever was going to unfold. She was getting the same sinking feeling that she had had in college when, flirting with the radical fringe, she opened a friend's closet and found a cache of guns. She knew that "my involvement was at a point where maybe I couldn't get out unscathed."

The rest of the meeting was a tactical discussion. What could they do to prevent this from happening again? From then on they had to take temperatures and blood pressures before the abortions to screen out anyone who was ill. How could they continue to serve women who needed them without jeopardizing the service itself? Obviously, Kris's apartment could not be used as a Front. Drivers had to follow a different route on each round-trip between the Front and the Place. They had to find places to work in parts of the city and outlying suburbs they had not previously used. In case their phones were tapped, they had to make service calls from pay phones, never home phones. If the police contacted anyone, she should not tell them anything.

The next meeting was significantly smaller. When confronted with this harsh reality, between a third and a half of the group dropped out. The remaining members were wary and paranoid. At meetings they repeated their tactical procedures: If the police come, don't say anything; don't think you can trade information with them. Their conversations on the phone were terse.

For a few weeks Kris was frantic, so she withdrew from Jane. By the time the police knocked on her door, she was beginning to relax her guard. Two homicide detectives introduced themselves; Kris invited them in. Bill was watching a football game on TV and the detectives sat down on the sofa with him. After a few minutes of small talk one of them asked, "Is this the house that was used in the abortion murder?"

Kris said, "I don't know what you're talking about."

They asked her if she knew Jenny and Julia. She denied knowing them.

The detectives pulled out a thick notebook and said, "It doesn't matter because we've been keeping surveillance on this group for many months. We know all about you, what cars you drive, where you go. We've followed your cars."

Kris said, "These are serious charges. If you have any further questions, I have to have a lawyer present."

Finally the officers got up to leave, "We'll be back within two weeks with a warrant and we will charge you, so I ask you again to cooperate with us because it will go much easier on you."

After the police left, Kris and Bill panicked. They called Deborah, whose husband, Marc, was a lawyer, and headed to the North Side to talk to him.

When they told Marc and Deborah what had happened, Marc said, "If they come back, say you won't talk unless your lawyer is there." He told them: Hang tight; do nothing; wait and see what happens. Kris asked him what she could be charged with and what kind of jail time she was looking at. He answered: Conspiracy to commit abortion: up to ten years.

The detectives went to Julia's but she wasn't home. They asked her husband, Herb, a few questions, left and never returned. Then they went to Jenny's. They said, "We want to talk to you about this case."

Jenny decided to ignore the lawyer's advice. She felt that "we're not going to lose anything by talking to them because we're as bad off as we can possibly be, so I'm going to talk to them. How can we be in worse trouble than we're already in?"

"Tell me what information you have, first," she said. "Before I answer anything I have to know what you have to say." She never admitted anything but, instead, asked them questions, which they answered, much to her surprise.

They told her what they knew, including that one of Delores's relatives said that she had previously taken some pills and gone somewhere unknown to have something done and had been running a fever. They let Jenny read their records. She said, "This sounds just terrible. Sounds like she was desperate and resorted to some pretty drastic measures. Isn't that true?"

They concurred, "We talked to her family and she was pretty desperate and took some risks."

Jenny responded: "That's a good argument for legalizing abortion."

The detectives launched into a description of Jane. They knew all about the group. Jenny said, "If what you are saying is true, I would think that an organization like that would be saving lives. Where do you think women should go? How would you feel, what would you do, if your seventeen-year-old daughter were pregnant?"

After they left, Jenny was amazed by how open the detectives had been with her. She hadn't expected them to be sympathetic. Her tactic had paid off. The police corroborated what their doctor contact had told them.

The group kept working. Everyone was on edge. Kris stopped counseling. At meetings she was almost as hysterical as Henny-Penny: "We've got to stop for a while. They're going to send a plant through. We're all going to get arrested. The world will end." Jenny met Kris's ravings with determination. She focused on the hundreds of women who depended on them. Deborah calmly repeated the steps each of them should take if the police came or if they got arrested. "Everything will be okay," Julia added, her mouth drawn tight. "We'll all be fine." The pressure was too much for Kris; she quit the service.

The new level of cautiousness in their practice complicated everything. Finding places to work was hard enough, but having to find them in neighborhoods outside of Hyde Park, away from their geographical and social center, was a real chore. Counselors were even more conscientious and scrupulous when following up with women. But Jenny felt it was a crapshoot, a matter of odds. Taking temperatures and blood pressures, she felt, was of limited value. She knew that sometimes people with temperatures and high pressures were just the ones who needed an abortion immediately. She turned over in her mind what they could have done to avoid this tragedy; one thing still haunts her: "Somebody should have taken her by the hand, directly to the hospital, but, then, she had some responsibility, too."

Time passed and nothing happened. Was it because, as Jenny suspected, the police were sympathetic and realized that prosecuting them would only put more women at risk of dying from incompetent abortions? But what part did racism play? A black woman, one more black woman, had died, so they weren't going to pursue it. Would the police response have been different if Delores had been white and middle class?

Regardless of how each of them came to terms with the young woman's death, the consequences of being underground, working without a safety net, without on-site medical backup, were clear. No institution sanctioned what they did. When problems arose, as they inevitably would, no one would defend them. They were on their own. Doctors and medical professionals had the power of an institution to protect them, but they had none. "There was no cushion," Deborah says. "Even though the police winked at us and the climate was in favor of us, for death there was no positive sanction. When New York legalized abortion and they had a mortality rate their first year, they were excused. We would not have been excused. We never would have excused ourselves."

CHAPTER 18

Since Delores's death Jane's membership had dwindled. For self-protection the group had suspended their monthly orientations for new counselors. Deborah and Lorraine were on maternity leave. After her daughter's birth Lorraine did not return to the service, but Deborah was looking forward to coming back to work when her baby was a little older. The women who had dropped out after Delores's death compounded the usual attrition rate, but the calls from desperate women kept coming. The remaining members were swamped. By mid-fall necessity forced them to plan an orientation for November.

The members were careful about whom they invited to the orientation. Every recruit had to have an established member who could vouch for her. One of the new women invited was Molly, whose abortion with Jane early in the spring had been so positive. Since then she and her counselor, Charlotte, had become friends. Molly often baby-sat for her. When any of Charlotte's counselees called while Molly was baby-sitting, she answered their questions and offered reassurances. Through Charlotte, Julia and Miriam got to know Molly. She was exactly the kind of person with whom the service was comfortable.

Ellen had been invited to join by Miriam, who lead the Women and Their Bodies class she was taking, which was based on the book *Our Bodies, Ourselves.* The class was part of the Chicago Women's Liberation Union's Liberation School, which offered courses around the city on everything from auto mechanics to organizing strategies. Miriam and a few other service members led the CWLU's "bodies" classes.

A few months earlier, Ellen had moved with her boyfriend to Hyde Park from New York where she had been a social worker. Abortions were legal in New York, so when she arrived in Chicago she was astounded that "in one state it was okay; in another it wasn't. I saw that as unfair. It was a real light bulb, radicalizing thing." When she mentioned her interest in abortion counseling to Miriam, Miriam told her about Jane.

Also at the orientation were two friends from the University of Chicago, Lynn and Gail. Lynn had just dropped out of college. One of her friends was a member of the group and had invited her. Lynn was floating, unsure of what she wanted to do. Her motivation for joining was personal: "I wanted to understand how I could be a grown-up woman. That was my real interest in the women's movement. There were a tremendous number of young women like me who had to find a way to be women that didn't make them feel humiliated."

Lynn asked her friend Gail if she was interested in going to the orientation with her. Gail had been reading about feminism; she and Lynn had been in a consciousness-raising group that had never jelled. Gail was looking for something concrete to do because she felt "detached from real action, which you definitely feel if you're a college student."

Gail had realized that "women were getting screwed and a lot of women were not in control of their lives. Every day on the South Side of Chicago I saw a lot of poor women whose lives were really out of control. Maybe if I hadn't been surrounded by such a poor area, abortion wouldn't have seemed as important. I wanted to do something to help empower women and I saw abortion that way."

When Lynn and Gail walked into the first training session it seemed to them that a hundred women were crammed into the living room. The counselor who was leading the session exploded. She wanted to know who Gail was and who had invited someone no counselor could vouch for. A heated discussion about Gail followed. It took place, Lynn recalls, "in that special way that service arguments always went on: in the other room with somebody else arguing and you don't know what's going on." The outcome was that Gail could stay, but, for the two friends, it was an unpleasant beginning. Lynn noticed that "the tension level was so thick I could almost see it in the room."

Once Gail's status was resolved, the counselor leading the training related the group's history: how initially women had had to wait on street corners to get picked up by strangers, how the group had taken control, and eventually had discovered that the doctor they used wasn't a doctor. Now, she explained, the abortions were performed by women paramedics. Since there was no way to know which of the people at this first session would actually join, she didn't want to jeopardize the group by giving too much information, so she did not say that those women paramedics were members of Jane. She also neglected to mention that men occasionally performed Jane's abortions. Near the end of the meeting, the new recruits were asked to think about how they would feel if someone died. They had to face the possibility of getting arrested for murder.

Julia, dressed in jeans and a pea coat, had arrived late for the orientation. Even though she was only trying to find a place to sit in the crowded room, everybody stopped what they were doing to greet her. Gail thought, She must be a central player here.

Gail and Lynn walked home together talking about the meeting. They hadn't liked the hostility directed toward Gail, but they were impressed by Miriam and Julia. These might be the people Lynn was looking for, women who could be her role models. It was clear to both of them that some critical piece of information about who was doing the abortions had been withheld. As they walked home through Hyde Park's quiet streets, Gail said, "If anyone there is doing abortions, I bet it's that woman Julia."

The second orientation session was at Charlotte's on the North Side. Charlotte had invited Kate to the orientation. A friend of Kate's from the University of Chicago had recently had a Jane abortion. She had been so excited by the experience that she had taken Kate to meet her counselor, Charlotte, and Kate had decided to join. Kate had missed the first session and, when she walked into Charlotte's, she was greeted with the same suspicion as Gail had been: "Who's she?" Kate mumbled something about her friend's abortion and turned to Charlotte to bail her out.

Kate looked around Charlotte's living room, which was full of white women with long hair, dressed, as she was, in work boots and jeans. Once the initial suspicion passed, everyone seemed amazingly warm and friendly. Kate had moved back to Chicago from New York the month before and she was used to New York's aggressive women. She thought, Who are all these sweet women doing this outrageous thing?

Kate had not responded to women's liberation when she first heard about it as a student at the University of Chicago. After she graduated and moved to New York her consciousness had been raised, but she can no longer remember the catalyst: "All I know is that one day my eyes were opened, like in 'Amazing Grace': Was blind but now can see."

In New York she marched down Fifth Avenue with thousands of others for women's liberation. At the rally, Betty Friedan spoke. "The gist of what Friedan said," Kate recalls, "was that you too, meaning we women, could be bank presidents. That wasn't why I was there. For me women's liberation wasn't about women having a bigger piece of a rotten pie. I never thought that just replacing men with women would make the world a better place." Kate didn't want to be in a consciousness-raising group or a study group. She wanted to do something that would have an impact on people's lives.

At the first Jane training that Kate attended, the second in a series of three, the trainer presented a mock counseling session, covering the information each counselor had to know. As she spoke, the instruments used in abortions were passed around the room. The trainer went over Jane's few rules: Explain everything fully and never lie; treat other women the way you want to be treated.

The third session, a few days later, was devoted to a discussion of induced miscarriages. At the end of the meeting the service's general procedures were explained, the index cards, *Big Jane*'s role, all the details of getting women from the first call through their abortions. Each of the new people was assigned a Big Sister whose counseling sessions she would sit in on for further training. Gail was delighted to find out that Julia was going to be her Big Sister.

When Gail arrived at Julia's for her first counseling session, Julia had the flu. "I walked into this messy house," Gail recalls, "with these children running all over the place and Julia lying on the couch." When the woman arrived, Julia pulled herself together; afterward she collapsed back on the couch. Gail was struck by Julia's "facility for making people feel welcome and comfortable so that they would start talking about their feelings. The thing is, she's really judgmental but she would be very nonjudgmental with the women she counseled."

Soon Gail was a regular visitor at Julia's. The more time Gail spent with her, the more she noticed that whenever another counselor had a problem or needed anything, she called Julia. It was clear to Gail that her hunch that first night about Julia's role was accurate. When Julia confided in her that the people who performed the abortions were actually women in the group, Gail said, "And you're one of them."

Gail's first few counseling experiences validated her reasons for joining the service. She was amazed by "how many people really live on the edge. They live from one little paycheck to the next. I'm not even talking about people on welfare who don't even live from one check to the next because the check isn't big enough. I mean working people." One of the first women she counseled had two small children and had managed, after much struggle, to find a job and get off welfare. She knew that, if she had another baby, she would end up spending two or three more years on welfare because she couldn't afford child care. That prospect terrified her. The next woman Gail counseled was a waitress whose boss was threatening to fire her for missing work because she was often sick from the pregnancy. For the people Gail was counseling having a baby would be a disaster.

At first Gail was uncomfortable with the women she counseled. Many were older than she, and even those who were her age usually had children and an entirely different range of experience. Most of them were poor black women from the South Side. She tried to overcome the race and class differences by focusing on the matter at hand. She noticed that "with some people all that stuff didn't matter. They just wanted someone to talk to."

Lynn was so shy that she was terrified of calling women she was going to counsel: "Hello, may I speak to Doris Carter . . . Oh, do you know when she'll be home? . . . I'll call back." She felt as if she were walking a tightrope: how much was too much to divulge to a woman's relative; how much was too little to get a chance to speak with her? She would "get those cards and go home and sit on those cards. I never made the call the first night." Lynn worried that the women who came to her for counseling would be frightened and wondered whether she could allay their fears. She was always "afraid they wouldn't come and hoped they wouldn't come, but once they were there it was always okay."

Because of the diversity of the women they counseled, the younger Jane members were being given an opportunity to learn from other women as well as teach them. Their youth and inexperience had not prepared them for the difficulties that people faced. In the early seventies wife beating was not publicly discussed; Molly knew nothing about it. While she was driving from the Front to the Place, one of the women in the car confided that she had been beaten by her boyfriend. She told the other women that it wasn't until he began abusing her kids that she realized she had to leave. Sometimes, she said, it takes seeing someone else hurt to realize you shouldn't be hurt, that none of us should be hurt. After she ended the relationship he had come after her and she had had to hide her pregnancy.

The five new counselors who joined in November accounted for almost one-quarter of the membership and were the largest single group ever to join Jane. They were like a wedge, opening up the service. It was only then that Cynthia was allowed to begin training as an abortionist.

Gail, Lynn, Molly, Ellen and Kate came into the service at a time when its membership was depleted. Along with a few similar women, like Donna, who had joined in the preceding months, they altered Jane's character. Rather than housewives, they were all under twenty-five, single and without children. They were used to living on very little and had time and energy to devote to Jane. Lynn, Gail and Ellen lived in Hyde Park. Like Donna, Molly and Kate were North Siders. They had been inspired by the moral imperative of the civil rights movement and used to the challenges to authority that the student and antiwar movements presented. None of them had been seriously involved in political activity before, so they carried no ideological baggage. They came into Jane as feminists, part hippies, part radicals, looking for a concrete outlet for their feminism. None of them were troubled that lay people, women, were performing abortions. Their mindset fit the service perfectly.

CHAPTER 19

By the fall of 1971 Jenny, Julia and Pam were adept abortionists. From their experiences they were able to recognize unusual correlations. For instance, they noticed that in some abortions the fetal and placental tissue was specked with dark blood clots. Upon questioning these women they found that all of them had taken quinine tablets in an attempt to self-abort. But, as skilled as the trio had become, their medical knowledge was limited. Most of it came from Nick. His expertise was confined to abortion and only to those techniques with which he was familiar. Even though an abortion was fairly straightforward, the human body was complex and interrelated. To do their work safely, they needed to know more than Nick could teach them.

That fall Miriam asked her doctor, who was a well-known progressive, to teach a few of them how to do bimanual pelvics, the basic gynecological exam. They hoped that with that skill they could judge the length of each pregnancy more accurately, and recognize other gynecological problems so that, as with Pap smears, they could provide basic gynecological care.

Miriam approached her doctor circumspectly: "She was feeling me out. She didn't want to tell me much if I was going to be negative. She said something about a group interested in self-exams and training others." He was sympathetic.

In the late 1940s he had been an intern at Cook County Hospital,

Chicago's public hospital. As part of his intern rotation he had spent twenty days on a ward for women with infections from abortions that were either self-induced or done by someone else. Each day he had performed D & Cs on between one and more than twenty women with incomplete abortions. He had become aware that "this was a huge problem. Cook County Hospital, by and large, was the hospital for poor people, but these were not just poor people. These were women from every social class who had botched abortions. It raises your consciousness about the plight of women, not only that they'd had to have it, but also the circumstances, the abuse they'd had during it. You don't have to be maudlin to imagine the impact it had on a young doctor."

Jenny, Miriam, Julia, Cynthia and Sarah, a graduate student who had joined the service the previous fall after working with the Chicago Women's Liberation Union, trooped into his office on a weekend. He demonstrated on Sarah how to feel a uterus. With two fingers, he reached into her vagina under her cervix, and pushed up while he pressed externally on her abdomen with the other hand. By shifting the position of both the internal and external hands, he felt for her ovaries. Then the five women practiced on each other while he answered questions. One of them asked him how to tell if something was wrong with a woman's ovaries. "If they're enlarged, then you can feel them," he said. "Otherwise, you can't feel anything."

Cynthia was astounded: "You mean all this poking around and prodding, they're not feeling anything? It's the absence?"

"Well," he replied, "if somebody experiences pain, then you can tell that something's wrong."

"Certainly that isn't the impression you get when you go for a pelvic," Cynthia says. "You think the guy's got eyes in the tips of his fingers." A pelvic exam didn't require a high degree of skill or a medical degree. They could teach it to other women. The only new equipment they needed was examining gloves. During an abortion only instruments, not the person's hands, are inside the woman's body. Nick never wore gloves because he found them awkward and they interfered with his hands' sensitivity, so, following his example, they never wore gloves.

It wasn't the only new skill they added that year. In September, Cynthia, and two of the suburban high school teachers in the service, Elizabeth and Irene, attended a NOW conference in California. There they met women from the California women's health movement who were promoting self-help groups in which women examined themselves with speculums. Two California women were about to leave on a tour of the United States to teach self-help. Cynthia said, "Gee, we're doing something very similar to what you're doing." She told them about Jane.

These women introduced the three Jane members to Jordan Bennett, who had invented a method for performing early abortions using a thin plastic tube, called a cannula, attached to a 50 cc syringe. The device worked like a vacuum aspirator, the machine used in legal clinics for abortions up to 10 weeks lmp, except that it created less suction. Jordan offered to come to Chicago to teach Jane his new technique.

Late in the fall of 1971, Pat and Monica, the two California women, stopped in Chicago on their cross-country tour promoting self-help groups. In these groups a woman learns to insert a speculum in herself and, with a mirror and a light, examine her cervix and vagina for changes or signs of infection. Pat and Monica were also demonstrating a method they had devised for removing menstrual fluid. To Jordan's cannula and syringe, they attached a shunt, some tubing and a mason jar to perform what they called menstrual extractions (ME). The shunt apparatus prevented the introduction of air into a woman's uterus, which could be fatal. The explanation for ME was that, rather than menstruating and cramping for five to seven days, a woman could have her period removed all at once. Jane members wondered why a woman would put something in her uterus and risk infection to avoid having a period. But ME had another purpose. With it, an early abortion, up to 7 weeks lmp, could be performed in a self-help group setting.

The women in Jane invited their visitors, with whom they seemed to have so much in common, to observe a work day. According to the service members who were there, the impression Jane made was not all that favorable. "They were appalled by our sloppiness," Julia recalls, "our casualness with the Kleenex and plastic sheets and no gloves." They were shocked that the service did not use an autoclave, a steam pressure machine, the proper way to sterilize instruments. Because the service moved from apartment to apartment, they couldn't carry around a cumbersome autoclave. Instead they relied on boiling and cold sterilizer, which was used in wartime by front line medical units. Rather than an easy connection, the two groups of women were wary of each other. Sarah felt that "we were doing something a little more important, serious, harder than they, and it took away some of their thunder."

After work a dozen Jane members met with Pat and Monica at Cynthia's. "We talked about what we did and they were aghast; they talked about what they did and we were aghast," Julia recalls. "What we were aghast at was their attachment to Jordan Bennett. They had a reverence for him that none of us would ever have had for Nick. They thought that he was, if not a man among men, then a man among women."

Then Pat and Monica demonstrated self-help, which the Jane members found fascinating. This was something, showing a woman her cervix with a mirror and a light, that had never occurred to them. "What they had to offer was really exciting," Sarah recalls. "It was another way of taking the knowledge that doctors had about women and using it for ourselves."

"They were really into getting arrested and we thought, Oh, we don't want to get arrested," Julia recalls. Pat and Monica viewed an arrest as a way to test the laws that prohibited lay people from providing gynecological care, while Jane wanted to avoid a confrontation with the police in order to keep providing abortions. Julia recognized that "they had a different vision of how to change the world. It was a whole different headset, and because we were so self-righteous—they as well as we—it came out as disapproval. We identified what we didn't like about them as that they were people who wanted to be stars. We were in a very hierarchical situation ourselves, which we weren't interested in acknowledging, but we understood it shouldn't have been that way."

Jane's anti-star bias was common in the women's liberation movement. In reaction to the hierarchy of male leadership, both in society and on the left, that relegated women to the bottom, radical women intended to create a movement without leaders or stars in order to share power and promote personal growth.

Jane members incorporated into their practice a challenge to special privilege. While the assistant prepped a woman, the person who was going to perform the abortion took the assistant's place, sitting by the woman's side and holding her hand. Then the two women switched places, as if there were no difference between the assistant and the abortionist. Service members wanted the women who came through Jane to understand that, with training, any of them could do it, so that they would not be intimidated by someone else's skill.

The secret nature of the service precluded the possibility of any member becoming a movement star. For security reasons, no one outside of the group knew exactly who was subsumed under the anonymous title Jane. As a result, the service attracted women who relished anonymity.

Although Julia instinctively reacted against people who sought special status, she understood the need for someone to take a public role: "If there aren't stars within the women's movement, then my daughter and that whole generation won't have heroes in the movement because it's made up of deliberate non-heroes. I want her to understand that being a star is not important; I want her to understand that what's important is for people to become empowered and do exciting things."

The week after the demonstration of self-exams, service members brought mirrors to work. At first they asked women having abortions if they wanted to see their cervix. When most of them declined, the women in Jane stopped asking and said, "Here, look at your cervix." This was self-knowledge that every woman needed. She would not opt out of it any more than she could opt out of the information they gave her about her body or abortion.

Cynthia and Elizabeth decided to learn more about ME. On Elizabeth's Christmas break from teaching, she and Cynthia went to California. During their training they realized that ME was not appropriate for Jane. There was so little suction with the shunt and jar in an ME that those abortions could take at least half an hour, twice as long as a D & C, too long for Jane's packed work days. In California Cynthia also became aware of a change in Pat and Monica's attitude toward Jordan Bennett. Although Cynthia never knew why, in the few months between the fall and Christmas their adulation had turned to contempt.

In January of 1972 Jordan Bennett came to Chicago to teach Jane to use his cannula and syringe. Service members met with him at Cynthia's house. She roasted a turkey which they ate as they sat around her dining room table talking.

Cynthia recalls, "Jordan's attitude was: 'I developed this wonderful thing and I'm sharing it with you because you are something special,' nudge, nudge, wink, wink. But I wanted to learn from him, pick his brains and know what he knew."

Julia was struck by how inflated his ego was: "He was such an odd person, a real star."

Jordan gave them cannulas and syringes to use and agreed to return to provide further training. Regardless of how they felt about him personally, his technique was useful. Over the years they had worked with other difficult personalities. Arrogance was a common trait among illegal abortionists. Nick, the best of the lot, wasn't easy to work with, yet they had managed to turn an adversarial relationship with him to their advantage and they could do it again. What struck Miriam "was how strong we were with the men. We took all the information from them that we could get. I've never seen it that way in any other group."

This new method provoked a series of discussions whose subtext had as much to do with personalities as techniques. The use of forceps and curettes was Nick's method and they were comfortable with it. "There was enough conflict between the hard-liners who felt that any change in the way we did things was de facto wrong, and those of us who simply rebelled against that attitude," Cynthia recalls, "so that neither side was really sitting down and saying, 'Let's look at this. Let's try to be as dispassionate as possible and take personalities out of it,' because it was very hard to take Jordan's personality out of it." But it was not only Jordan's personality that was the problem. Since Cynthia had had the initial contact with Jordan and was instrumental in bringing him to Chicago, the cannulas and Cynthia were linked in the group's assessment.

Julia viewed this new method as "sort of a technological revolution. More people learned because it felt much less invasive. Since the cannula's diameter was small, you didn't have to open the cervix with a dilator as much. Because the cannula was plastic and not metal, the fear of hurting the uterine wall was less. It was like learning on an automatic instead of a stick shift." Unlike ME, with the cannula and syringe an abortion took no longer than a D & C did. In cannula abortions, Jane members finished each one with curettage to make sure the uterus was clean. Some women who performed abortions used cannulas and some did not, a matter of personal preference. Cynthia remembers another abortionist in the group commenting with disdain, "Cynthia? Oh, she uses a cannula."

Adding new skills wasn't the only change in Jane's operation that winter. The lease on their Hyde Park Boulevard apartment was up at the end of the year. The group decided they needed two new apartments, one for assisting women with miscarriages and one for a work place. Cynthia rented a three-bedroom apartment in which to perform abortions. It was in a high-rise overlooking Lake Michigan on South Shore Drive, about ten blocks south of Hyde Park. The group rented the second apartment, for assisting with miscarriages, on Dayton Street on the North Side.

Late in the fall of 1971 Jane had decided to offer more organized support for women going through induced miscarriages. Previously most women who had been induced had either gone to a hospital to miscarry or had miscarried on their own with the help of a parent or friend, depending on their counselors only for advice. Some women had miscarried alone, with no one to help them but their counselor on the other end of the phone. The members decided it was essential to have fulltime midwives available to help these women miscarry safely.

Two members volunteered to midwife miscarriages as their primary responsibility. One was Robin, who had joined in early 1971 after her own abortion with Jane. The other was Nora, one of Deborah's former high school students, who had just joined the service in the summer. They were among the youngest of the new Jane members. Nora was nineteen; Robin twenty-three.

Nora moved into the apartment on the North Side which was to be used for miscarriages. Counselors advised the women who had come to Jane for induced miscarriages that any who wanted to use the midwife services should go to Nora's apartment when their contractions were five minutes apart. Nora and Robin were each on call for alternate twenty-four hour shifts. Robin went to Nora's apartment whenever she was needed.

Robin and Nora were taught to manage miscarriages by other counselors who were experienced. They learned to recognize bleeding that was dangerous, to apply emergency measures and to determine when it was necessary to send a woman to the hospital. Perhaps because of the group's ambivalence about induced miscarriages, Nora's and Robin's training did not follow the step-by-step pattern that abortionists' assistants went through. When a problem arose that they had not previously encountered, they called someone in the group who had more experience.

When the service moved out of the Hyde Park Boulevard apartment at the end of 1971, Nick's tenure with Jane was over. There was a new openness during work, with more women coming in every day for training, which was not his style.

"When we moved," Nick recalls, "it was over for me. The beginning was interesting, but the end was really nice. I would have sold my soul to the devil to have done it. Fortunately, it just fell into my lap; I certainly can't take any credit for it. I came out of this nothing childhood and then had this marvelous experience and I ended up better for it. There was a movement and I was a part of it; I liked that."

CHAPTER 20

While Jane was performing between sixty and ninety abortions a week, the Clergy Consultation Service, a network of clergymen in Chicago, continued to counsel and refer women to local and out-of-state sources. Their moral authority gave them the opportunity to speak about abortion in venues that were not receptive to women's liberation. Jane and Harris Wilson, the Baptist minister who organized the Chicago clergy group, shared a mutual respect. Both groups had been organized around the same time in 1969 and, from the outset, Miriam and Harris met regularly to keep each other informed of each group's progress, any problems they encountered and the doctors they used. Miriam had put Harris in touch with one of his most reliable local referrals. Although the clergy had decided as a matter of protection to refer people to sources other than Jane, Harris admits, "I turned to Jane a few times if the person simply had no money at all. I never had a complaint." At one of their informal meetings late in 1971, during a discussion of the clergy's reliance on a few doctors to describe the procedures to the network's members, Miriam said, "Not only can they explain it, but they can teach us how to do the procedures."

Harris thought he had misunderstood her. "What?" he asked.

"Well, we have someone who can not only describe the procedure to us but instruct us how to do it. This is a male-dominated profession and we don't think women should have to be helpless and dependent. We should be able to take care of ourselves."

Now he understood. All he said to Miriam was, "Oh." "I got the message. I didn't probe with her. She'd given me the information that she thought I ought to have," he recalls. "By that time I was convinced that you didn't have to be a physician in order to do an abortion. But, inside, I thought, My God, how much risk are these women willing to take? If they get caught they're going to get clobbered. Yet I had such admiration for the group that I left it there."

Harris Wilson was feeling some heat himself. Early in 1971 he had been invited to speak on abortion before a general session of the Illinois state legislature. He had begun his presentation with his usual format: that outlawing abortion had never prevented it, but had only put women at risk. He reeled off the statistics, the number of women who had died or been injured. None of it was new. If he continued in that vein he knew that he wasn't going to get any press attention, so he said, "Let's not talk in generalities. You people have a heavy responsibility to formulate the laws for this state and you've got to be humane. I personally know thirteen physicians doing abortions in this state. We estimate that between fifty and sixty thousand illegal abortions are performed in Illinois every year. These are the facts of the situation and we've got this prohibitive statute and it really doesn't make sense."

Henry Hyde, then a state legislator, stood up and thundered, "I want to know the names of those physicians."

"I cannot give you the names because it would violate the confidential character of my pastoral ministry," Harris responded.

Henry Hyde tried to have him cited for contempt of the legislature for not handing over the doctors' names. The attempt failed, but the information was sent to the state's attorney who subpoenaed Harris Wilson before two grand juries. Then Harris realized "that my great effort to be honest and open and get a little publicity for this thing was really going to get a little complicated."

He stuck to his position with the grand juries, repeating that it would violate the confidential character of his ministry to divulge the doctors' names. "It was a ploy but psychologically it worked," he says. "They finally decided to drop it because the state's attorney said he thought that to put the dean of Rockefeller Chapel at the University of Chicago in jail for not giving names of physicians doing abortions would only make a martyr of him." Harris knew he had the support of university officials and that bolstered his courage: "If I hadn't had that real strong base of operations, I probably wouldn't have been anywhere near as outspoken as I was." The president of the university told him he had complete confidence in him; members of the law school faculty had set up a mock grand jury to help him prepare. Harris's commitment to abortion rights never wavered. When Miriam told him what Jane was doing, his only concern was for Jane's safety.

By early 1972 the newer counselors were being integrated into the service. There were two routes for moving into positions of trust and responsibility in Jane. One was through friendship with someone in the inner circle and the other was through a paid position in the group. Miriam asked three of the counselors who had joined in November, Molly, Kate and Ellen, to take on three of the four *Call-Back Jane* positions. Each *Call-Back* was on for two weeks and off for two weeks. One picked up the messages every four hours, alternating with another, so that the machine was cleared every two hours. By the spring each of the new counselors had observed abortions during a work day.

The new members were beginning to understand the dynamics at meetings. Between a half and two-thirds of the membership regularly attended service meetings where they selected women to counsel. Gail, one of the young women who joined in November, thought that process was "like getting picked for volleyball. This huge stack of cards would come around. The North Side cards always disappeared first. North Side counselors were always looking for North Side women to counsel so those women wouldn't have to travel far. There were hundreds of South Side cards and thousands of West Side cards, of women who lived in those mostly poor black neighborhoods. The stack would go around once and then *Jane* would say, 'We have a lot more people who need to be counseled this week.' And the pack of cards got passed around again."

Since confrontations at meetings were usually frowned upon, problems with individual members were converted into questions of practice. At first Gail "didn't understand what the debates were about because a lot of it wasn't about issues but personalities. If you actually took the argument at face value and gave an opinion, you might be supporting some side on a meta-argument that was going on, which no one had told you about." For instance, the discussion might be centered on problems associated with scheduling work days, but it was actually about Cynthia, who was handling *Big Jane*.

Pam, like Jenny before her, decided she was not going to counsel anyone. Pam felt too exposed performing abortions on women she had counseled. But what was acceptable for Jenny was not acceptable for Pam. Pam tended to look down on service members she thought were not as radical as she. Miriam and Julia suspected that Pam, by choosing not to counsel, was setting herself above the group, as if her skill exempted her. But no one at a meeting said directly to Pam, "I don't like the fact that you're not counseling. I think that's bad for the group and you."

Kate picked up that something more was going on, but she did not know exactly what it was. She said, "Why don't we just talk about what's really happening and get this stuff out into the open." After a few minutes of silence, Miriam, in her soothing, motherly tone, said, "Oh, we don't do that here," implying, you don't know what you're suggesting, so drop it. In their attempt to keep the group unified and on track, the members had long before decided to limit extraneous discussion. But the distinction between what was divisive and what was valuable was a judgment call. Inevitably, it was influenced by the leaders' desire to maintain control. At meetings, Julia recalls, "we pretended we operated by consensus but that's because we never talked about anything."

· · ·

At an antiwar demonstration in the Loop Molly ran into people she knew from Revolutionary Youth Movement II, the radical group she had briefly belonged to in college. When they asked her what she was doing, she responded vaguely. Molly didn't tell them about Jane. There was hardly anyone she confided in beyond the closed world of the service.

Like Molly, many of the other service members for whom Jane was their central activity found themselves withdrawing from acquaintances outside the group. They gravitated to each other for support and to socialize. Since they were breaking the law, they couldn't talk about their work with other people, but more than that turned them inward. Who besides Jane members could relate to their worries about a sixteen-year-old who refused to tell her parents, or a woman who had called all night after her abortion, suffering with cramps, crying and frightened? Their daily routine would be incomprehensible, if not appalling, to most people. And certainly no one else would be amused by the humor they used to cope. Jane was its own world.

Their work separated them from the rest of the women's movement, even their umbrella group, the Chicago Women's Liberation Union. Their distance from the CWLU was deliberate. It protected the union from Jane's illegality.* Someone from Jane was supposed to attend every CWLU meeting, but no one was eager. They hardly had patience for their own meetings, so their tolerance for union meetings with their political debates and theoretical discussions was minimal. Like other Jane members, Julia "really didn't think that anything else going on would interest me very much. I thought those people at the union should do their deal and we should do our deal and, if they felt threatened because what we were doing was illegal, then we just won't tell them." But that separation isolated Jane

*The Chicago Red Squad files include detailed reports of union meetings, courtesy of police informants.

members further. Although Cynthia continued to be involved in NOW, without a larger context the others felt so far out in left field that they weren't even in the ballpark.

There was a difference in philosophy between Jane and the CWLU that added to the distance. Sarah, who had been working with the union when she joined Jane, sensed that union members thought: Jane is just solving individuals' problems, whereas we, at the union, are going to change the system.

Julia supposed that there was also a difference in perspective: "The women active in the union came to feminist concerns with a very heavy political orientation, so they felt the appropriate work to do was radicalizing and organizing women. The practical work was another level down and not so interesting. I don't know much about organizing, but I feel as though, if the reality of the situation doesn't change people's heads, then nothing's going to change their heads. Marches and those things are not the work of it. The work of it is whatever the work is."

For members of the service, the split between organizing and service work made no sense. It wasn't only what they did but how they did it that mattered. A year earlier they had debated whether to inform women that the person doing the abortions was not a doctor. Now, Julia felt, "It was manipulatively useful to say it's not a doctor." Simply hearing that forced some women to reevaluate their expectations. "For the people who did not care about that," Julia continues, "then you had to find a different way to tell them: This is really yours to do and not ours." They wanted women to view their abortions in a larger context. They hoped women made the connections, as when a middle-aged Irish Catholic woman from Mayor Daley's neighborhood commented to her counselor, "If they're lying to us about abortion, what else are they lying to us about?" When women refused to take that step they were using the group rather than putting the group to good use. As one counselor put it, "I got angry whenever women didn't rise up angry."

CHAPTER 21

When Lois contacted Jane for a friend, she thought the only choices for young black women were either have the baby or die from an abortion. She had heard the horror stories of coat hangers and hemorrhages. Another friend gave her Jane's number and said, "Listen, call these women. It's a white women's group but, if you don't have the money you don't have to worry about it. I only paid fifty dollars."

Because her friend had to keep the abortion secret, Lois made the arrangements and went with her to Donna's for counseling. At Donna's Lois's friend "was terrified of being asked questions because she was in a white atmosphere and she didn't know how to respond," Lois recalls. "She was very uncomfortable and I thought, If my girlfriend feels like that, then how do other black women feel?"

When Donna called Lois to give her the address of the Front, Lois said she was interested in joining, but she wanted to know why so few women of color were in the group. She came on with an accusatory attitude that "you guys are the white angels that are going to save everybody and where are the black women at?" Donna hesitated; Lois took the edge out of her voice and said, "Maybe I can identify with black women a little better."

Donna said, "Oh great. When do you want to start?"

"Let me see how it goes with my girlfriend and then I'll call you."

The Front was crowded with women, most of them black. A few

asked Lois questions, assuming she was a counselor. It was disturbing that total strangers turned to her only because of her color. "That's why I actually joined," she says. "I wanted to be there for women to see. To me Jane was a movement and black women at that time were not interested in that movement because our movement was different. When people talked about the women's movement, they talked about women burning bras. We were trying to: one, deal with being black women; two, deal with prejudice; three, deal with the structure, being single parents and staying alive. That was our struggle."

After her friend's abortion, Lois mentioned to her that she was thinking of joining the group. She tried to talk Lois out of it: "You've got three children. My God, what would happen if you got arrested? Those white women would get out of it, but not you. Girl, you could go to jail. They'd take your kids away."

Lois was more concerned about being involved in something that she couldn't talk about with her friends and family. She was mulling over whether to join the group when, a few months later, she discovered she was pregnant. She was twenty-two, in college, married, and had three children. She had to decide whether to have the baby. One part of Lois was "sorry that I knew Jane, that they were there, but the other side of me was happy as hell." She called Jane.

Her uterus was too large at thirteen weeks of pregnancy for a D & C abortion and she had to be induced to miscarry. She had not expected that, but she was "geared toward being part of the group and I wanted to see what was going on." After she got dressed, she asked if she could observe.

One of the workers said, "You have to get permission from the women having abortions. It's their bodies." After sitting in on several, Lois felt that "even though I was going through my own thing, I was hooked. I knew that was what I wanted to do."

She liked the informality of Jane's setup, "the laid-backness, the closeness of the one-to-one basis, the lack of the sterile scene and white walls," she recalls. "I didn't get the attitude that, I'm the doctor and you're the patient. I'd had a baby when I was sixteen. If I'd known Jane I might not have had it. That's what I was thinking: Maybe the next sixteen-year-old doesn't have to have a child because she doesn't have an alternative."

Two days later she miscarried alone in her apartment and whatever lingering ambivalence she had vanished. She felt "a wave-of-gratitude thing, that this was a choice that I had to make and I made it and thank God for those women. Thank God for Jane."

"When I have experiences in my life I don't like to forget them," Lois says. "I wanted to deal with this one. I wanted to make something out of it. God, there were a lot of women out there who needed the same thing that I had. I thought, Let me be here. Let me help those women." She called Donna: "When can I start?"

When she told her husband, Keith, what she was going to do, he said, "They're probably a bunch of lesbians." She gave him a withering look, as if to say his comment was irrelevant. As far as the illegality and the risks, she figured the only way to deal with them was to put them out of her mind.

The night of the orientation Miriam's living room was filled with young white women with long hair, in jeans. Lois did not look anything like them. Not only was she black but she dressed in stylish outfits with matching nail polish. But those differences did not dissuade her because she "had been through the hippie scene. I'd worked with CORE [the Congress of Racial Equality, an integrated civil rights group], so a white environment did not terrify me. I wanted to break the prejudices, the images they had been taught to believe the same way we had been taught. I was not saying I was coming into a white woman's movement. I was saying, I can render service. When I got into the group I didn't look at them as white women. I saw them as sisters." Even though her background and experiences were different, she recognized a similarity: They were all strong women and "They all had big mouths," she says, "just like me."

Lois wanted to broaden the women's movement. She felt it had to be "for women of color to be able to identify who they are and what they are about. Black women are here. We're part of the change. This is not just about you guys. This is for all of us."

Gregarious and open, she settled into Jane comfortably and made friends in the group. Lois often joked, "Okay, guys, I'll add some color to the joint," referring more to her fashion sense than to the color of her skin. Even though there were few other women of color in the group, Lois never felt intimidated, nor did she feel like a token. Her warmth and competence were quickly recognized by the leaders.

New counselors, like Lois, came into Jane with enthusiasm and energy, but the most experienced abortionists in the group, Jenny, Julia and Pam, felt the pressure of working with minimal medical backup, without societal sanctions. Pam could no longer juggle graduate school and Jane, so she dropped out of school. She worried that she didn't know enough about medicine but she didn't have the time to learn more.

Since Jenny rarely attended meetings, Julia and Miriam ran them. The younger counselors looked up to Julia and turned to her for advice. Always calm and approachable, she inspired confidence. She was consumed with worry about how everyone else in the group was managing. Her teeth reacted to the stress. For the first time in her life she was getting cavities.

But most of the responsibility for the abortions was still Jenny's. She would have liked to shift it onto someone else, but she could not. She had more experience, skill and knowledge than anyone else. She trained the other abortionists. "People thought it was such a privilege to do the abortions," Jenny recalls. "They thought it was power-tripping. I never liked to do it. Sometimes, on a work day, I would get impatient and say, 'Goddamn it, I can't teach any more people today. We have fifteen more abortions still to go and it's already four o'clock.' Because of that, people thought I was jealously guarding knowledge, but that was not the case."

Over the winter the strain took its toll on her. Still suffering from

Hodgkin's disease, her health was eroding. That summer she had contracted hepatitis and never felt fully recovered. Physically and emotionally she was exhausted. She confided in Julia and Miriam her dreams filled with blood. Her short fuse was shrinking. She lost her temper with clerks in the grocery store. In the group, the target of her outbursts was, most often, Miriam. "As Jenny got sort of strung out she used to blame Miriam for everything that went wrong, an interesting deal between the two of them, like an old married couple," Julia recalls. "If we didn't have the directions to a Front, Jenny would always blame Miriam. Or, if we got to a work place and there weren't any syringes, it would be Miriam's fault." Those close to Jenny watched as she stretched to the breaking point; they felt helpless to do anything. Jenny's looming collapse had a mythic quality. She was the one who had broken a taboo, stolen fire from the gods, and she was paying for it.

Some days more than thirty abortions had to be completed, stretching the work into the night. That only increased the pressure on Jenny. She snapped at the assistants over real or imagined delays or mishaps. On one work day, an assistant walked into the kitchen and found Jenny leaning over the sink, weeping.

On another hectic day, Sarah, who had joined through the Chicago Women's Liberation Union, was driving women from the Front to the Place. En route to the Place the driver collected the money from women for their abortions. Jenny asked Sarah for $20, explaining that she had a doctor's appointment downtown and needed to slip it to the cop on the block so she could double-park. Self-righteously Sarah replied, "I thought we never pay off the police. Is that going to come out of your daily pay?"

Jenny blew up: "What right do you have to tell me anything in this group, especially about money? You're just the driver. Keep your nose out of it."

On another day, one of the last people was a teenager who had said she was ten weeks pregnant. When Jenny began the D & C, she realized that the pregnancy was more advanced. The abortion dragged on. In the middle of it, without saying anything to either the assistant or the girl, Jenny walked out of the room, too exhausted to continue. After a few minutes she returned and completed the abortion, neither apologizing nor explaining. The assistant thought, Jenny's not behaving the way we say we want to.

Finally, even Jenny recognized what was happening to her: "I was sick, physically sick. I needed a rest. I couldn't tell one color from another. I couldn't tell words apart." In the middle of March, she signed herself into a psychiatric ward. She felt as if it were the only way she could get a break from the service.

Without any formal acknowledgement of it, the role of lead abortionist passed to Julia. But Jenny's absence from the group did not alter its structure. "For me," Julia says, "Jenny carried so much power that, as long as she was in the group, there would be a power skew. I tried to absorb Jenny's burden, because that's how I defined it: I can do her part now and she can withdraw because this is obviously making her crazy. But what good would it do if I were in the position that she was? Then the group is in the same circumstance in that one person carries an enormous amount of power, which is not the way you want it to be, whether you're the bottom or the top."

As the spring progressed, the relationship between the group's two midwives, Nora and Robin, deteriorated. After assisting with a miscarriage at Nora's, Robin went home without cleaning up. Sometimes, just as her shift was about to begin, she called from out of town to ask Nora to cover for her. Then, Nora recalls, "She would apologize so profusely, go through this 'poor me' routine that I'd feel like a terrible person." The final straw for Nora was when, before dawn, she called Robin for her shift to notify her that a woman was on her way to miscarry. Robin answered the phone barely awake, said she'd be there, then fell back asleep with the phone off the hook. Lately everything Robin did was like a neon sign flashing: Burned Out.

Nora, too, had had enough, but she recognized it and started training another counselor to take her place. The lease on the Dayton Street apartment was ending on May 1 and Nora picked that as her quitting day. On May 3 she was going to move to Colorado.

Nora's midwife work had turned out to be much more stressful than she had expected. Even on the days no one came to her apartment to miscarry, it was a strain. Since personal beepers were unheard of, she had to be home for the full twenty-four hours. By April she was tired all the time.

The last few weeks seemed to drag on forever. One woman, in the process of miscarrying, threw up and, out of sympathy, Nora went into the bathroom and vomited. The last woman she helped started running a fever. When Nora said, "I'm sending you to the hospital," the woman began to cry. She had planned on keeping the abortion a secret from her husband; in the hospital that would be impossible. Then Nora started crying. She knew "it was all over for me at that point because I wasn't separated at all." When she began assisting with miscarriages five months before, she knew so little that her fears distanced her from the women she was helping. The more she learned, the more her competence and comfort level increased; then, the emotional barrier her fear had erected toppled, and she was vulnerable. The medical profession's deliberate distancing of practitioner and patient, subject and object, served a purpose, self-protection. But Jane members believed that objectifying the people who turned to them would only breed arrogance and callous treatment. The women in the service walked an emotional tightrope stretched between empathy and professionalism and, clearly, Nora had lost her balance.

While Nora was preparing to leave the service, the new counselors who joined in the fall were ready to get more involved. In the spring Gail, the college student who spent free time at Julia's, mentioned to the inner circle sitting around Julia's kitchen table that she wanted to start assisting. Nobody reacted. She waited a few weeks and then repeated her request, assuming that the inner circle had discussed it. She had the benefit of Julia's friendship. Julia was receptive to training the young women who visited her and baby-sat for her children. She knew she had "a great deal of difficulty separating out the people I liked from the people I trusted. I know it's wrong. But there's this thing of personality which intrudes." She told Gail she could begin training as an assistant on Wednesday, May 3.

CHAPTER 22

On Wednesday, May 3, 1972, Gail's first day as an assistant-in-training, the service was working in the South Shore Drive high-rise apartment that had a view of Lake Michigan. Deborah had had her baby in the fall and had rejoined the group a month or two before. She was the driver that day, ferrying women between the Front in Hyde Park and the apartment on South Shore Drive. Julia and Cynthia were performing the abortions; Donna and Sarah were assisting. Lynn, Gail's friend, was at the Front, expecting to be relieved by another counselor in the afternoon.

One of the workers had bought a selection of pastries to give to each woman as a treat after her abortion. Cynthia was cooking a pork roast for lunch, thinking that if they had to work hard they should eat well. By midday they had completed more than a dozen abortions. For the first time in ages, it looked like they were going to be finished at a reasonable time. Cynthia was thinking, Gee, I'll be able to go pick up my kids at school and be home in time for supper.

One of the women had bled heavily during her abortion and was resting in the spare bedroom with ice on her abdomen, the bleeding under control. Shortly after one-thirty Sarah and Gail took another woman into one of the bedrooms to prepare her for her abortion. In the third, Cynthia was inducing a miscarriage with Donna assisting.

Deborah arrived with five more women from the Front. She

decided to drive back immediately because the one woman whose abortion was completed needed to leave. Her son was having surgery that day and she was anxious to join her husband at the hospital. She and Deborah left the apartment, walked down the hall, and rang for the elevator. The woman wasn't feeling well. "I think I'm going to throw up," she said.

"Can you wait until we're downstairs?"

"I don't think so."

At that moment the elevator doors opened. There stood five huge white men in trench coats and shiny shoes. It struck Deborah that "they looked so much like cops that they could have been from *Dragnet.*"

She stepped aside. They started to walk past her. Then, Deborah says, "They stopped and literally put the arm on us. The woman with me freaked. I was very scared, too."

The men asked, "What apartment did you come out of?"

"Who are you?" Deborah demanded.

They were detectives from the homicide squad. They showed her their badges: "We know who you are and what you're doing. What's your name?"

The woman with Deborah burst into tears. She was nauseated, her son was being operated on, her husband was waiting for her. A group of officers took her to the other end of the hall to question her.

Deborah called out, "You don't have to talk to them. You don't have to tell them anything," but the woman, surrounded by detectives, was terrified and upset and she blurted out the apartment number.

Deborah yelled toward the apartment, "Don't open the door," but she knew that no one could hear her.

One officer immediately took both women down in the elevator to a bench in the lobby. The woman was still crying. She kept repeating to Deborah, "I'm sorry, I'm sorry."

Deborah comforted her, "It's all right, just don't say anything else. It'll be okay. Don't worry." Deborah felt a heavy weight settle on her. They had talked about what to do and how to act if they got arrested, but she was completely enervated.

Meanwhile, up on the eleventh floor, the officers rang the apartment's doorbell. Cynthia said to Donna, "It's okay. I'm basically done. Go answer it."

Donna opened the door a crack, and, as soon as she realized who it was, she tried to close it, but the detectives shoved past her into the apartment. She shouted, "It's the cops! It's the cops!"

Julia heard the commotion. When she saw the detectives, she tried to stop them: "You don't have a search warrant. You can't come in." Her mind screamed: It's happening, what we've been worried about is happening. And who's taking care of my kids?

While Julia argued with the police, Donna went into the living room and said to the women seated waiting for their abortions, "These are the police, but none of you were doing anything wrong and you don't have to talk to them. Nothing you did is against the law."

Cynthia heard Julia yelling. She was expecting the janitor and, for a second, she couldn't figure out why the janitor needed a search warrant. Then it hit her who was out there. She helped the woman on the bed get dressed and walked out of the room. When Cynthia saw the policemen, she thought she was going to faint. One of the men turned to her, "Are you all right? Are you a customer or one of them?" When she didn't reply, he said, "Just sit down."

Because Donna and Julia were the ones trying to impede them, the cops assumed they were the ringleaders, so they took them into the kitchen and handcuffed them. For Donna, who considered herself shy and insecure, it was a shock to be singled out. The officers kept demanding, "Where is he? Where's the doctor?"

One of them asked Donna what was in the oven. She answered sullenly, "Pig," which didn't endear her any further.

In the other bedroom, Sarah and Gail heard what Sarah describes as "a lot of noise, like a roaring in your ears." Donna and Julia were screaming, "You can't come in." Sarah and Gail quickly locked the bedroom door, helped the young woman on the bed get dressed, and hid the instruments. Sarah was terrified, her pulse racing. The three women sat down on the bed and waited. They heard a man's voice telling them to open the door. Then he kicked it in and herded them into the living room. The detectives kept asking, "Where's the guy? Where's the doctor?"

When the officers demanded everyone's name and only the Jane members refused, they quickly figured out who was who. Other than the five workers at least eight other women were in the apartment. There was a lot of milling about while the officers questioned each of these women separately. Gail felt her whole life shifting. She wanted to distance herself from what was happening, so she picked up a copy of *The Martian Chronicles* that happened to be lying around and sat down to read. Time passed. The three women who had had abortions were taken to the hospital, examined and released. Everyone else was going to the police station.

Julia, Donna and Deborah were chained to the side of a paddy wagon for the ride to the station. Deborah, as the driver, had been collecting money from women all day and she had wads of it stuffed in her pockets. The three of them decided to split it up. Julia had the list of women scheduled for abortions that day with the name of each one's counselor noted on it. They ripped up the paper into tiny pieces and scattered it in the back of the paddy wagon.

Cynthia, Gail and Sarah, daisy-chained together, rode in another paddy wagon. Cynthia had in her handbag at least thirty duplicate three-by-five-inch index cards, each for a woman who had contacted Jane. Gail said, "If the police get hold of these they could harass those women." They tore off the corners which had the names, addresses and phone numbers and ate those. By the time they arrived at the police station at Ninety-first and Cottage Grove, they had swallowed the identifying information. For three hungry women expecting a pork roast for lunch, index cards were a poor substitute.

At the police station, Cynthia, Gail and Sarah were ushered into an office and left alone. There was a phone on the desk, so they started calling everyone they could think of. The detectives put Deborah in a room by herself and handcuffed her to a ring in the wall. Julia and Donna were in another room together, also chained to a wall.

At the same time that the police were in the South Shore Drive apartment, Miriam arrived at the Front. Early that morning, before work, Julia had stopped by Miriam's house in a funk. After she left, Miriam went to visit Jenny in the hospital. Jenny was in good spirits and said she'd be getting out soon. Miriam decided to cheer Julia with that news, but, when she called the apartment, there was no answer. She was a little worried, so she went to the Front.

When Miriam arrived, Lynn had her hands full. One of the women she had counseled, an eighteen-year-old with four children, had brought three of them and left them in Lynn's care while she went for her abortion. Lynn told Miriam that, as far as she knew, everything was fine because Deborah had just picked up five more women. Miriam, her mind at ease, informed Lynn that her relief had cancelled, dropped off a bag of snacks for the Front and left.

As Miriam headed down the building's hallway, she saw two big men talking to a nervous little man standing in the doorway of the next apartment. She thought, maybe I should help this man; on second thought, maybe I should just go home. After she walked out of the building the officers realized they were at the wrong apartment and knocked on the door Miriam had exited a few minutes before. When Lynn heard the knock she assumed it was Miriam returning. She opened the door to a huge hand attached to a gigantic man.

Lynn had just turned twenty-one; with her long blond hair she looked younger. Only slightly over five feet tall, she was overwhelmed by the huge detectives, but, trying to remain calm, she walked into the living room which was crowded with women and their support people and announced, "These are the police. You don't have to say anything." Everyone, including Lynn, was terrified into silence. The officers asked Lynn, "What are all these people doing here?"

Lynn replied, "Ask them." She refused to give them her name. The detectives proceeded to question everyone else. The other people kept turning to her for advice. She repeated, "You don't have to say anything. There's no reason for you to tell them anything but your name. You haven't done anything wrong." The detectives took everyone at the Front to the police station, where they kept Lynn in an outer room by herself.

In all, there were at least forty people from both the Front and the South Shore apartment—women, men and children—wandering around the police station. The seven members of Jane had the distinct impression that this collection of people was not what the police expected. They kept asking where the man was. They seemed perplexed, out of their element, and didn't know what to make of the Jane members who, Deborah says "were too smart, too white, too middle-class and we gave them a lot of lip." The hours dragged on as the women waited—hungry, bored and terrified in equal measure.

Deborah had been chained to a wall in a room by herself for over an hour. She thought, Nobody knows I'm here; nobody's coming back. Finally an officer unchained her and took her to the room where they were keeping the instruments, the drugs, everything they had confiscated from the two apartments. One of the officers, a young man in a short-sleeved shirt, casually asked her, "What did you do before this?"

"Before what?"

"Oh, come on."

"Do you really expect me to have this conversation with you?" Deborah asked, and then thought, What the hell. "Well, I was a high school English teacher," she said. He had been a biology teacher, so they spent a few minutes chatting about teaching. Then he asked, "What made you go wrong?"

Deborah couldn't believe her ears. "Did you really say that? Look, this may seem melodramatic, but I'm not going to say anything to you. I haven't made a phone call yet. I'm supposed to be able to call a lawyer."

Deborah called her husband, Marc, who was a lawyer. Marc's partner, Dan, informed her that Marc had gone to New York for a meeting, exactly what she had asked him not to do: "Molly will be with the baby and, if something happens, you'll get back too late," to which Marc had responded, "Oh, nothing ever happens." But Marc was wrong. Something had happened.

Deborah said to Dan, "Guess where I am."

"What were you doing today?"

"I was working."

"You've been arrested."

"That's right, toots."

He started to lecture her, "I told you—"

"Look," she interrupted, "Now is not the time. I'm in the police station. Call Molly."

Dan called Marc in New York. He caught the first flight back to Chicago. Then he called Molly, "Can you stay with the baby for a while, for a long while?"

Meanwhile, Donna and Julia were in another room handcuffed to the wall. Julia had her period and was out of Tampax. She was hungry, she was irritated and no one had a Tampax. When she got a turn at the phone she called home and asked her babysitter to contact her husband, Herb, at work.

Now that she wasn't chained to a wall, Deborah's terror lifted. At some point, she and Donna were in the bathroom together. She asked Donna what they should do with the cash they had between them. Donna said, full of anger, "One thing's for sure, we're not letting them have it." They tore up the money and flushed it down the toilet.

One of the people Cynthia and Sarah reached by phone was a woman labor lawyer, who came down to the station. Sarah's husband arrived with bread and bananas. Cynthia's father called: Did she need money? Was she okay? Finally one of the detectives realized they were using the phone and took it away. Gail remembers that "Cynthia kept chattering endlessly. Sarah was freaked out, very tense and completely silent, every once in a while saying, 'Oh shut up, Cynthia,' and then the police would come in and they'd get real quiet, even Cynthia."

For Gail there was "a certain banality to the whole thing. You sort of realize that you're in their hands and you can't do anything about it. They make you wait endless amounts of time." Out of boredom she opened the desk drawer in the office and found, in the nearly empty drawer, an S/M magazine with pictures of bound women being whipped. When the next officer walked in she showed it to him and said, "Great stuff you guys read." Obviously annoyed, he snatched it from her.

The detectives continued to question the people from the Front and the South Shore apartment. At one point one of them, with a puzzled look on his face, asked Lynn, "How much did you charge?"

"For what?"

"Oh, come on. What's the fee?"

"Didn't you ask all those people?" Lynn asked.

"I did, but everyone said a different amount."

"Well," she said, "that must be what they paid."

The detectives took photos of the seven women in Jane for the other people to identify. They insisted that the police take a group photo. Somewhere there is a picture of those seven Jane members, standing in a row, their arms around each other's necks, like a chorus line.

By the time they were driven to the women's lockup at Eleventh and State, it was almost midnight, nine hours after the raid began. They had mug shots taken, they were fingerprinted, booked and left in a holding cell with whomever the night had brought in. They were tired, giddy and scared, making sarcastic comments about one of Miriam's favorite pronouncements: "We're such nice people, we do such good work," Miriam used to say, "we'll never get busted."

Deborah struck up a conversation with the other women in the holding cell. Most of them had been picked up for prostitution, drugs or theft. When the name Jane came up, they had heard of it. One of them had a friend who had come through the service. Most of the prostitutes kept to themselves except for one who, Gail recalls, "was talking about great moments in prostitution." The woman knew a prostitute whose specialty, since she had no front teeth, was blow jobs. That kept Lynn amused through the night. Lynn thought that "they were as out of our experience as we were out of theirs."

The joking ended as soon as the seven women walked into the jail. None of the special treatment they felt they had been given at the station was in evidence here. They were seven criminals, nothing more. The steel doors clanged shut behind them.

As she led Deborah to the cell Lynn was in, the matron said, "I'm going to put you in with your partner." Lynn threw herself into Deborah's arms. Deborah looked around. The cell, she recalls, "had a wooden plank about six feet long stuck into the metal wall. There were three metal walls, one grid wall and the whole top was covered with mesh. The floor was not quite damp but there was a cold wet wind blowing across it that made it horrible like a dungeon (and we were eleven stories up). There was a little triangular toilet/sink arrangement with water you couldn't drink. The first thing we heard was this pounding and moaning and shrieking that never stopped, a shrill keening sound, women screaming, and it never stops." Deborah thought, Oh Jesus, look at this. Look where we are. Because she was still nursing her baby, her breasts ached. She went over to the sink and expressed her breast milk into it.

Donna and Julia were in a cell together. Julia looked around her in horror. Instantly, she understood "how tenuous our freedom is.

Radicals say everyone should spend a night in jail because it's a mind-expanding experience. Well, it is, but only on a level of unbelievable fear. You really felt stripped naked as if you had none of the protections that make you a human being in this society. They had all of them and could give them to you or not, as evidenced by the fact we never got fed."

Gail and Cynthia were in an adjacent cell. Cynthia "wanted a pillow or at least some coffee. We were told we were supposed to get coffee in jail. We didn't. It's stupid to be resentful about things like not eating, but we hadn't." Gail spent the night sitting on the floor, listening to women scream.

Sarah was in a cell by herself. She was thinking, What are my parents going to say now. She was jumpy. Every time she heard a sound she thought, What is that? Is it going to affect me? Questions tumbled through her mind: Can I get a drink of water? What happens, what physically happens, in the courtroom downstairs? What time do they get you up? Do they feed you breakfast? Even in the women's lockup, they were still focused on food.

At about three in the morning a matron took Deborah out of her cell. She and Lynn looked at each other in anguish. What was this about? Deborah yelled down the corridor to the others, "They're taking me out."

The matron took Deborah and Sarah to the attorney's room, where Deborah's husband, Marc, his partner, Dan, and a lawyer friend of Sarah's were waiting. One of the lawyers said, "All right, this is the deal. There's no time to get all of you out tonight. They will take one and the one we think we have the best chance with is you, Deborah, because you're a nursing mother and your husband is here and he's a lawyer and the judge downstairs is a lawyer. What do you think?"

Deborah said, "No deal. I'm not leaving them."

"Now look, here's why we want to do it. We know this judge; we've been before him. You are going to get the lowest bond this guy has ever given. If you get out tonight, then tomorrow morning, when they try to set a high bond on the other women, they won't be able to. You will help them if you leave tonight."

Sarah's attorney friend looked at her sternly: "Was it worth it? Do you think all those women are glad you did this for them? Are they going to come and help you?" Back in her cell, Sarah rolled up her coat for a pillow and tried to sleep. She thought, They ought to give a course in high school called What to Do When You're Arrested.

Deborah, in her cell, yelled the attorneys' plan down the corridor to the others. They called back, "Go, you should go, for the good of the group."

Deborah started to cry. "It was so intense in there," she says. "Even when conditions are terrible, when you're with your people, you don't want to leave them."

A matron put Deborah in a holding pen, like a barred cage, with two teenaged white girls, both drunk. They had been arrested for stealing a television set. One of them was dressed up, teetering on high heels. The other, wearing jeans, was five months pregnant. Her arms were scarred from needle marks and stitches where she had slashed herself in suicide attempts. For what seemed like hours the three women talked and waited in that cage.

Eventually they were taken down to night court in an iron elevator. As Deborah walked into the courtroom Marc and Dan whispered to her, "You are Mrs. ________, the wife of a lawyer. You're going home to your baby. This man is going to let you go home to your baby if you are nice to him." She couldn't believe that these two men she had known for years were talking to her as if she were a two-year-old.

The judge said, "Mrs. ________, how are you?"

"I'm not too well. I've been locked up upstairs and I'm very tired. I was in the police station a long time. How are you?"

"Well," he said, "I hate night court."

Deborah thought, How bizarre, he's talking to me as if we're sitting at the same table at Cousin Sophie's wedding.

"I think we can get you out of here very quickly. You'll go home to your baby." And then he set a low bail, just as the lawyers had predicted.

Deborah sat down and the judge started the next case, the two teenagers. He bellowed at them, "All right, what about you girls." He noticed Deborah still sitting, and, once more the kindly uncle, said, "Mrs. ________, you don't have to sit through this. You can go."

As the doors closed behind her, Deborah went into a kind of shock: "They fucked the teenager over and they let me go, which was a very interesting lesson for me. She was real small and she was wearing cheap clothes and had a Southern accent. She was a kid and pregnant, for Christ's sake. There's nobody there to help her and there's me with all these lawyers, nursing mother of the year. I was so ashamed. I hated the judge for that."

That afternoon, when Sarah called Miriam from the police station, Miriam felt suddenly alone. But she had no time to dwell on that. She began calling everyone in the service who had Jane money and everyone else she could think of who could raise money. She phoned Elizabeth, one of the suburban schoolteachers in the group: "Do you have any money?"

"I've got a couple of thousand dollars in the freezer."

"You need to bring it to me right now."

That's all Miriam had to say. Elizabeth understood exactly why Miriam needed it. Elizabeth also knew that it was her name on the South Shore Drive apartment's lease. For days afterward she expected the police to show up at her school and arrest her, but they never did.

In a few hours on the phone Miriam managed to pull together $10,000. She contacted the two *Call-Back Janes* on duty, who started calling the women who had left messages for Jane. They encouraged anyone who could possibly dig up the money to go to New York. To women who had no where else to turn, they said, call us back in a week. Molly, one of the *Call-Backs* and Deborah's baby-sitter, had to shake the misery she felt. She forced herself to make those calls because "there was that thing that you just kept going. You were competent. You did it, no matter what."

While the news spread from service member to service member, Nora, the nineteen-year-old who had been one of the group's two midwives, was at O'Hare Airport about to get on a plane for Denver, excited about the life ahead of her and relieved. She was leaving at a perfect time. She had discharged her responsibilities competently, without screwing up. As she waited in the airport she heard her name paged. It was the other midwife, Robin, calling to tell her about the bust. Well, Nora thought, as she boarded the plane, no longer so cheerful, I almost got out free.

Day begins early in jail. The six remaining Jane members were wakened and put in a holding cell along with an assortment of other women whose arrest stories were all connected to a boyfriend.

Julia noticed that "a lot of them were people who had this typical-black-person-in-Chicago-who-got-fucked stories: A woman who said she was out with her boyfriend and he ran a red light and didn't have his license so he got thrown in jail and so did she." One woman had been involved in a drug-related shooting and advised the others to turn state's evidence before their partners did. Another tried to be reassuring: "You know, it's not so bad in jail. You get three squares and you don't have to hustle like you do on the streets." Gail thought, Here's someone who thinks jail is better than being on the outside. What can her life be like?

The courthouse at Twenty-sixth and California was filled with Jane members and supporters. Miriam brought the money she had raised for bail. When Julia saw her husband, Herb, she started to cry.

As the lawyers predicted, the prosecuting attorney asked for a high bail, noting that the state considered four of the defendants risks for flight, since they had been born out of state. A young black feminist attorney, who had volunteered to help, objected: "That's ridiculous. These women have families and mortgages. They're not going anywhere." Deborah's husband, Marc, used the ploy they had planned, citing the low bail that had been set for Deborah. Bail was set at $2,500 each. The six women walked out of the courthouse, into a May morning that could not have felt sweeter.

C H A P T E R 2 3

When Miriam got home from the courthouse she called Jenny in the hospital: "Okay, you've had a long enough vacation."

Jenny agreed. The service needed her. She said to her psychiatrist, "Listen, it's time for me to get out of here. I'm well enough."

"Fine," he said. "How about leaving in a week or so?"

"No, I thought I'd leave today."

"This doesn't have anything to do with what I've been hearing on the news, does it?"

The arrests were reported in the media. The *Chicago Tribune,* in an article headed "Lib Groups Linked to Abortion," quoted a homicide detective: "We also believe there are other abortion clinics operating in Chicago by the same type of women's liberation groups . . . I don't think we put them out of business. They will probably pop up elsewhere."

The bust had been on a Wednesday, the first day of Jane's three-day work week. Other than the fifty to sixty women scheduled that week, another two hundred were waiting for appointments. Jane had an obligation to every one of those women.

Miriam wished she "had been busted. My life would have been a lot easier. I would have been with my friends. We had two hundred fifty women waiting for abortions and they had to be taken care of. We couldn't call them up and say, 'We're sorry. You can't be taken care of now because we don't exist any more.' I thought that *I* had to make sure the women got abortions and *I* had to keep the group together. I couldn't let it fall apart." An unwanted pregnancy could not be put on hold, waiting for events to sort themselves out. Time was the critical factor. For Jenny that "was so compelling that it really overshadowed everything else."

Jenny and Miriam called an emergency meeting for that same night. The turnout was enormous; even women who had not been active in months were there. Jenny and Miriam laid out what little they knew. At that point, they had more questions than answers. Was there a plot to get Jane? How did the cops know where to go? Was there an informer in the group? Who was being followed? Whose phones were tapped? They couldn't deny it any longer: they were breaking the law and that had consequences; they could wind up in jail. So much for Miriam's dictum—We're too good; we're too nice; they'll never arrest us.

In the middle of the meeting, the seven women who had been arrested arrived together. They were greeted with silence. No one applauded or rushed to embrace them. Everyone else was too lost in her own worries to offer them any support. The seven filled the others in on their next steps. A few of the women who had been arrested argued for closing Jane down for a few weeks. They assumed that the police were going to keep raiding the group until they had arrested everyone. Gail, who had felt her life turn upside down the minute the police barged in, said, "The heat is on. The service should just lie low for now."

Jenny exploded, "But there are all these women who need abortions. What will happen to them?" It struck Gail that Jenny said it as if she could see an endless line of desperate women stretching before her.

Since the seven assumed the police were watching them, they said, "We better not have anything to do with you."

As closure to that discussion, Jenny announced: "We're going to keep on working and anybody who's not going to do that should leave right now."

The women who had been arrested, Julia, Donna, Cynthia, Sarah, Deborah, Lynn and Gail, got up and left. Lynn felt that "we were invited to go away. We were going to be followed and they didn't want to talk in front of us. We had expected hugs, kisses, some show of solidarity. Instead we were met with the same paranoid atmosphere that had greeted me at my first meeting."

The remaining Jane members were grim and frightened, but they had work to do. Miriam had contacted Harris Wilson of the Chicago Clergy Consultation Service and arranged for some women to go through the clergy's network. She had also contacted abortion clinics in New York and Washington, D.C., who knew about Jane. Several of the clinics instantly responded, "If your women can get to us, we'll give them free abortions." The service set up a system for calling the hundreds of women waiting for abortions to lay out the alternatives and make sure each one had some place to go. Jane counseled them and made the appointments.

One of the women scheduled for an abortion the week of the bust was Maria. When her counselor called her the night before her appointment and said, "We've been busted. Can you get enough money together for an airline ticket to D.C.?" Maria panicked. Her girlfriends had barely managed to scrape together $100 for her Jane abortion.

Maria was in her second year of college when she discovered she was pregnant. She was the oldest in a large, strong black family for whom education was a priority. As the good girl, in college, she was setting an example for her siblings. When she was growing up in the sixties, she felt that the black community viewed young black women as either good or bad. The good ones went to college, became teachers or married ministers; the bad ones had babies at fifteen and were indelibly marked. The disgrace she felt she would bring to her family was unbearable.

A friend suggested she go to a doctor at the Cabrini Green Housing Project. "They have crooked doctors there," she said, "and they'll probably give you something." Cabrini Green was notorious. Decrepit and dangerous, it symbolized the worst aspects of urban poverty. Maria went to the doctor, determined to get an abortion. When he confirmed her pregnancy, she pleaded, "Isn't there something you can give me to bring my period on?"

"No, you find that guy and you tell him that you're going to have a baby and he'll be very excited and proud. I know how these guys feel about you girls having babies."

After she left the doctor she was hysterical. She could not have this baby. She thought, I wonder how they do it with knitting needles or quinine. Someone told her that castor oil and a laxative would bring on her period if she wasn't "too far gone." Maria was ready to commit suicide when a friend gave her Jane's number.

The week before the raid Maria met with a counselor who prepared her and warned her about common post-abortion problems, saying, "If you can't get hold of me and you do have to go to the hospital, tell them what happened, but that you don't know where you had it. You've got to be honest because it's your body we're talking about."

Maria felt that "here's a person I can trust because she's being honest with me. She really emphasized the educational aspects of having an abortion, letting me see the two sides of it and working things out, asking me if I was comfortable with the decision I had made."

When her counselor called her May 4, the night before she was supposed to have her abortion, and suggested she go to D.C., Maria said she didn't have enough money for airfare. Her counselor responded, "You can use what you have toward the plane ticket and we'll give you the rest. Here's the flight you need to take and directions to the clinic. They'll be expecting you."

Maria flew alone to Washington and took a bus to the clinic.

Other people got off at the same stop. They had all been sent by Jane. After their abortions they went to a private home in Georgetown where Jane had arranged for them to spend the night.

That group of women shattered Maria's stereotypes of good girls and bad. They were both married and single women, black and white, poor and middle-class. One woman was her mother's age. Another was Maria's age; she felt exactly the way Maria did: Now that this is over, I can get on with my life. Maria felt that "reading about abortion in the newspapers, looking at statistics, was not as effective as being with a group of women to say, 'Hey, we're all in this together. I'm going to support you.' "

Her contact with Jane "helped me sort this whole thing out. I felt that Jane was really saving me, beyond the abortion. I no longer perceived it as I'm disappointing my parents. I felt they were helping me to see my future, to realize the seriousness of relationships and childbirth and birth control. It isn't just a momentary thing. It's about making this real solid decision: I'm making this decision; nobody else is."

While Miriam organized the referrals to clinics, Jenny's task was to get the service operating again. She and Pam had agreed to begin performing abortions as soon as possible, but all of their instruments, equipment and medications had been confiscated by the police. For the next few days Jenny made the rounds of medical supply houses and visited her pharmacist connection to replenish their supplies.

The bust forced the group to restructure. Some of their most reliable assistants had been arrested, and, although one other counselor was advanced in the training process, Pam and Jenny were the only experienced abortionists left. One thing was very clear: more women had to begin training, and quickly. They also had to change the way they handled work days. They stopped setting up Fronts. Performing their usual twenty-five to thirty abortions a day was out of the question. Instead, they limited themselves to five abortions at a time. A counselor either picked those women up at a public location, such as a street corner, and drove them to the apartment they were using, or had them meet at her house and then took them directly to the work place. Counseling immediately preceded the abortions.

Between the abbreviated work days that Jenny organized and what Miriam was able to arrange elsewhere, the service could provide abortions for most of the two hundred fifty women who had contacted them before the bust, and for the women who continued to call Jane. But there were other women who posed a bigger problem. They had no money and their pregnancies had advanced past the point where clinics normally performed D & Cs or vacuum aspirations. In New York, where abortions were supposed to be legal up to twenty-four weeks of pregnancy, few hospitals provided saline abortions, in which saline solution is injected into the amniotic sac, the medically preferred method for inducing miscarriages. Where they were available, they were very expensive. Jane members felt that because of the time involved and the increased possibility for complications, for the present, inducing miscarriage was too risky for Jane.

Four months earlier, in January, when Jordan Bennett, the California abortionist who taught them the cannula method, came to Chicago, he also demonstrated a technique he had developed for inducing miscarriages. He used large IUD-like coils, called super coils, which when inserted into a uterus initiated labor within twenty-four hours. Once a woman was in labor he removed the coils in the same manner that IUDs were removed. Labor and delivery continued normally. He had used the technique on women who had been raped during the recent civil war in Bangladesh. Because it was outside official medical practice, there was no data on the effectiveness or safety of the super coil method. Sheryl, an abortion rights activist in New York who was in contact with Miriam, offered to arrange super coil abortions in a hospital in New York. Jordan agreed to fly in from California and perform them for free.

Although service members were wary of Jordan Bennett and his incessant self-promotion, they used his cannulas regularly. They were desperate to come up with a way to help these women. Using super coils had to be better than abandoning them.

Counselors contacted those women to let them know what they were planning to do. They described the method, explained that it was highly experimental and that Jane had no track record with it, so they could not give any assurance as to possible problems. The group felt that, if they were completely honest with each woman, and gave her every bit of information they had, then she could make her own decision.

About twenty women agreed to go to New York for the experimental procedure. The service rented a bus to take them. At the last minute Sheryl called Miriam to say the hospital in New York had backed out, but she had located an alternative in Philadelphia. In 1971 a judge had struck down Pennsylvania's restrictive law and the state had not appealed that ruling. Since then the status of abortion was nebulous and some Pennsylvania doctors were openly providing abortions. Miriam assumed that Sheryl had found a hospital, so she never checked it out. But it wasn't a hospital. It was a clinic whose doctor performed vacuum aspirator abortions and had agreed to host the super coil event. Miriam felt it was too late to rethink the whole thing. She had to trust Sheryl and Jordan.

A week and a half after the bust, about twenty pregnant women, all of them poor and more than half of them women of color, boarded a charter bus for Philadelphia. Miriam, Robin, one of Jane's members who midwifed miscarriages, and another counselor traveled with them. The counselors spent the trip reviewing the technique with the other women. It seemed to Robin that "everybody was very up and enthusiastic on the way there."

When the women arrived at the clinic in Philadelphia late that night, there were TV cameras waiting for them. Sheryl, the New York activist, had called the press to get publicity both for Jordan and for abortion, but had neglected to tell the Chicago women. The women from Chicago, the counselors and those coming for abortions, had been on a bus all day and most of the night and they hadn't planned on going public. The counselors from Jane said to each woman, "Nobody has to talk to the press, but, if you want to, go ahead."

Jordan used this opportunity to teach his super coil method to a gynecologist who had accompanied him from California and to the clinic's doctor. Upon examination, Jordan and the doctors determined that several pregnancies were less advanced than the women had estimated. On those they performed D & Cs. Into the early hours of the morning, training the two doctors, Jordan inserted the super coils in the remaining women. Miriam watched Jordan teach the doctors and she was astounded: "He actually gave them the information which he never did with us because he wanted us to be dependent on him because we were women. I could not describe the difference or write it down, but, if you made a movie of it, you could see it because it all had to do with ways of relating."

Also with Jordan was a Scandinavian couple who were writing a book about him. They cooed over Jordan, extolling his virtues to the pregnant women. The Jane counselors thought their behavior was outrageous, nor did they approve of the attention being showered on Jordan. It was the pregnant women from Chicago who deserved attention.

At two or three in the morning, after the coils were inserted, the women went to private homes to rest. When they returned to the clinic later that morning, a demonstration was brewing. An abortion rights group, having heard about the super coil event in progress, came to protest and close down the clinic. They believed that women were being experimented on without their knowledge. The phone kept ringing with threats of police action. Sheryl, the New York activist, more frazzled by the minute, tried to talk to the demonstrators while Jordan's support people lavished praise on him inside. Between what was going on outside the clinic and what was happening inside, the whole scene felt to Miriam "like a Salvador Dali painting, all absurd."

The demonstrators threatened to call the district attorney. They pounded on the clinic doors. The women from Chicago, the clinic staff, the doctors and Jordan and his entourage locked themselves inside the clinic, barricaded the doors and did not venture out again. The counselors from Jane were worried about the Chicago women's response to the protest, but each of them said, "If you all can keep them away from here, I'll be fine. Don't worry about me." They saw themselves as a team. Robin was impressed that "their sense of participation and choice about what they were doing was very strong." They had traveled all the way from Chicago to get abortions and they were furious. If there were risks, it was their choice because Philadelphia was their only hope. Who were these people outside and why were they interfering? They hadn't offered to help.

To complicate matters further, Jordan was having problems. A few women were not miscarrying. The pressure to get everyone done and en route to Chicago increased with each passing minute. The demonstrators were relentless. At any moment the police might arrive. Someone let the air out of the bus tires. The tension escalated. The clinic was under siege. Jordan used drugs to encouraged labor and performed a few late D & Cs. The whole event, which had started out on such a positive note, had turned into a nightmare. One woman was hospitalized in Philadelphia and had a hysterectomy. Another's back problems were exacerbated by her miscarriage and she had to return to Chicago by plane. The other women rode the bus back to Chicago in silence.

That was not the last the service heard about Philadelphia. The hospital in Philadelphia, to which one of the women had been taken, contacted the CDC (Center for Disease Control). The CDC began an investigation of the super coil abortions in Philadelphia. Since there was no research data on the coils, they wanted to find out who got sick and why. The next week, through Jane, the CDC doctors offered the women who had gone to Philadelphia post-abortion examinations in Chicago. All but two went to Cook County Hospital for follow-up. Miriam accompanied them. Although the CDC determined that the morbidity rate was unusually high (60 percent of the women suffered some form of complication, either minor or major), their report published in the *Journal of Obstetrics and Gynecology* notes that the atmosphere, the threats of prosecution and other factors beyond the method itself may well have contributed to the unusually high problem rate. In Philadelphia Jordan was eventually charged with eleven counts of performing illegal abortions and eleven counts of practicing medicine without a license. He was tried and convicted on two counts and fined $500.

A year later a position paper entitled "The Philadelphia Story: Another Experiment on Women" was circulated at women's conferences around the country. It portrayed Jordan as a charlatan, Jane as his dupes, and the women seeking abortions as ignorant poor women of color, guinea pigs experimented on without their knowledge or consent.

Before writing the paper the authors did not contact counselors in Jane or any of the women who went to Philadelphia for abortions. Jane members found out about it by chance when it was distributed at conferences they attended. They were horrified. The women who had had abortions in Philadelphia were already outraged by the demonstrators at the clinic. They were even more upset by their portrayal in the position paper. To assume that they were ignorant victims, just because they were poor and of color, smacked to them of racism. Here, again, were people who had given them no help, attacking those who had helped them. Two of the women from Chicago who had had super coil abortions went to Philadelphia and testified at Jordan's trial in his defense. One of the others joined the service and several sent relatives through Jane.

The "Philadelphia Story" unleashed a series of charges and countercharges in the feminist press. Jane suspected that the California women, who had come to Chicago to teach them self-help, were behind the paper and were using it to attack their archenemy and former ally, Jordan.* But the debate raised larger questions: What does experimentation and informed consent mean in a situation where people are barred from access to established medical practice as these women were in May of 1972? And who is to decide?

*For more on Philadelphia see Ruzek, *The Women's Health Movement.*

CHAPTER 24

When Jenny told Nick about the bust, he felt "the hair stand up on my arms 'cause I knew I was going down with it. That's the way it goes, names named and grand juries. I knew it was going to be a lot of trouble for me." And, when Jenny mentioned that they were back at work, he was shocked: "It's one thing to be covert," he says, "but, when it's time to fold . . . I was just amazed that the whole thing didn't fall apart. They were like Raskolnikov. They had no concern for the law."

Even after having worked closely with the service for two years, Nick thought like a criminal, but the women in Jane did not consider themselves criminals. Performing abortions was, they believed, "a high calling." Besides, for the women who were arrested, Nick was not an issue. He had served a purpose and now he was gone. "Giving him up" to the authorities did not even occur to them.

The seven women who had been arrested had much more on their minds. Donna, the shy redhead, had planned to take over Nora's job, midwifing miscarriages, and had rented an apartment for that purpose. Now she was out of a job and a place to live. Gail, the University of Chicago student who had begun assisting on the day of the bust, worried that pending criminal charges were going to affect her standing in school. At the end of the spring term, her boyfriend was leaving Chicago for Oregon; she decided to go with him. Cynthia, whose marriage had been deteriorating for years, filed for a divorce shortly after her arrest. Sarah and her husband were waiting to adopt a baby. A week after the raid the adoption agency called with a baby girl for them. Sarah and her husband agonized over what to do. Since Sarah's future was uncertain—she might spend years in prison—it was no time to bring a baby into their family. They declined the adoption. For Julia, the legal limbo provided a break from the pressures of work. The service had taken over her life and had interfered with her family. Gail, who spent time at Julia's, noticed that, "in a funny way, it was a time of incredible freedom for her because she wasn't working sixty hours a week anymore. She hung around with the kids and, even though the court stuff was tense, she was very relaxed compared to what she had been."

The seven felt they had to unify quickly, but there was little basis for solidarity. Gail and Lynn were school friends and had joined the service together. Deborah barely knew either of them, since she was on maternity leave when they joined. Deborah and Julia were close. Donna, Lynn and Gail were Julia's protégés and looked up to her. Cynthia, however, always resented Julia's rise to power in the service and her own exclusion, and her resentment was palpable.

Sarah's parents were another source of friction. They flew into Chicago soon after the arrests and came to one of the seven's meetings. Donna remembers Sarah's mother "throwing her two cents in on what she thought, which was all pretty conservative." Julia thought it was good that Sarah's parents supported her, but she objected to their attitude: "We want to get you a separate lawyer because you don't want to get stuck in jail with *these* people, people who did this bad thing to you," as if the innocent Sarah had been misled by the others. Julia felt that Sarah should have told her parents to back off.

The seven of them differed about the approach they should take. It was clear to Donna that "some of them didn't want to talk to the press at all; they didn't want to do anything; they wanted it all to go away. I thought it would have been okay to talk to the press, but we were together and I wouldn't have gone against what the group wanted."

Miriam became a source of tension, as well. Although the women who had been arrested felt that they had to become a cohesive unit, Miriam kept showing up at, and participating in, their meetings. But the seven was just that, the seven. They had to make the decisions that directly affected their futures, not hers. Especially Cynthia was annoyed by Miriam's insinuating herself into their group. Cynthia believed that she had been excluded from the inner circle because Miriam did not like her. Miriam had kept her out of that group and now Cynthia was determined to keep her out of this one.

The seven agreed that all major issues would be decided by consensus. They discussed how public they were going to be, whether they should use the arrest to educate people about abortion and to make a case for legalization. In Gail's view, "Sarah didn't want to do any publicity and, I suppose, she kept us all careful."

The Chicago Women's Liberation Union set up the Abortion 7 Defense Fund and that became another cause for contention. They had disagreements about the money. Should they pay for Gail's trips to Chicago from Oregon? Should the money be spent on gifts for the lawyers who had come to the police station, the jail and the bail hearing? Even though these were minor issues that did not require consensus, Cynthia resented that Julia and Deborah, sometimes in consultation with Miriam, who cosigned the Defense Fund checks, arbitrarily decided those things. As in the service itself, it was not the decisions per se that Cynthia objected to, as much as the way those decisions were made.

When it came to hiring a lawyer, they took Deborah's husband's advice: "Find yourselves the best criminal lawyer you can and don't screw around making yourselves into a cause." They made appointments with Chicago's most respected criminal lawyers who handled political cases.

Day after day, dressed in cutoff jeans and T-shirts, they sat in wood-paneled attorneys' offices. Almost all the lawyers were men who kept referring to them as girls. Most seemed sleazy and slick, and none of them had any understanding of why these women had been providing abortions. Just like the police, the lawyers wanted to know where the man, the doctor, was. They could not even conceive of women acting independently. For one lawyer, Lynn remembers, "We were a cause, and he was ready to fight for our bodies as we lay bleeding in front of him. We all came out of there and felt the same: we don't want to be a cause; we just want to be out."

Then the seven interviewed Barbara. She was one of the top criminal lawyers in Chicago and someone Jenny had consulted in the past. She had defended other radicals and her position was clear: There's no reason for any of you to go to jail. My job is to keep you out of jail, not to fight the issue of abortion.

They picked Barbara because she was straightforward, she was a woman, and because, of all the attorneys, she came closest to understanding the group's motivation. And Deborah felt "completely knocked out by her apparent power. I'll never forget the way she looked when we went to court. She was wearing canary yellow pants and a sleeveless canary yellow sweater and she had a canary yellow patent leather briefcase. She had big silver bracelets that clanked up and down her arms and great big earrings; hair and makeup perfect but outrageous, and a mind like a steel trap. I loved it that she could walk in there looking like that and play their game and win."

Few of Jane's members, as engrossed as they were in their work, paid much attention to what was going on nationally vis-à-vis abortion. Until Barbara told them about it, they were not aware of the Supreme Court's pending decision in *Roe* v. *Wade*. The case, originally filed on behalf of Jane Roe, a woman who could not get an abortion, challenged the constitutionality of Texas's prohibitive statute. It had been brought before a Texas federal district court in 1970. The three-judge panel had struck down Texas's law, ruling it unconstitutionally vague, but had not imposed an injunction against enforcing it. Based on the lack of an injunction, Jane Roe's attorneys appealed to the Supreme Court. A ruling in the case could affect abortion laws throughout the country. Since the oral arguments in December of 1971, the Supreme Court had been deliberating. Barbara informed them that the Court might very well legalize abortion and that would have a positive bearing on their case.

The seven women went on a weekend retreat to a friend's farm in Door County, Wisconsin, hoping that time together would help them feel closer. For Lynn it was her "second grand failure with group process (the first was my college rap group). We didn't have anything to talk about. It was hilarious. Many of us did not have enough respect for each other to listen. Sarah basically wanted it all to go away. She had nothing but contempt for Gail, Donna and me, the hippies in the group."

None of them knew how to confront without attacking. Sarah noticed that their "only way of dealing with how to put a point across was to hurt somebody else, so there was some pretty unpleasant stuff." As a married woman without children, she felt caught between the three women with children and the three younger, single women. Her point of view was usually much more conservative than the others'.

Deborah remembers that all of them "were nervous and scared. Cynthia and Julia had a very bad scene. It was a strange little group of people but, even with all of that, just like in the service, we did what we needed to do." Their legal defense was the task before them, not their personal issues.

The arrests underscored a problem in Jane that was inherited from Nick. He had resisted training more women because he wanted the fewest possible people to be able to identify him. Even after he no longer worked with Jane, the women abortionists, not the group as a whole, selected the people they wanted to teach. The difference between liking someone and trusting her constantly blurred. Although

Jane members saw the training to perform abortions as a promotion, being an abortionist and having power in the group were not synonymous. There was one trained abortionist who had no authority, while Miriam, who was inept at medical skills, had a great deal of power and control.

The selection process had led to a shortage of trained people, which the bust had exacerbated; it had to be scrapped. Rather than wait until one of the leaders thought she was "ready" to begin training as an assistant, all counselors were encouraged to do it. Not everyone did. Some women didn't have the time; others were not interested. On top of that, only fifteen counselors were still active. About ten counselors, a third of the group, dropped out after the bust. The arrests, like the revelation of Nick's status and Delores's death, sheared off another layer of people who, no longer able to ignore the risks, could not accept them. Lois, the young black woman who joined that winter, felt that "the women who stayed were for real. Those who weren't didn't hang around. They couldn't because the reality would eat them up."

Over the next month, the group learned what was behind the raid. The newspapers noted that the police had acted on a complaint from a woman whose sister-in-law was scheduled for an abortion. She had given them the address of the Front and the police had followed Deborah, the driver, to the South Shore Drive apartment. There was no grand plan to get Jane. The seven's lawyer, Barbara, concluded that the raid was a fluke. Her sources told her that, if a certain higher-up had been on duty that day, the bust would not have happened.

Once the members realized that the police did not plan to close Jane down, their paranoia dissipated. In less than a month and a half they resumed their former method of operation, using Fronts, counseling women with their support people in advance in the counselors' homes. But that news did not alleviate the stress of an overworked skeleton crew of counselors, assistants and abortionists.

Less than two months after her arrest, Cynthia returned to the service. She felt "very traumatized by the bust. It had the sense of my relationship with my parents: somebody telling me what to do. I felt, if I was going to exist with myself, I couldn't have the Chicago police telling me what to do, so I went back." At first the leaders responded to Cynthia's return cautiously, worried that she might be followed, but soon she was back at work, performing abortions.

The service was not only short on people, but on Fronts and work places as well. Even though the raid was a fluke, the group felt it would be safer if they worked in neighborhoods outside of Hyde Park. Sally, one of the few Jane members over forty, lived with her husband and four teenage children in Oak Park, a suburb west of the city, in a house designed by Frank Lloyd Wright. She asked her husband if the service could use their place for a Front. He said, "No way, I'm already involved in controversy. If anything happened it would be really bad for me."

He was the chair of the local Open Housing Committee, trying to integrate the neighborhood, which had made him enemies. So many times Sally or her husband had answered the phone to an anonymous, "How'd you like to have your house burned down?" that they had to get an unlisted number. Sally considered his objections for a few hours and thought, Why is it okay for me to take risks for his work, but not him for my work? She went back to him and said, "I think I will use the house for a Front, anyway." Reluctantly, he assented.

For the remnants of Jane, that summer was gray and oppressive. The counselors who had begun to assist with the abortions got over their initial terror at performing medical tasks through constant practice. Molly, one of the young women who had joined in November, felt as if all she did that summer was work: "It was exhausting. That whole period didn't feel easy anymore. I don't remember getting much of a break at all."

Some counselors had to face more that grim hot summer than overwork. On a summer night Lois was dragged off the street by four young men. All night they held her prisoner in a basement, raping her repeatedly. In the morning they threw her out on the street. She called home and she called the police. Fortunately, the investigating detectives believed her. Her husband scoured the streets to find out what he could. Not only was he able to discover the identities of the four young men but he also found out something that was alarming: These four friends had raped many other women. Lois was the only one who had reported it to the police.

The detectives picked up the young men; Lois recognized them in lineups. Throughout the trial the courtroom was packed with feminists. Seeing their faces gave Lois the strength she needed. The defense's strategy was to try to prove that Lois was a whore. She not only had to contend with the emotional grief of any rape victim undergoing a harsh cross-examination, but also she felt torn. She was a young black woman, sending young black men into a brutal prison system. What kept her going was the information her husband had uncovered: They had raped women before and they would do it again. If they were locked up, another black woman would be spared her nightmare. The four young men were convicted and sentenced to prison terms.

The preliminary hearing for the seven Jane members was held in August. The three women whose abortions had just been completed when the police barged in had given statements. Since then, two of them had had second thoughts. At the hearing, one, a working-class white woman, testified that she could remember nothing. The second, a black college student whom Gail had counseled, refused to say anything and was treated as a hostile witness. After the hearing she said to Gail, "The cops tried to push me around, but fuck them. I wasn't going to tell on you." What Jane provided, she added, was a service that was needed and that she felt great about.

The third woman was a teenage mother of four living on welfare who had brought three of her children to the Front that day. She had been induced and had miscarried long before the hearing. She told the court everything, but she could identify only two women. She turned around and pointed at Gail, "That one sitting there." Gail found it "sort of depressing that a welfare mother of four was willing to testify against us." Donna felt "bad for her because she had so many pressures, so many things that could get used against her."

Julia was infuriated by the woman's testimony: "She wasn't one of the people who didn't get done that day and so might have had some bitterness about it." Jane members felt that the women who came to the service had a responsibility to protect the group, just as the service members had a responsibility to them. Their lawyer, Barbara, had told the seven that the police use any ploy they can to get someone to testify. Perhaps in this case, they had brought toys for her kids or something for her to make her feel important. Julia didn't feel "sorry for her, though. I was rather resentful, as a matter of fact."

One moment in the preliminary hearing was particularly amusing to the seven women from Jane. The prosecutor seemed embarrassed to talk about an abortion. Instead of directly asking, "Did any of these people do an abortion on you?" he asked, "Did any of these people touch you in the vicinity of the vaginal area?" Among the seven Jane members, that became the joke: the vicinity of the vaginal area. What could that possibly mean?

After the hearing, the case was bound over for grand jury indictment in September. Barbara's strategy was to delay as much as possible, knowing that the Supreme Court was about to hear a second round of oral arguments in *Roe* v. *Wade* and that a decision was expected shortly thereafter. If the Court decided to legalize abortion, the seven women might never have to go to trial.

In the service, another crisis was building that August. Jenny was on the edge again. Being the most competent and experienced of the abortionists, Jenny felt as if everything in their medical practice depended on her. She felt that the other abortionists, Pam, Charlotte and Cynthia could not shoulder the responsibility on their own, and no one else had advanced that far in training.

On one more sweltering August day, the service was working in a comfortable suburban house in Evanston, just north of Chicago. Thirty-one women had come for abortions and the women working knew they would not be finished until well into the night. Toward the end, Jenny was with a young woman who became hysterical as soon as she got on the bed. Inserting a speculum in her was almost impossible. Jenny stopped to talk to her. It was not the first time that someone had behaved this way. This kind of reaction usually meant that the woman did not want the abortion, so her body was refusing to allow it to happen. At that point whoever was with her would say, "You know, your body is telling us you don't want this abortion. Maybe you should go home and think about it some more because we can't do it now."

Jenny took that tack with the frantic woman on the bed, but she protested. She had to get an abortion. She just had an extremely low tolerance for pain. She begged Jenny to continue and Jenny acquiesced. The abortion went on interminably, with Jenny stopping every few minutes to give the woman a chance to regain her composure. The assistant tried to make it easier, breathing with her, soothing her. After it was over, Jenny was drained.

The last abortion that day was with a teenager who had said she was eight weeks pregnant. Once Jenny examined her she realized that she was four months pregnant. Jenny explained that she was going to induce a miscarriage. That was all she could do. Jenny prayed: Let me get through this one, please. She knew that was the last abortion she could do. "I couldn't stand to watch the suffering anymore," she says, "of this endless line of women stretching into infinity who got pregnant because they got fucked at the wrong time of the month. It was just too much. I couldn't do it anymore."

She went to Julia and begged her to come back: "I can't handle it anymore. I know this is an unbelievable sacrifice to ask you to make, but I've made all the sacrifices I can make. Physically and emotionally, I'm totally beat." Julia agreed to come back to Jane.

As opposed to the early spring when Jenny went into the hospital, this time Jenny transferred her authority and power to Julia directly. It was clear that Jenny expected her to be the lead abortionist. Julia felt that she "could not refuse this request. Jenny talked as though she felt endangered. I would not have gone back if she had not said that to me. Did my heart sink? Yes. Did I have a sense of being chosen? Yes. I felt I had to. I really didn't feel done with the service. I had this feeling that, I'm not going to let the bastards grind me down. So what, you get busted. Fuck that." She wasn't worried about being rearrested. Barbara, their lawyer, had reassured them, "You're on the cutting edge of a Supreme Court case that's happening right now and it's probably going to fall your way." Julia never believed any of them would go to prison. They were too white, too middle-class, not the sort of women who spent time in prison.

She talked it over with her husband, Herb. Herb felt that, even if he objected, it was Julia's decision. He had always believed that what Jane was doing "was a good thing for humanity, providing a service that people needed." Although he thought that going back to the service was a crazy thing for Julia to do, he, too, never believed she would go to prison. "I couldn't possibly see what she had done that could warrant going to jail," he says. "All she did was a good abortion."

When Julia came back to work, Donna and Lynn returned, too. Part of their reason for coming back was to support Julia, their mentor. Donna had another interest. Julia was going to train her to perform abortions. To Donna, using curettes and forceps didn't feel like a dramatic change: "It was a fluid thing, assisting the abortionist and doing the abortions. You learn one step, then the next; before you know it, you know the whole thing."

Lynn went back partly to support Julia and partly to learn the assistant's skills. For her, the bust was the moment in which she grew up. It taught her that actions had consequences, which had not crossed her mind when she joined the group a year before. "This time I was really choosing," she says. "I felt my eyes were open and I was doing this because it was important to do and the right thing for me to do."

Gail had moved to Oregon with her boyfriend. Sarah never considered going back: "Nobody invited me. Should I have to risk my life twice?" Sarah had felt separated from the other women arrested. In Lynn's view, "It was always the six of us and Sarah." Deborah felt that the service was no longer the same group she had known. In the past two years she had been fired from her teaching position, worked with the service, had a baby, and been arrested. She needed a break to sort all of it out. She was not going back to Jane.

CHAPTER 25

Through the summer and fall women continued to join so that by the end of 1972 Jane's membership was back to its usual complement of thirty plus. Since the police raid in May, new members no longer waited for six months to attend abortions and learn medical skills. As soon as a new member completed counselor training, she was encouraged to begin assisting with abortions. Once she attended abortions, nothing was secret. Out of expediency, the power that knowledge held became more equal. Because the assistant's tasks were fairly easy to learn, the pool of trained people expanded. But doing abortions required months of training; there were still only four women in the group who had mastered that skill. Within the larger group, though, the balance of power shifted from the Hyde Park housewives to the younger, single women, who were determined to open up the group's decision-making process.

In September Miriam asked two of them, Molly and Kate, who were *Call-Back Janes,* to take over *Big Jane,* the main administrative position, referred to in the group simply as *Jane. Jane* was supposed to be on call twenty-four hours a day. For the past year and a half the position had been shared by two women, alternating two weeks on and two weeks off.

Molly and Kate's first task was to get organized. They set regular work hours. Between three and five in the afternoon and after eight in the evening, neither of them was available, except for emergencies.

They bought *Chicago Tribune* maps of the city on which they marked each counselor's location.

By September, a third of the phone calls to the Chicago Women's Liberation Union were women looking for Jane's number; each week the service had three hundred women waiting for abortions. Since Jane could only accommodate one hundred a week, many had to wait up to three weeks for an appointment. To complicate matters, anyone whose pregnancy was approaching the cutoff date for a D & C, around 12 weeks lmp, had to be pushed to the top of the list to avoid induced miscarriages. Through some magical process *Jane* had to select just the right number of people for a work day even though it was impossible to predict how many women would actually show up. Kate sat in her tiny apartment, the cards spread out in piles on the living room floor, deciding who had to be done that week and who could wait. No matter how many times she rearranged the stacks of cards, she could not fit three hundred women into the one hundred slots available each week.

Kate's and Molly's phones never stopped ringing. They felt as though the telephone was permanently attached to their ears. Counselors called to report on women they counseled or to reschedule someone who had been a no-show the week before. The *Call-Back Janes* called in several times a day. At the end of each work day one of the workers contacted *Jane* with the list of women they'd seen and specifics about their abortions, which *Jane* recorded on each woman's three-by-five-index card. *Jane* was responsible for contacting the women from out of town. *Jane* had to call the counselors who hadn't attended the last meeting to assign women to them. Molly and Kate were always begging counselors to take one more woman. It was up to *Jane* to make sure every counselor knew the location of the Fronts so she could notify her women. Some crisis, such as a last-minute change in the Front's location, always seemed to arise just as either Molly or Kate was walking out the door for a movie or dinner. Both of them counseled women and, on their two weeks off, they worked at Fronts, drove and assisted.

For Molly it was a turning point. "It came at a time when I was getting high a lot and in an irresponsible relationship," she recalls, "part of a whole culture of heavy irresponsibility: What the heck, let's trip." But in the service not only was she responsible for other women's lives, but now she and Kate were accountable to the entire group. Through handling the pressures of *Jane*, Molly's self-perception changed. She felt "like a much more competent person and I liked myself a lot better. Before the service I never thought that I had the concentration to do anything, but, as *Jane*, I would stay up and work all night."

Molly had initially taken an instant dislike to Kate, but sharing *Jane* brought the two women closer. They kept in touch daily to assure continuity, and started spending their free time together. On afternoon breaks they went out for treats; at night, with their boyfriends, they went to movies. They discovered that not only could they work together but that they enjoyed each other. For Molly it was the primary lesson she learned in Jane: Liking someone is not a prerequisite for working well together. She also learned, "Through work, sometimes you get to like people you thought you wouldn't."

One night Molly called Kate: "You're working tomorrow, aren't you? I counseled this teenager tonight. Her mother did all the talking; the kid never said a word. She wouldn't even look at me. Try to find out what's going on, what she wants. Her name's Angela Nolan, she's fifteen."

Kate and the other women who were working that day met at the apartment early and cleaned it. They boiled instruments, filled syringes and set up the bedrooms. They made the beds with fresh linen and covered them with heavy plastic sheets. At the foot of each bed they positioned a small table covered with a clean towel and on it placed a box of tissues, syringes and instrument trays filled with cold sterilizer. By the time the driver arrived with five nervous women, they were ready.

The women who volunteered to have their abortions first went into the bedrooms and instantly the work day found its own rhythm. After each abortion, the used instruments were scrubbed and boiled again, the plastic sheets washed with alcohol.

In the middle of the day, another worker notified Kate that Angela was in one of the bedrooms. Kate knocked on the door and went in. On the bed was a stocky girl. Kate introduced herself. "Molly, your counselor, called me last night. She's worried about you. She told me she didn't know how you felt about this abortion. I want you to know we're not going to do anything to you that you don't want."

Angela looked at Kate and said, "I want this baby, but my mother won't let me. She says I'm just a baby myself."

"If you have the baby, what are your plans? Are you going to finish school?" Kate asked.

"Yeah, and then my boyfriend and I can be together."

"And how are you going to take care of the baby while you're in school?"

"That's the problem. My mother she says she won't do it. She says she raised her kids and she's not raising mine. She's saved a little money and she says she wants to spend it on new furniture."

In this situation, Kate had to admit, her sympathies were with the mother. She said. "You can't really blame her, can you? But, look, it's up to you. It's your body and it's your life. If you don't want an abortion, we won't do it."

Another assistant opened the door, anxious to get started. Kate asked her to wait a few more minutes. Turning back to Angela, she asked, "What do you want to do?"

"I've got to have the abortion. I can't have this baby. I can't take care of it myself. Go ahead. It'll be okay."

"You're sure?"

"Yeah, I'm sure."

Kate sat with Angela through the abortion. Angela hardly said a word. When it was over, Kate said, "Please call Molly. I know she wants to hear from you and I'm going to ask her how you're doing."

When she left Kate thought, What is any fifteen-year-old doing having a baby. But if everyone has a right to make her own decisions, where does that leave Angela? Will she regret this for the rest of her life and hold it against her mother?

A few weeks passed. Then one night Molly called. "I just heard from Angela Nolan, remember her? She called to thank me. Can you believe it? She found out her boyfriend was just using her to get to her friend. What a jerk. She just wanted to let us know she's glad she had the abortion."

In the fall of 1972, with an increasing workload, the group had to reexamine their counseling method. Up until then Jane members had counseled women one-on-one, in private sessions. In order to prepare one hundred women each week they decided to abandon individual counseling for group counseling. While group counseling was dictated by their current circumstances, it had some benefits. Going through counseling with other women in the same situation alleviated a woman's feelings of isolation, and group counseling could encourage women to turn to each other for support instead of depending on the counselor. Women traditionally interacted in groups, kaffeeklatsches and quilting bees. The only difference in Jane's groups was the topic. The downside was that group counseling diluted the attention given each woman, which meant that a counselor could miss a subtle sign of an unresolved problem.

Week after week Jane counseled and performed abortions. The counselors coped with the pressures of work with varying degrees of success, but a few had more to deal with than stress and overwork. That fall Lois attended the sentencing hearing for the young men who had raped her. Kate's father was dying of cancer in New York. And, in September, Cynthia's youngest child was killed in a freak accident while playing at a neighbor's. It was almost inconceivable that such a tragedy could happen to anyone, least of all Cynthia, who was facing criminal charges and going through an ugly divorce. Within hours everyone in Jane knew about it.

As Kate was about to leave for Cynthia's son's funeral, the telephone rang. It was a young woman she had counseled who had had an abortion a few days earlier. As Kate had instructed, she had been watching her temperature and it had risen to 102. Kate quickly called Julia, who advised: either send her to the hospital immediately, or try to cure the infection with Ampicillin, which the service kept on hand for such emergencies. Kate picked up the antibiotics and rushed to the young woman's apartment. By the time she arrived, the woman's temperature was 103. Kate administered the medicine according to Julia's instructions. After waiting for the antibiotics to take effect, she handed the woman a thermometer, "If your temperature hasn't gone down, you'll have to go to the hospital immediately." Kate said a prayer and read the thermometer. It was slightly below 101 degrees. The two women hugged each other. Laughing, the young woman said to Kate, "Boy, when you gave me that thermometer, you looked worse than I felt." Kate waited until the young woman's temperature had returned to normal, then raced to Cynthia's son's funeral.

At Cynthia's Kate updated Julia, adding, "Lately it seems like everyone I counsel has problems. Maybe I should take a break for a while." Kate had been counseling three to five women a week for almost a year and not one of those women had had medical problems. Suddenly that September several women she had counseled had had complications. Julia reassured her that problems seemed to pass from one counselor to another; this month it was Kate's turn. Within a week, Kate left for New York to help care for her father through the final stage of his illness. A month later, after his death, she resumed her work with Jane.

While Kate was dealing with medical problems, Molly was discovering that she was more exposed than she had thought. She was living in an apartment whose entrance, hidden on the side of the building, was difficult to find. One evening a black woman, conspicuous in Molly's white neighborhood, was searching for Molly's door. A squad car pulled up; an officer leaned out the window and said, "If you're looking for Molly, she's in the side entrance."

The woman was not surprised. She had assumed some collusion between the police and Jane, so she commented to Molly, "Oh yeah, this cop really knows you." Molly had a sinking feeling. She thought, Oh no he doesn't, but he knows where I live and what I'm doing. But she did not consider stepping back from the service because "nothing else had that intensity. What can you do that has more immediate gratification than help someone get an abortion? They're taken care of. They're able to make choices and go on with their lives. I loved when my counselees would call me just to say, 'Thanks, just wanted to let you know I'm okay.' "

In October questions that had been simmering for months about Pam, one of the group's first abortionists, boiled over. For Julia, Pam's behavior was an eerie replay of Jenny's preceding her hospitalization the winter before: "One way we knew Jenny was falling apart was that she was not such a good abortionist for a short period of time. We who knew her said, 'Oh, Jenny is falling apart.' I consider it our fault that nobody protected her. Nobody said to her, 'You have got to stop working.' Then it started happening to Pam. Pam would be real shaky and she would explode at people for nothing; she would get into doing things that were like a proof of competence that indeed endangered people. It was the same thing that had happened with Jenny. I said to myself, 'This is not going to happen. She's not going to hurt anyone and there's no reason for her to hurt herself.' "

Pam was totally committed to the service, but she never participated in the informal afternoon sessions around Julia's kitchen table and did not get along with either Julia or Miriam. Julia felt that Pam viewed her skill as affording her special privileges. Pam felt that the married women with children resented her single life.

It was Pam's judgment, not her skill, that members questioned. Julia felt that Pam was overreaching her competence, performing abortions that were heroic feats, late D & Cs at the end of the day when everyone, including Pam, was tired. A late D & C saved a woman from having to go through a miscarriage, but it took up to three times as long as one at 10 weeks lmp. Because of the thinned uterine wall and the amount of material that had to be removed, the later the D & C the more the dangers of hemorrhage and the woman's discomfort increased. For borderline pregnancies, between 12 and 14 weeks lmp, whether to induce a miscarriage or do a D & C was a judgment call. The administrators, *Jane,* scheduled these borderlines early in the morning when the workers were fresh. Pam seemed to be trying to rescue these women, a situation that could result in problems for them, for Pam, and, by extension, for the group. When Julia tried to talk to Pam about it, Pam responded, "You're just jealous of my skill."

Since there was no mechanism within the group for dealing with these kinds of problems—neither personnel issues nor details of work days were discussed at meetings—service members grumbled to each other privately. By the time a story was repeated several times, it had been blown out of proportion.

Through the summer and early fall, even the newer workers had problems with Pam. Lynn, the young woman who had returned in September after her arrest, was assisting on a day when Pam started a late D & C and ran into trouble. Without explaining what was going on, Pam left the room and made a phone call. Lynn was frantic: "I'm talking to this woman and I have no idea what's going on. Something's wrong but nobody's telling her; nobody's telling me." Then Jenny arrived and finished the abortion.

Finally, in October, at a meeting that Pam did not attend, all the troubling stories about Pam were laid out for discussion. The group scheduled another meeting, one at which Pam's attendance was mandatory, to confront her.

No one remembers much about the meeting except that, by the end of it, Pam was in tears. When asked, she denied that she needed a break. Then a torrent of accusations were leveled at her. The meeting turned into an attack. Pam noticed that some of her most vocal accusers were women who had rarely, if ever, worked with her, and had never performed an abortion themselves. One of Jane's members, back after a year and a half absence, suspected that the attack on Pam was about something other than her work. With Jenny absent there was a power vacuum. She thought this meeting was part of a struggle for power between Miriam and Julia, on one side, and Pam on the other.

Firing Pam had consequences. Robin, one of the group's midwives who had been burned out and on leave through the summer, decided to quit before she, too, was kicked out. Julia thought, If we can fire Pam, then, for sure, someone can fire me because they'll see I'm burned out before I see it. Not a woman in the room thought she was exempt from dismissal. Jane no longer felt like an inclusive group. Whether or not Pam had to be fired, the viciousness they unleashed shocked them.

The attack on Pam served an important function. It was an outlet for the tension, anger and frustration that had built up in the group since the arrests in May. But there was more involved than judgment questions or scapegoating, and that had to do with attitude. Service members were neither heroes nor martyrs. They worked with Jane because they got personal satisfaction from it. The service wasn't about self-sacrifice or rescuing anyone; it was about being a responsible person.

CHAPTER 26

Although service members believed their abortions were the best available, they had no way to prove it. For security reasons and to protect the confidentiality of the women who needed Jane, they never kept records. Even if they had, counselors could not reach some women after their abortions. Women simply disappeared; others refused to talk to them: It was over; they wanted to put it out of their minds. Counselors advised every woman to get a post-abortion checkup, but the group never knew how many did or what the results were. Without follow-up services that the service controlled, they had no way of documenting the quality of care that the women received. Late in the fall of 1972 Miriam and Julia had an opportunity to set up that kind of program.

At the University of Illinois Medical School in Chicago, a group of progressives organized a one-semester course, the Urban Preceptorship. The course was open to medical students and community health activists. By bringing medical students in contact with activists, the organizers hoped to raise their awareness of the social and political dimensions of health care in the United States, specifically in Chicago. At the end of the course each student was required to submit an independent project.

As Jane's representatives, Miriam and Julia took the preceptorship in the fall 1972 semester. For their project they developed a formal follow-up program. Through it not only would they be able to document Jane's success but they could also make sure that women had their checkups and access to contraceptives. Miriam approached a sympathetic gynecologist. She asked him to provide, at Jane's expense, post-abortion examinations for the women who came through the service.

Before agreeing, he contacted his lawyer: "If a woman has had an illegal abortion and she comes to me and I treat her, am I liable?"

His lawyer responded, "You are not liable for what went on before you saw her." With that assurance he was willing to examine the women Jane sent him at a charge of $10 each, which the service paid. Obviously money was not his deciding factor. What led him to agree, he says, was, "my intellectual curiosity which, to me, would have been more than payment."

In the early sixties, before Jane existed, he was a staff doctor at Cook County Hospital, a public hospital that primarily served poor people of color. There he realized that "the real tragedy of the poor black women I took care of was not that they were poor, not that they were black, but that they couldn't control their reproduction. Without that control they were no more than chattel. Without it you've got nothing. Voting? So what? Stocks, bonds, money? So what? If you can't turn that off, that's fundamental.

"You didn't have to be too brilliant to figure that out, spending four years in the Department of Ob/Gyn at Cook County Hospital. I had seen so many times where women had resorted to criminal abortions. Appalled isn't the word, shocked, angry, furious, that patients had to resort to a criminal procedure that put them at incredible risks, whereas a woman who was rich could avoid those risks. If I could send some woman to London for a legal abortion, what about her maid who couldn't go to London? Why should she have a lesser quality of care only because the color of her skin was different and she wasn't rich?" Not only did he agree to examine the women from Jane and provide birth control, but he had no problem with Miriam's and Julia's suggestion that service members attend the examinations.

For several months in the late fall and early winter of 1972, every woman who came through the service was offered a free post-abortion checkup. Julia and Miriam developed one form, which the workers filled out at the time of the abortion, and another for the doctor's use. On Saturdays Jane's counselors met women at his private downtown office. They were impressed by the amount of information he was willing to give them and the women he examined. "At that time I had seen the newsprint edition of *Our Bodies, Ourselves,* a fabulous book," he recalls. "In the introduction it says 'These are our bodies. Why shouldn't we know about them and control them?' It just made sense to me. Why not share the information? What was the big secret? Patients do much better when they're informed, and I think lots of people have come to that opinion years later."

He treated minor vaginal infections, prescribed birth control pills, and inserted IUDs. Julia thought he had a personal mission to get tubal ligations for poor women who had as many children as they wanted. A few times he actually set up the surgical appointment.

When he was examining someone who had had six children, he asked, "Have you ever thought about having your tubes tied?"

If she said, "Yes, but I can't afford it," he replied, "I'm sure we can work something out."

He never pushed. Not once did he try to talk someone into anything, either sterilization or contraceptives, she did not want.

Neither Miriam nor Julia told him explicitly, but he figured out that physicians had not done these abortions. He thought of Jane as extralegal rather than criminal: "From everything I knew at that time, from my examinations, these women were not maltreated and had no ill effects. Their periods had returned; they were in good health; they had no complaints. All that says is that one does not need to be a doctor. You only need good training to do an abortion. I think I developed that belief at that time. I would have had to be psychotic or asleep to have come to the conclusion that these women were showing evidence of something bad; ergo, the people who did it didn't do a bad job. The level of expertise required for certain things is not as great as some of us make it out to be. Jane was a particularly adept group of women, well motivated, well trained and careful." The results of his post-abortion examinations indicated that the service had a problem rate for D & C abortions approximately equivalent to New York's legal clinics.

Although their independent project was a success, Julia thought that she and Miriam failed in the role the course organizers wanted them to play. In her estimation "the whole point of the preceptorship was to educate those two medical students who happened to be sitting there while you're ranting and raving at them. Well, Miriam and I just weren't interested in doing that. I was quite burned out. I didn't have a lot of energy for that kind of polemic stuff. I remember one speaker coming up to us afterward and saying, 'I'm real disappointed in you two. You didn't bring up any feminist concerns.' And I thought, This is obviously my role here and it doesn't interest me."

When the preceptorship ended late in the winter, Julia and Miriam quit the service. Miriam had played a central role in the group from its inception. Julia had looked over everyone's shoulder, thinking, If I don't pay attention to everything, something terrible will happen. When Miriam and Julia left they discovered that they were no more indispensable than anyone else.

By late 1971 the women who turned to Jane included teenagers and women without access to their family's money, but the majority were poor women of all races. By 1972 at least half were public aid recipients. The service helped people no one else would. "The more we got into the community that really has no alternatives," Julia recalls, "the more I thought we were sort of getting at the root of the problem." These were women whose needs had been ignored. They lacked decent medical care, and poor health is poverty's handmaiden. There were women who were so obese that even the largest size speculum opened fully could not expose their cervix. Some had high blood pressure, anemia, and other problems related to the bad nutrition that is often a consequence of poverty. They had no regular medical care and sometimes were unaware of existing health problems. Since it took everything they had just to survive, their lives were apt to be out of control. As a result, more women whose pregnancies were borderline, between 12 and 14 weeks lmp, were contacting Jane, and the number of women needing induced miscarriages or late D & Cs grew.

When Julia first learned to do an abortion she thought that "it didn't seem that hard to do, but at the end, as our population got poorer and poorer, I really began to worry." Given how unhealthy many of these women were, the number of difficult abortions increased, and Julia began to feel that no one in the group had enough medical knowledge or emergency skills. She never talked about that at a meeting because she felt that "if we talk about it, that will immobilize us from doing it." The women who performed abortions confided in each other how terrified they were. What enabled each of them to continue was knowing that the entire group stood with them. Julia did not feel "What in the world am *I* doing, but what in the world are *we* doing. I felt supported by the other people who were doing abortions, but also by the people in the group who weren't, who were carrying the brunt of it anyhow."

Over time, it had only become more obvious to the women in the service that educating themselves and other women was one of their primary responsibilities. Service members spoke about abortion, birth control and women's health to college students and community groups. From 1971 and for many years following that, Jane members led Women and Their Bodies classes in all kinds of venues, from the CWLU's Liberation School to Illinois's women's prison. Women's organizations and informal rap groups asked them to lead self-help groups. The aim of these groups was to promote health self-education as a tool for control. Self-help groups were often held as the culmination of a Women and Their Bodies class. After eight weeks of talking about physiology, pregnancy, birth control, and the alienating images of women's bodies in the culture, the class was comfortable enough with their own bodies to examine themselves and each other in a group setting. While the rest of the group watched, each woman inserted a speculum in herself and examined her cervix and vagina with a mirror and a light. Service members also taught women to do bimanual pelvic exams, to feel the uterus and ovaries, and take Pap smears, sharing what they had learned in order to demystify medicine.

At one of these classes, held in the leader's living room, during her self-exam a woman said, "You know, for years I tried to reduce my thighs, but in this class I have decided that these are my thighs, these are my thighs." She said it with acceptance not resignation; the other women gathered around her laughed and applauded.

Elizabeth, the suburban high school teacher, led a self-help session at a NOW conference in Minneapolis. After looking at her own cervix, one woman said with surprise, "Oh, it's pink and it's nice."

Elizabeth asked, "Well, what did you think?"

The woman burst into tears: "I always thought it was ugly and diseased. My doctor always sighed when he looked at it. All my life I've used a separate washcloth to wash my genitals because I thought they were filthy." Elizabeth was horrified. She thought, How many other women feel that way? How many other women think of their bodies as ugly or shameful?

Early in 1973, Jane had a chance to introduce their educational perspective into the public schools and reach teenagers whose pregnancies and abortions had been so heartbreaking for the group. Ellen, one of the younger women who had joined the service in the fall of 1971, had been accepted into the master's program at the social service school (SSA) at the University of Chicago for the fall term of 1972. During her first year of graduate school, each student had to participate in a project involving groups. Ellen thought that if she developed something similar to Women and Their Bodies classes, but geared toward teenagers, the service could reach girls before they became sexually active. They might be able to help girls build self-awareness and self-esteem, or, at the least, prevent unwanted pregnancies.

Miriam, as a social worker and a graduate of SSA, supervised Ellen's project. Miriam was also a parent of a student in one of Hyde Park's public schools and knew the principal. He shared their concerns about teen pregnancy, but he did not want to be told the course's specific content. Parents had to sign permission slips before their daughters could attend. Ellen drew up a brief, generalized proposal for a ten week course:

> As a woman I have been . . . concerned with women's issues, particularly those pertaining to women and health . . . I am proposing a group of 7th and 8th graders to discuss "women and their bodies" because it is at this age that girls are so particularly aware of their bodies—the changes occurring . . . and the consequent fears, questions, doubts, and social effects that might arise from these changes. . . .
>
> We feel the small group setting, led by people who are not teachers or in any pre-ordained authoritative role, would be most conducive to a free and open atmosphere in which the girls could most easily express their fears and questions and concerns, something they might not be able to do in the ordinary classroom setting. . . .

The first class that Miriam and Ellen led was of thirteen-year-olds. It turned out to be the perfect age. Unlike older teens, thirteen-year-olds do not presume to know everything and, consequently, are not embarrassed to ask questions. Once Miriam and Ellen passed the girls' initial testing period, to discover if, indeed, these adults were going to be frank with them, the kids opened up. They seemed hungry for someone to answer their questions. By the end of the first class, they were asking about masturbation. Ellen was amazed by "how open they were with each other and with us."

The first series of classes went so well that Ellen and Miriam repeated it for another group. The next fall they expanded the program to two additional schools and recruited other Jane members to lead those classes. The only credentials the service members had was their willingness to respond honestly and nonjudgmentally to any questions asked. And the kids asked everything. They wanted to know how their bodies worked and about birth control, sex and homosexuality.

Miriam remembers that "once in awhile we'd get parents—not of the kids in the class because they signed releases, but others—who would say, 'You mustn't tell kids about birth control because you'll be encouraging them,' and you still hear that today." From years of counseling teenagers for abortions Miriam knew that not having the information never stopped anyone from having sex.

Lois always encouraged her children to talk to her. When her oldest daughter was twelve she said to Lois, "Guess who's having sex?" Lois stocked up on books about sexuality written specifically for children. Her friends warned her, "You're crazy. She's going to end up pregnant." Lois, pregnant herself at fifteen, was not dissuaded: "The reason I became pregnant was that I was ignorant because what I heard was, 'Keep your dress down and your panties up.' Out of curiosity I wanted to see what happens if I raise my dress and pull my panties down. Well, I found out." Unlike Lois, her daughter never became pregnant as a teen.

CHAPTER 27

On the morning of January 22, 1973, the Supreme Court announced its decision in two abortion cases: *Roe* v. *Wade* from Texas, and *Doe* v. *Bolton* from Georgia. By a 7–2 majority, the court struck down Texas's restrictive law for violating both the ninth and fourteenth amendments' implied protection of personal privacy.

The *Roe* v. *Wade* opinion, written by Harry Blackmun, reviewed the history of abortion laws in the United States, noting that abortions before quickening, that is, discernible fetal movement, had not been prohibited until the mid-nineteenth century. He wrote that, while the American Medical Association (AMA) had pushed for that prohibition to protect women's lives, now, a hundred years later, medical technology had progressed to such a point that early abortions were safer than childbirth, so the justification for the ban no longer existed. The AMA, the American Public Health Association, and the American Bar Association all now supported lifting it.

Blackmun traced the right to privacy, citing cases as far back as 1891, including *Griswold* v. *Connecticut* in 1965 which gave married people the right to contraception, and *Eisenstadt* v. *Baird* in 1972, which extended that right to single people. Both of these decisions were based on a constitutional right to privacy in matters of sex and procreation. Blackmun concluded that, "the right to personal privacy includes the abortion decision but that this right is not unqualified and must be considered against important State interests in regulation." He noted that the fetus before birth had never been considered a person in a legal sense and that neither medicine, philosophy nor theology had agreed on when life begins.

The Court explicitly stated that a woman does not have an absolute right to abortion. She may not do what she wants with her body. Pregnancy is different from other sexual privacy issues because of fetal development. The State has an interest at two key points: after quickening, for the mother's health and safety, and again at viability, when the fetus can live outside the womb, to protect potential life.

Then Blackmun went on to describe the State's changing interest as it relates to gestational trimesters. During the first trimester, approximately before quickening, "the attending physician, in consultation with his patient, is free to determine, without regulation by the State, that in his medical judgment the patient's pregnancy should be terminated . . ." In the second trimester of pregnancy, after quickening but before viability, the State may, in the interests of the health of the mother, "if it chooses, regulate the abortion procedure in ways that are reasonably related to maternal health." In the third trimester, approximately after viability, in the "interest of the potentiality of human life," the State "may, if it chooses, regulate, and even proscribe abortion except where it is necessary, in appropriate medical judgment, for the preservation of the life or health of the mother." Blackmun wrote that this decision "vindicates the right of the physician to administer medical treatment according to his professional judgment up to the points where important State interests provide compelling justification for intervention. . . . the abortion decision . . . is inherently, and primarily, a medical decision, and basic responsibility for it must rest with the physician."

In *Doe* v. *Bolton,* the Court struck down Georgia's therapeutic abortion reform law that required hospitalization, approval by a committee, and two concurring physicians. Between the two cases, the

Court invalidated the statutes of thirty states that limited abortion to those necessary to protect the woman's life or health, and the therapeutic reforms of another fourteen states that had been enacted since 1967.

The breadth of the Court's decision was astonishing even for those who had been fighting for abortion rights. To many it seemed to have come out of nowhere, though, in fact, it was the logical outcome of a progression of rulings by courts throughout the country. It was the result of a concerted effort on the part of many people, from various regions and segments of society. Legal scholars, those who had brought and argued court cases, professionals, activists who led broad-based community education efforts and those who lobbied legislators all played a part. And in quiet clergymen's offices, hectic women's liberation centers, and countless women's living rooms, women desperate for an abortion had found understanding and immediate help.

Radicals recognized that *Roe* v. *Wade* and *Doe* v. *Bolton* were a culmination of efforts to change society's attitudes regarding abortion. Since the thalidomide tragedy of the early 1960s the media had publicized abortion. Over the past six years leading national professional and religious organizations had backed repeal. The women's movement had brought abortion into the streets, with demonstrations and speak-outs, mobilizing thousands of women. Through the movement, women were beginning to identify themselves as a class and abortion as a class issue, part of a challenge to male authority and essential for their own liberation. By the early seventies women's violation of abortion laws was no longer seen as a shameful secret, but as a woman's right. Clergy active in referral networks used their moral position in society to defy the law. Women's liberation groups, without the clergy's protective standing, helped thousands of women get abortions.

On the other hand, *Roe* v. *Wade,* as much as it was a culmination, also undermined the grassroots efforts to confront the social authority that had kept women in their place and the medical profession firmly in control of women's health. Abortion had become a catalyst for criticizing the omnipotence of doctors. As one of the women who came through Jane wondered, "If they're lying to us about how dangerous and complex an abortion is, what else are they lying to us about?" Faced with unsympathetic and patronizing medical treatment, women were demanding control of their own health care, demanding information, forcing a shift in power between doctor and patient. Unfortunately, *Roe* v. *Wade,* written emphatically in terms of physician's rights, not women's rights, revalidated the medical profession's control of women's reproductive health. The Court had bent the laws regarding abortion just far enough to reassert the authority of the State.

The night of the Supreme Court's decision, Jane members held an impromptu celebration at Julia's, snacking on the spread of exotic cheeses and breads that Julia had quickly assembled. The celebration was more subdued than jubilant. Although their reaction to the decision was ambivalent, the overwhelming feeling in Julia's living room that night was one of relief. They would no longer have to risk their freedom and women's lives. They had accepted responsibility for themselves and other women and had discharged that responsibility competently and caringly. Once abortions were legally available, they would no longer have to be terrified of injuring someone or worried about going to prison. The pressure was exhausting. They had made it through and soon they could stop.

A few people were far from exhausted. Grace, who had been in the group less than two months, felt "so disappointed that Jane was ending. I remember kind of not saying it because everybody else was just ecstatic."

She was not the only one less than thrilled. Lois, on the day of her own abortion a year before, had watched the abortionists at work and thought, I want to do that. Now she felt that "it was a selfish thing with me that, when it became legal, I felt like I had been cheated. I was so close to learning the procedure. Damn, I almost did it. I was so glad it was legal. My God, we don't have to hide in corners anymore; abortions aren't a social taboo, but I felt personally cheated."

For several years service members had talked about starting a women's health clinic. The Chicago Women's Liberation Union had tried to organize one and early in 1971 a few Jane members had met to work toward that goal, but nothing ever came of their efforts. At Julia's, the night the *Roe* v. *Wade* decision was announced, the discussion of setting up a clinic to provide health education, birth control, and health care resurfaced. Miriam noted, "If we do a clinic we'll have to come up against stuff that will be a bitch, like licenses and malpractice insurance." Having operated outside the law, they thought those things were meaningless. The only accreditation they valued was their own competence and meeting women's needs. Jenny smiled, "The service is a hard act to follow."

Underlying their relief at the Supreme Court decision was a nagging doubt. What had women really won? The right to more callous treatment by the medical profession? Women would still be objectified as patients, alienated from abortion as a life-determining experience. They would be acted on, not acted with. Jane members knew that the medical profession was not going to use the opportunity to educate women. *Roe* v. *Wade* had won the war, but the battle for decent care and respectful treatment was still a long way from over.

Roe v. *Wade* did not take effect in Illinois immediately. The state was still under an injunction issued by the Supreme Court in early 1971, after a federal district court ruled Illinois's law unconstitutional. It would be weeks or months before the legal issues were resolved and abortions available in Chicago. Even after the injunction was lifted, the women who came through Jane, poor women and teenagers, were not going to be served by private doctors in their Michigan Avenue offices. It might be some time before clinics opened that served these women. In the meantime, Jane had to keep working. The calls from desperate women never stopped.

On March 2, 1973, the courts lifted the Illinois injunction. Regulations and guidelines for clinics were debated, but private doctors began performing abortions; clinics would open soon. "If not Jane, then a butcher" was not a valid contention anymore. Members dropped out of the service, but the calls from desperate women did not stop; more of the work fell on fewer Jane members.

On March 9, the case against the seven Jane members who had been arrested the previous May was dismissed and their court records ordered expunged. Donna read the Abortion 7's statement to the press.

> . . . We feel abortion should be available to all women in Chicago who desire it. But in fact abortions though legal are expensive, available only in a few places and restricted to the first trimester. Even more important for the woman who fights through the obstacles, the attitude of society and of the professionals she deals with often make an abortion an unhappy experience. There should not be any legislation on this issue; it would be as inappropriate as laws governing appendectomy. Hospitals and doctors who are waiting for guidelines from the legislature are only avoiding their obligations to their woman patients.
>
> To insure abortions being not only medically safe but comfortable and human, these things must be done:
>
> *Outpatient abortion clinics—freestanding as well as hospital-attached be set up.
>
> *Cost of an abortion be cheap—$100 maximum—and covered by Public Assistance and all other health insurance.
>
> *Abortions be available without restriction in the second and third trimester.
>
> *Paramedics, not only M.D.'s, be providing this service.
>
> *Supportive counseling done by women be part of each procedure.

*Consent to the operations coming only from the pregnant woman—not hospital boards nor her parents nor her husband.

That spring a doctor who had long worked for abortion reform contacted Jane. She was planning to add abortions to her clinic's services and wanted to explore the possibility of Jane managing that department. She brought her lawyer to a meeting. When service members asked if she intended to allow Jane women to do the abortions, she said yes, while her lawyer vigorously shook his head no. "Absolutely not," he said. "Within the law that would be impossible." The women in Jane declined her offer. They did not want to revert to the role of handmaidens to abortionists, whether or not they were physicians, and have to put up with behavior and procedures they did not approve of, but could not control.

Instead, they wanted to continue to share what they had learned and expand their skills. They began planning for a women's health center, based on a self-help model that emphasized education, and held the first meeting at Julia's for women interested in starting a clinic. Her living room was packed with not only Jane members but also women from all over the city. Over the next six months the working group evolved into the Emma Goldman's Women's Health Center, a well-woman health clinic. The services they eventually provided included gynecological exams, Pap smears, breast self-exams, pregnancy tests, diaphragm fittings, gonorrhea cultures, hematocrits, vaginitis diagnosis and treatment (using the teaching microscope Nick had given them, women saw what the clinic worker was looking for in diagnosing their infections), and eventually they learned to fit cervical caps. As public speakers, they continued to promote their view of woman-centered health care.

The service held a special meeting to decide Jane's future. Julia came back for that meeting and spoke forcefully for closing the service: Now that abortions are legal, whatever protection we had from the police will be gone. The city might have tolerated Jane's existence as a safety valve, but that benign neglect is going to end. Once abortions are available through outpatient clinics, the service might be considered a financial threat to doctors and clinics. That would put them in greater jeopardy. For all those reasons it was too dangerous to continue.

Nora, the group's former midwife, who had returned from Colorado in the fall, was furious that Julia, who still had a powerful influence even though she was no longer a member, had returned to argue for closing Jane. Nora was the most vocal proponent of continuing the service: What we offer is unique. No one will get this quality anywhere. Although she agreed with Nora on that score, Kate was annoyed. Nora was no longer willing to do any medical work. What right did she have to demand that other people do something that she herself would not do? If you want something done, then you should be willing to do it.

Most of the women sitting around the living room floor that night were just plain tired out. Since her son's death in September, performing abortions had become an emotionally wrenching experience for Cynthia. She needed to stop. Another abortionist's marriage was crumbling. Several members were barely speaking to one another. None of them disagreed that abortions provided by medical professionals would not measure up to Jane's standards. Women would probably be subjected to the same insensitive medical care they always got, but, for the members of Jane, the benefits of continuing did not outweigh the costs and risks. They had had a mission: while it was illegal, they had made sure that abortions were available. They had completed their mission. As soon as the first legal clinics opened, Jane would fold.

The last *Call-Back Jane* listened to the disappointment in women's voices when she told them Jane was out of business and offered referrals to Chicago clinics. Only a few women showed up to clean out the apartment they had rented that fall on the North Side. As they moved furniture and packed up their supplies, they bitched about the lack of interest. No one remembers scheduling a last work day. No one remembers working a last work day. There was no fanfare, no fireworks. Jane was gone.

In its four-year history Jane members estimate they performed over eleven thousand abortions.

On May 20, Sally hosted an end-of-Jane party at her elegant Frank Lloyd Wright house in Oak Park. The invitation read:

You are cordially invited to attend
The First, Last and Only Curette Caper
The Grand Finale of the Abortion Counseling Service
RSVP Jane 643–3844

Everybody who had ever had anything to do with Jane was invited, all the former members and the people who had offered their houses or apartments for Fronts or work places. Jenny talked Nick into going to the party. Still guarding his identity, he was reluctant. It was the only time he saw the majority of the women who made up the service. He had half expected wild-eyed revolutionaries dressed in motorcycle jackets and combat boots. Instead, gathered on Sally's brick-walled terrace in the sunshine, was a group of ordinary women in sundresses and shorts, eating and talking. They did not fit the image he had in his mind. They looked too normal, too straight. He thought, This is really strange: all these straight women doing this illegal thing.

In the middle of the afternoon Sally picked up her guitar and, to the tune of John Prine's "Your Flag Decal Won't Get You Into Heaven Anymore," sang a song she had written especially for the occasion, her ode to Jane:

I woke up one bright morning
About the middle of May.

I had some kids and a good old man,
Things were going my way.

But I looked at my calendar
And there I read my fate.
Five pounds here and a bigger brassiere—
I was about seven weeks late!

Chorus:

643–3844 is a number you'll adore
The women in the service
Know what you're calling for.
They'll give you an abortion
No matter what the reason for.
And 643–3844 is a number you'll adore.

I sidled up to my best chum
I tried to tell her why—
I was getting fat and my breakfast sat—
And then I started to cry.

"Don't you worry, don't you fret,"
She said to me so plain.
"I'll give you a telephone number
And you can tell it all to Jane."

Chorus:

I called this lady on the phone.
She sounded really great.
She asked my name and telephone

And then my l.p. date.*
"A counselor will call you,
Just put your mind to rest.
We'd like $100
But we'll take your best" (quietly)

Chorus:

It's another bright May morning
My problem's all resolved.
But my heart is heavy laden
'Cause I hear that Jane's dissolved.

No more o.o.t.'s, 6pp's
3 ks, abs, or misc.*
'Cause when you dial the number
The message sounds like this—

Chorus:

643–3844 can't help you anymore
We're already out of business
From your dirty legal war.
We gave you an abortion
No matter what the reason for.
But 643–3844 can't help you anymore.

---

*These are the abbreviations Jane used on the index cards:
l.p.: last period
o.o.t.: out-of-town women
pp: number of previous pregnancies
ks: number of children
abs: number of previous abortions
misc: number of previous miscarriages

EPILOGUE

Jane, like the women's liberation movement it was part of, grew out of the social and political upheavals of the 1960s. The civil rights movement confronted immoral laws, while the antiwar movement challenged blind obedience to the State and the student movement questioned all hierarchical authority. Those three vehicles for social change, known collectively as The Movement, began with the conviction that individuals must have a voice in the decisions that affect them. The Movement shook the social structure and, for a brief period, fissures opened. Some people pushed through those cracks. In the process, like the members of Jane, they transformed themselves.

In 1973, while organizing the Emma Goldman Women's Health Center, Jane members began to recognize that the service was more than a product of the 1960s social revolution. It was part of a tradition older and deeper than any of them had realized. In the introduction to the pamphlet *Witches, Midwives, and Nurses*, published in 1973, the authors, Barbara Ehrenreich and Deirdre English, state:

> Women have always been healers. They were the unlicensed doctors and anatomists of western history. They were abortionists, nurses and counselors. They were pharmacists, cultivating herbs and exchanging the secrets of their uses. They were midwives, travelling from home to home and village to village. For

> centuries women were doctors without degrees, barred from books and lectures, learning from each other, and passing on experience from neighbor to neighbor and mother to daughter. They were called "wise women" by the people, witches or charlatans by the authorities. Medicine is part of our heritage as women, our history, our birthright. . . .
>
> To know our history is to begin to see how to take up the struggle again.

For the members of the service, recognizing their historical roots was grounding. But they had learned more than that medicine was their birthright as women. Through their work they realized that, in order to equalize power, it was essential to base medical care, or any kind of service, on respect for the people needing that service. The focus belonged not on the person with expertise, but on the person needing it. The first time Lois gave an intramuscular shot, she was so wrapped up in the technique that she forgot about the woman on whose body she was learning. She caught herself and thought, I'm missing the whole point here. Then she looked up at the woman, rubbed her leg, and said, "How're you doing?" She understood that what was important was "the communication, being with the woman, making her feel secure, letting her know what was going on when you were doing it."

After Jane, some of the group's members thought that they could apply this perspective to a medical setting. But they did not anticipate just how difficult that would be. In medicine's rigid hierarchy, patients were relegated to the bottom rung. When Molly began nursing school with Donna, one of the group's last abortionists, she was struck by the extent to which patients were viewed as the objects of medical care, not the subjects. On her surgery rotation she saw a D&C performed under general anesthetic. She was horrified "to see this woman knocked out cold, roughly treated. I remembered how we positioned people's legs. We were so gentle, so careful."

When Molly graduated she got a job at a respected abortion clinic. The doctor who ran the clinic hired other physicians on a per diem basis to perform the abortions. In the clinic Molly saw doctors and nurses replicating the same behaviors that she had found appalling in the hospital: "I never had nightmares in the service, but, working at the clinic, I would wake up in the middle of the night with nightmares because of the way people were treated. People were just put in a cold sterile room and expected to be good."

During clinic abortions she explained to each woman what was happening as she had in the service. The doctors looked at her quizzically, wondering what she was doing.

After their abortions women rested in the recovery room alone. Whenever Molly had a spare minute she kept them company, offering graham crackers, taking blood pressures, and talking. On one of those stolen minutes, a woman called her over and said in a whisper, "You don't remember me, do you? You assisted at my illegal abortion years ago. I don't see how you can work here after what you did. You guys spent a lot of time with people and the counseling was so different. It must be hard for you to work here." Molly knew she had to quit. Molly now works as a visiting nurse and is a member of her local school board. She lives with her husband and two children.

A year after the service folded, the alternative Catholic high school where Kris taught closed. She got a job at an abortion clinic, first as a counselor, then, later, as a consultant to teach nurses self-help techniques for follow-up care. She wrote a manual and trained the staff but "it came out looking just like it always did. Everybody had this body hysteria. The nurses made jokes about specula and all sorts of things. I realized that there was something very different about the service, which was not just providing illegal abortions. That had obscured the very important experience women had—that it was done by other women in a situation where they were not objects. They were forced to be accomplices and, because they were forced to join in, they had to take responsibility for what they did. It made them autonomous. Legalizing abortion allowed women to have a service provided. They gave up their power, the way you always do in a medical situation. Consequently, women were really not growing and they had a lot of unfinished business about the abortions."

Kris witnessed the same unsympathetic treatment Molly did. She felt that had an effect on how women came out of their abortions: "The more roughly they were treated, the more they lamented and complained of unhappiness and cried in the recovery room." No matter how much she and the other counselors tried to change the atmosphere by painting the walls bright colors and even counseling in groups, they could not lessen women's isolation and powerlessness. For Kris, that was a product of standard medical attitudes: "In that concept somehow you separate yourself from the disease and do battle with it. That notion of separateness is what the male model is. It's not just medicine. It pervades the culture. When women are forced into that environment they lose their base of caring, of providing a transformational service where the people come out of it better than when they came in. We can train all the women doctors we want, but, in that context, it's all going to be the same."

For Kris the only inherently transforming part of the service was that the knowledge to do it was both hidden and forbidden: "Once you've done four hundred Pap smears there's nothing empowering about it, which is, of course, the whole myth of medicine anyway: It's all very boring. The violation of the ritual is what, I think, made the service experience important. Women need to have these transforming experiences. They need to do something that's hard for them, that violates some rule. For my kids, who are eleven and seven now, I want them always to be bumping up against their own competence and the rules of society." Kris and Bill are raising their adopted daughters. Kris teaches aerobics. She is a breast cancer survivor.

Over its four-year history, more than one hundred women were members of Jane. Most of them have never spoken publicly about Jane and rarely discuss the past with friends or coworkers.

Of Jane's original members, Lorraine chose to stay home when her first child was born and "got involved in a cooperative nursery program, community projects and the PTA." Now that her children are grown, Lorraine, in her early fifties, works in administration in a public school. Looking back on the service she says, "One single one of us wouldn't have gotten any of it done. We all did this thing together."

Jenny has survived Hodgkin's disease. She lives a few blocks from her daughters, with whom she is very close. She grooms dogs for a living, while still devoting time to political activism. Looking back, though, she feels that nothing has compared with the intensity of the service: "People forget how horrible and sordid it was for women trying to get abortions back then. That was the situation we wanted to do something about. Things have to be pretty terrible to force you to act. It had to be done, but what we did was an evolutionary process. At first we had doubts about what we could do. We had been raised to believe that women couldn't take care of themselves, but we figured it out. We started out completely dependent on men, but, little by little, we became less and less dependent. When we saw that women could act on their own, it was, even for me, a revelation. It couldn't have happened unless everyone did her part well. It was great, it was such a relief, to work with dependable people, to know I did not have to do it alone, and I mean not only the people in the group, but the women who came through. Before the service my faith in women was theoretical, but through the service it became part of me, so that when someone didn't act responsibly it was shocking. We went from seeing ourselves as secondary to knowing that we could make things happen."

"I wasn't that middle-class Jewish housewife for very long after being involved with Jane," Karen, who joined the group with Jenny, comments. She is now the director of a women's employment organization and involved with her local lesbian community. What she learned in Jane was that "legality is relative; women's needs always come first. I learned how powerful a group of women can be. It's always fueled me. We can change people's lives because of our activism."

Miriam's children are grown. She teaches crafts and volunteers at her local public radio station. She was involved in Jane longer than anyone: "Jenny and I grew into doing this thing. It wasn't like we started out doing it. In the beginning we didn't even know we'd be friends. We were heavy duty people, very strong personalities. Before the women's movement there was no acceptable place for women like us. But in the service there was all kinds of room and lots of other strong women. So much of who I am now is because of the service. It allowed me to be the person I was meant to be."

Carol, who was a student at Roosevelt University when she joined at the end of 1969, is a psychotherapist. She learned from Jane that competence doesn't depend on credentials: "If I want to learn something, I find someone who knows how to do it. You take the shortest distance between two points to get something done. It was the best opportunity I had to put into action what I believed. Even though the service was on the edge of the women's movement, it captured more of the essence of the best of it than anything else. I often think how life-affirming it was in the context of death and destruction. That was an important juxtaposition for me."

Now that her children are grown, Cynthia lives alone. For her an important aspect of Jane was that the group took something that seemed completely abnormal—women performing abortions in their bedrooms for more than twenty-five strangers a day—and made it seem not only normal but comfortable: "We created our own reality, not in the big world but in the little world: You're pregnant, we'll fix it. You can't always change the big world. You've got to have a lot of help on that, but, on a smaller level, you can generally change your own reality."

Elizabeth, the suburban high school teacher, still teaches and is happily remarried: "The service made me much stronger. I was able to leave my husband and raise my son alone." For the first few years after Jane folded, Elizabeth talked about it compulsively. Now she never talks about it at all: "I look at myself as this English teacher. That's what I am and nobody knows the rest of it. When people say, 'If you don't like something you should do something about it,' I say, 'Well, I did.' I never elaborate on it. You do these things not just for yourself and your people, but for the future."

After the service, Julia returned to what she loves most, being a full-time mom. Through Jane she developed a constant awareness of power dynamics, not only in intimate and professional relationships, but in every interchange between people: "I would think about my children in school in terms of power, what it's like for the teacher, the amount of power the teacher holds, and how powerless the children feel. Once you have the revelation of the inherent skews in power in the world you can't get past it. You apply it everywhere. You can't stop and unpoliticize yourself. But that doesn't mean that in a group where you are a functioning member you can take the power inequities away.

"One thing I learned was that I don't do very well in groups. I was in a food co-op for years and the only thing I could do there was run it. In the service I carried most of the power, but I couldn't share power in a reasonable way. I never figured out how to pass it on. The only people I ever figured out how to empower are my children and I had twenty years to do it."

Although the service helped thousands of women, looking back, some of Jane's members are stunned by the medical risks they took. Even with all the goodwill and care in the world, serious problems could and did arise. Julia is one of those who is still troubled by the group's limited medical knowledge which she believes put women at risk. She feels that "if women came to me to start another service, I'd say, 'Good luck to you. I'll talk with you, but I can't teach you.'"

Deborah, who joined the inner circle with Julia and was arrested in May of 1972, is a scholar and a writer. The service taught her the value of responding in the present: "Here are these women. They need abortions. Yes, it's good to collect petitions and it's good to go to the state capitol, but I want to do this right here and now. There are some places where you actually can make it happen. You have to try to live towards the good, and, as much as you can do that in a world which is designed against the good, good for you."

Sarah, who joined through the Women's Liberation Union and was also arrested, lives with her husband and two adopted children and is active in NOW. Jane gave her "a greater appreciation of poverty and racism and the health care system screwing up all the time, and how far people are willing to go to help women, or not willing to go. It made me much more able to do everything I can to get around rules and laws if they're just screwing up people's lives. Knowing that I could do something that made such a difference in other women's lives gave me the energy to go further and keep pushing."

Now in her late sixties, Sally, who lived in the Frank Lloyd Wright house, thinks that without the service she "might have gone to my grave sweeping the floor and vacuuming. My life is better for it. It was an important experience for me in terms of my own growth and self-awareness. I like to think that while I was gaining that I was also doing something good for other people. Taking responsibility for others makes you do a better job. Because of that expectation you rise one level above where you thought you could."

After the service ended Nora, who was one of the group's midwives, came out as a lesbian and worked as a paralegal: "That's been my whole life, impersonating a professional." Later she worked in a family planning clinic. A few years ago she became frustrated that Jane was hidden history and started adding a few sentences about the service when she gave speeches on birth control and abortion. Reflecting on the lessons of Jane, she adds, "I think it's foolish to expect the State to end oppression given that it's the source of institutionalized oppression." Nora directs her state's AIDS coalition and writes articles on lesbian health issues.

Lynn, one of the younger women who was arrested, has five children between the ages of nine and nineteen. She is working towards her Ph.D. in science: "I look back and I was twenty. When I think of that person I'm amazed she did anything at all. Because of the service I began to think about my life in terms of making choices and of those choices having consequences. It gave me what I was looking for when I joined—an understanding of how to be grown up and respect myself. I'm grateful for that."

Ellen, the social worker who organized the Women and Their Bodies classes in the public schools, never saw herself as a leader: "but you start walking and you just keep walking and there you are in the middle of it." She lives with her husband and child and runs a program for pregnant teens: "The service affected how I approach things, that you're the person who's ultimately responsible for what you do. You can't turn around and say, 'Oh yeah, he told me to do it; she told me to do it.'" She struggles with power within her organization: "Even though we're not operating as a collective, are there ways of evening things out? Am I falling too much into that boss role and, therefore, they're waiting for me, waiting to be told? How do you help people take ownership and become more responsible in their work?"

Lois, who joined after her own abortion, is the only former member of Jane who currently works in an abortion clinic: "The service was getting me out, easing some of the tension between me and my husband because I was putting my energy someplace else. It got me to see myself in a whole different way, not just as a mother trying to go to school and hold her family together. A lot of the women I was counseling had two or three children and their husbands were not there. They were saying, 'I can't do it by myself; I can't handle it.' And I was saying, 'Oh yes you can.' I'm telling these women, 'Forget him,' and I was thinking, I can do the same thing, so it was like a total identity. I said to myself, You're stronger than what you thought. That's part of the change that occurred because of the identity I was creating through my work with Jane, the strength I was gathering as a woman. I was breaking away and it was great."

Grace, who joined two months before the *Roe* v. *Wade* decision made abortion legal, lives in an old farmhouse and teaches public school. What has stayed with her is "that true anarchist process of walking into a room with a group of people, talking it out, fighting it out, just doing what you think is right."

Kate is the pseudonym I've used for myself. Jane put me on a path I have continued to follow as a grassroots community organizer, working on projects that provide people with the tools to take control of their lives. I have applied the lessons of Jane, both what I want to replicate and what I want to avoid, to all of them. I learned that self-transformation happens through what I choose to do: I've become the person I wanted to be by acting as if I were that person.

The service embodied a shift in consciousness, from asking for something to doing it ourselves. Deborah told me that she tries to convey to her students that if a thing needs to be done, we can do it, figure it out, step by step. We in Jane learned that social change is not a gift given by leaders and heroes, but is accomplished by ordinary people working together. We make it happen by what we choose to do.

ACKNOWLEDGMENTS

My primary debt of gratitude goes to the women and men I interviewed for this book, especially the former members of Jane. They unstintingly shared their memories and put up with my neverending follow-up calls, even when they were tired of talking about the past. All of them, including those whose stories did not survive the final edits, have nourished me.

My family has been a source of strength: my mother, Rena, for her generosity and good humor, my sister, Hoda, for her unfailing faith in my ability and my uncle Oscar for being himself.

I want to thank "Jane," the author of "The Most Remarkable Abortion Story Ever Told," for allowing me to draw extensively from her articles; Linda Strothman for permission to excerpt from her unpublished vignettes; Pauline Bart for copies of the interviews she conducted in the mid-1970s with former Jane members.

Others who participated in the women's liberation movement talked with me and dug through their files. Of those I especially want to thank Naomi Weisstein, Amy Kesselman and Carol Hanisch.

Faughn Adams, Martha Scott, Susan Kimmelman and Ann Williams did essential legwork for me. Marlene Fried supplied the resource list at the back of the book. Thomas McQueen and Alan Sussman were generous with their time.

I want to thank my agent, Kristine Dahl, for recognizing the value of this story and believing in me. My editor, Linda Healey, pushed me to take hold of the manuscript and shape it intelligently.

Of the many people who offered useful suggestions, I want to list just a few: Jamie Kalven, Jamie Robinson, Maureen Brady and the people I met through her writers' workshops. I have been fortunate to be part of a group of writers that has met weekly for the past few years. They have listened and responded to the book, section by section. The diehards are: Tana, Val, Debra, Nora and Alix.

James Polk, Debra Moskowitz, Eileen Smith, Sunny Fischer and Ninia Baehr read early drafts of the manuscript. Their comments helped me rethink important aspects of this story.

Thanks to Hank, Jone, Martha and Norby, Susan and Tem, Marie, Brad, and Ann and Andy for their hospitality while I was on the road, conducting interviews.

I feel blessed by my friends whose love and understanding have carried me through the highs and the lows, especially those who have been there throughout the process: Barbara, Alice, Susan, Joe, Peaches, Geoffrey, Roz, Judy, Donna, Dennis, Jim, Tona and Cristina, Heshie, Doug and Jane, Mark, Janice and Janine.

This book would not have been possible without the help of foundations and individual donors. I am grateful to the Boston Women's Health Book Collective for their support, including fiscal sponsorship of the book. Thanks to Judith Simpson and Stephen Viederman for their help. Sunny Fischer, the former director of The Sophia Fund, the first funder to recognize the importance of Jane's story, was always willing to contact people for me and to offer funding suggestions.

Many thanks to the following foundations: The Sophia Fund, The Funding Exchange, The L. J. Skaggs & Mary C. Skaggs Foundation, The Astraea National Lesbian Foundation, The Ellen Fox Foundation, Human Rights for Women and The Open Meadows Foundation.

Some of the individuals who generously donated to my work wish to remain anonymous. My heartfelt thanks to them and to the others: Marjorie Craig Benton, Jean Hardisty, Maya Miller, Marcena Love, Ruth and Joel Surgal, Lucia Woods Lindley, Vivien Leone, Edith F. Muma, Barbara B. Dow and the Reverend Beatrice Blair.

SELECTED BIBLIOGRAPHY

BOOKS

Baehr, Ninia. *Abortion Without Apology: A Radical History for the 1990's.* Boston: South End Press, 1990.

Boston Women's Health Collective. *Our Bodies, Ourselves: Women and Their Bodies,* first edition. Boston: New England Free Press, 1971.

Chafe, William H. *The Unfinished Journey: America Since World War II.* New York: Oxford University Press, 1991.

Echols, Alice. *Daring to Be Bad: Radical Feminism in America 1967–1975.* Minneapolis: University of Minnesota Press, 1989.

Ehrenreich, Barbara and English, Deirdre. *Witches, Midwives, and Nurses: A History of Women Healers.* Old Westbury: The Feminist Press, 1973.

Evans, Sarah. *Personal Politics: The Roots of Women's Liberation in the Civil Rights Movement & the New Left.* New York: Vintage Books, 1980.

Fried, Marlene Gerber. *From Abortion to Reproductive Freedom: Transforming a Movement.* Boston: South End Press, 1995.

Friedan, Betty. *It Changed My Life: Writings on the Women's Movement.* New York: Dell, 1991.

Garrow, David. *Liberty & Sexuality: The Right to Privacy and the Making of Roe* v. *Wade*. New York: Macmillan, 1994.

Gitlin, Todd. *The Sixties: Years of Hope, Days of Rage*. New York: Bantam Books, 1987.

Gordon, Linda. *Woman's Body, Woman's Right: Birth Control in America*. New York: Penguin Books, 1990.

Hole, Judith and Levine, Ellen. *Rebirth of Feminism*. New York: Quadrangle/New York Times Books Co., 1971.

Koedt, Anne; Levine, Ellen; and Rapone, Anita. *Radical Feminism*. New York: Quadrangle/New York Times Books Co., 1973.

Lader, Lawrence. *Abortion II: Making the Revolution*. Boston: Beacon Press, 1974.

Mohr, James C. *Abortion in America: The Origins and Evolution of National Policy 1800–1900*. New York: Oxford University Press, 1978.

Morgan, Robin. *Sisterhood Is Powerful*. New York: Vintage Books, 1970.

National Women's Health Network. *Abortion Then and Now: Creative Responses to Restricted Access*. Washington, D.C.: National Women's Health Network, 1989.

Paris, Ginette. *The Sacrament of Abortion*. Dallas: Spring Publications, 1992.

Petchesky, Rosalind Pollack. *Abortion and Woman's Choice: The State, Sexuality & Reproductive Freedom*. Boston: Northeastern University Press, 1990.

Ruzek, Sheryl Burt. *The Women's Health Movement: Feminist Alternatives to Medical Control*. New York: Praeger Publishers, 1979.

Sale, Kirkpatrick. *SDS*. New York: Vintage Books, 1974.

Starr, Paul. *The Social Transformation of American Medicine: The rise of a sovereign profession and the making of a vast industry*. New York: Basic Books, 1982.

Students' Society of McGill University. *The Birth Control Handbook*, 2nd edition. Montreal, Canada: McGill University, 1969.

ARTICLES

Bart, Pauline B. "Seizing the Means of Reproduction: An Illegal Feminist Abortion Collective—How and Why it Worked," *Qualitative Sociology*, Winter 1987.

Bart, Pauline B., and Schlesinger, Melinda Bart. "Collective Work and Self-Identity: Working in a Feminist Illegal Abortion Collective." In *Workplace Democracy and Social Change*, edited by Lindenfeld, Frank and Rothschild-Whitt, Joyce. Boston: Porter Sargent, 1982.

Berger, Gary; Bourne, Judith; Haber, Richard; Keith, Louis; Knisely, Kristine; and Zackler, Jack. "Termination of pregnancy by 'super coils': Morbidity associated with a new method of second-trimester abortion," *American Journal of Obstetrics and Gynecology*, June 1, 1973.

Elze, Diane. "An Ordinary Group of Women," *Our Paper*, Portland, Maine, December 1987. Reprinted as "Underground Abortion Remembered," *Sojourner: The Women's Forum*, Boston, April 1988.

Hurst, Jane. "Abortion in Good Faith: The History of Abortion in The Catholic Church," *Conscience: A Newsjournal of Prochoice Catholic Opinion*, Catholics for a Free Choice, Washington, D.C., March/April 1991.

Jane. "The Most Remarkable Abortion Story Ever Told," *Hyde Park/Kenwood Voices*, Chicago, June–November 1973.

Reagan, Leslie Jean. "When Abortion Was a Crime: The Legal and Medical Regulations of Abortion, Chicago, 1880–1973," Ph.D. dissertation, University of Wisconsin, Madison, 1991.

Rockey, Linda. "Guidance for women in trouble," *The Chicago Sun-Times*, December 14, 1969.

RESOURCES

The following is a list of organizations to contact for more information on abortion access, reproductive rights and women's health. These organizations can steer you to others with a specific focus, such as breast cancer or AIDS.

The Abortion Access Project (Boston Reproductive Rights Network [R2N2]). P.O. Box 686, Boston, MA 02130, (617) 494-1161.

Asian Pacific Islanders for Choice. 310 8th St., Suite 30, Oakland, CA 94607.

The American Civil Liberties Union (ACLU) Reproductive Freedom Project. Contact the ACLU National Headquarters, 132 W. 43rd St., New York, NY 10036, (212) 944-9800.

Boston Women's Health Book Collective. P.O. Box 192, W. Somerville, MA 02144, (617) 625-0277.

Catholics for a Free Choice (CFFC). 1436 U St. NW, Suite 301, Washington, DC 20009, (202) 986-6093.

The Center for Reproductive Law and Policy, 120 Wall St., 18th Floor, New York, NY 10005, (212) 514-5534.

The Civil Liberties and Public Policy Program, Hampshire College, Amherst, MA 01002, (413) 549-4600, ext. 645.

The Federation of Feminist Women's Health Centers, 633 E. 11th Ave., Eugene, OR 97401, (503) 344-0966.

The Feminist Majority Foundation, 186 South St., Boston, MA 02111, (617) 695-9688.

The Fund for a Feminist Majority, 1600 Wilson Blvd., Suite 704, Arlington, VA 22209, (703) 522-2214.

International Women's Health Coalition, 24 E. 21st St., New York, NY 10010, (212) 979-8500.

Montreal Health Press, P.O. Box 1000, Station Place du Parc, Montreal, Quebec, Canada, H2W 2N1, (514) 282-1171.

Native American Women's Health Education Resource Center, P.O. Box 572, Lake Andes, SD 57356, (605) 487-7072.

The National Abortion Federation (NAF), 1436 U St. NW, Washington, DC 20009, (202) 667-5881. HOTLINE: (800) 772-9100, M-F, 9:30–5:30 E.S.T. In Canada: (800) 424-2280.

The National Abortion and Reproductive Rights Action League (NARAL), 1101 14th St. NW, 5th Floor, Washington, DC 20005, (202) 408-4600.

National Asian Women's Health Organization, 440 Grand Ave., Suite 208, Oakland, CA 94610.

The National Black Women's Health Project (NBWHP), 1237 Ralph David Abernathy Drive SW, Atlanta, GA 30310, (404) 753-0916. The Public Policy/Education office is at 1133 15th St. NW, Suite 550, Washington, DC 20005, (202) 835-0117 (or 0118).

The National Latina Health Organization (NLHO), P.O. Box 7567, Oakland, CA 94601, (415) 534-1362.

The National Lesbian and Gay Health Association, 1407 S St. NW, Washington, DC 20009, (202) 939-7880.

The National Network of Abortions Funds, c/o Civil Liberties and Public Policy Program, Hampshire College, Amherst, MA 01002, (413) 582-5645.

The National Organization for Women (NOW). Check your local phone book for area chapters or contact National NOW Action Center, 1000 16th St. NW, Suite 700, Washington, DC 20036, (202) 331-0066.

The National Women's Health Network (NWHN), 514 10th St. NW, Washington, DC 20009, (202) 986-6093.

Planned Parenthood Federation of America, 810 2nd Ave., New York, NY 10021, (212) 541-7800.

The Pro Choice Resource Center, 174 E. Boston Post Rd., Mamaroneck, NY 10543, (914) 381-3792 or (800) 733-1973.

The Religious Coalition for Reproductive Choice (RCRC), 1025 Vermont Ave. NW, Suite 1130, Washington, DC 20005, (202) 628-7700.

The Reproductive Health Technologies Project, 1601 Connecticut Ave. NW, Suite 801, Washington, DC 20009.

Students Organizing Students (SOS), 1600 Broadway, Suite 404, New York, NY 10019.

Women of All Red Nations (WARN), 4511 N. Hermitage, Chicago, IL 60640.

The Women of Color Partnership Program (WOCPP), 1025 Vermont Ave. NW, Suite 1130, Washington, DC 20005, (202) 628-7700.

I N D E X

abortion(s):
as act of responsibility, 131, 132, 144
AMA's ban on, 137–38
availability of, in Illinois, 276
bond between women undergoing, 85, 151, 236
cannula technique for, 197, 200, 201, 237, 238
Catholic church's position on, 65, 88, 134
as civil rights issue, 8, 21, 58, 81, 93
cost of, 42–43, 75–76, 77, 99–100, 120, 131, 135, 148, 149, 175, 178, 234
D & C method of, 35, 40, 56, 90, 106, 126, 127, 148, 152, 157, 158–59, 174, 196, 201, 211, 214, 237, 239, 256, 262, 267
illegality of, 12, 15, 26, 31, 32, 46, 52, 70, 87, 88, 91, 110, 122, 127, 141, 164, 166, 177, 181, 183, 190, 208, 233, 248
increased demand for, through Jane, 95–96, 120, 256
Jane counselees' roles in, 108, 136
Jane's follow-up program on, 264, 265–67
lack of lay information on, 26, 33, 57, 137
in long-term pregnancies, 153–57
ME device technique for, 198, 200, 201
medical complications of, 105, 150, 181–83
as medical issue, 5, 16
medical problem model of, women's problem model vs., 23, 24, 25, 274
miscarriage form of, 148–58, 211–12, 237–38, 239, 240, 241

abortion(s) (*cont.*):
physiological effects of, 78–79
as political issue, 5, 6, 16–17, 128, 129, 130, 132, 141–42
positive experiences of, through Jane, 134, 144–47, 168, 191, 236, 250, 257–59
preparatory work for, 126
Protestant position on, 64–65
steps in performing, 114, 126–27, 128
supercoils technique for, 237–38, 239, 240, 241
teamwork of Jane and Nick at, 121
teenagers and, 102, 144, 151, 155, 252
vacuum aspirator technique for, 197, 237
"Abortion—a woman's decision, a woman's right" (pamphlet), 27–28
abortion clinics:
New York, 98–99, 106, 116, 135, 234, 267
Washington, D.C., 234
Abortion Counseling Service of Women's Liberation, The (ACS), *see* Jane
"Abortion in Good Faith: The History of Abortion in the Catholic Church" (Hurst), 88*n*
abortionists, 37–38, 39–43, 53–60, 65, 70, 74–75, 78, 82, 83, 84–85, 90–91, 92–94, 148, 156, 161, 178, 237
arrogance of, 200–201
attitude of, toward patients, 39, 85, 90, 101–2
non-physician status of, 109–11, 112, 115
stigmatization of, 137
abortion legislation, 22–23, 79, 116
repeal vs. reform, 24, 80–81
Abortion 7 (arrested Jane members), 243–47
changes in lives of, after arrest, 243–44
lawyer for, 245–46, 248, 251, 253
preliminary hearing for, 250–251
sources of tension among, 244, 245, 247
statement of, 277–78
strategy meetings of, 244, 245
Abortion 7 Defense Fund, 245
Abortion II: Making the Revolution (Lader), xiv
abortion underground:
Claire's role in, 6–8, 9–13, 14, 15–16
role of clergy in, xiii-xiv, 61–65
Alaskan abortion reform bill (1970), 116

American Law Institute (ALI), 23
American Medical Association (AMA), 117, 137, 272
American Public Health Association, 117, 272

Baird, Bill, 34
Belous, Leon, 32*n*
Bennett, Jordan, 197, 198, 237, 238, 239, 240, 241, 242
arrogance of, 200–201
Big Janes, 96, 120, 162, 166, 178, 179, 192, 255
Billings Hospital, 63
Birth Control Handbook, The, 34–35, 106, 139, 140, 141, 146
Blackmun, Harry, 272–73
Boston Women's Health Collective, 139, 140

California Supreme Court, 79
Call-Back Janes, 96, 116, 154–55, 166, 178, 179, 206, 255, 256, 279
cannulas, 197, 200, 201, 237, 238
Catholic Church, abortion position of, 65, 88, 134
Centers for Disease Control (CDC), 240–41
Chicago, University of, 6, 15, 61, 63, 68, 77, 90, 135, 148, 191, 206, 243
social service school (SSA) of, 269, 270
Chicago Civil Liberties Union, 6, 101
Chicago Women's Committee on Abortion, 67–69
Chicago Women's Liberation Union (CWLU), 44–46, 50, 67, 68, 71, 93, 117, 125, 163, 188–89, 209
Abortion 7 Defense Fund of, 245
Jane as member of, 46, 208
Cisler, Lucinda, 80–81
Claire, 5, 132
and abortion underground, 6–8, 9–13, 14, 15–16
baby shower for, 48–49
as organizer of CWLU, 45
clergy:
as abortion counselors, 62–64, 204
in abortion underground, xiii-xiv, 61–65
Jane and, 64, 204
Clergy Consultation Service (Chicago), 63–65, 68, 204, 234
Clergy Consultation Service on Abortion (N.Y.), xiii, 61, 135
Comstock, Anthony, xiv, 34
Congress of Racial Equality (CORE), 212

consciousness-raising groups, 19, 67, 117, 189, 191
contraception:
counseling at Jane, 34–35, 77, 106
IUD form of, 141
laws about, xiv-xv, 33–35, 272
Cook County Hospital, 68, 105, 151, 195, 241, 265
counselee(s), Jane, 108, 120, 133–36, 188, 193
Angela Nolan, 257–59
Betty, 173–74
Celia, 144–47
Delores, 183–84, 187
family pressures on, 143
hospital treatment of, 150–51, 154, 177–78
Maria, 234–36
counselors, Jane:
Carol, 50, 51–53, 55, 86, 95, 117–18, 154, 288
Charlotte, 135, 188, 191
Cynthia, 73–74, 163, 166, 194, 197, 201, 245, 259–60, 288
Deborah, 103–5, 106–7, 111, 115, 118, 129–30, 132–33, 158, 160–61, 289–90
Donna, 140–41, 194, 210, 253, 277, 284
Elizabeth, 87–88, 96, 197, 200, 269, 288–89
Ellen, 188–89, 194, 206, 270–71, 291
Gail, 189–90, 192–93, 194, 206, 216–17
Grace, 171–73, 292
Helen, 77–79
Irene, 197
Karen, 17–18, 29, 30, 47–48, 95, 287–88
Kate, 191–92, 194, 206, 255–57, 260, 292
Kris, 123–25, 144, 163–64, 170–71, 184–85, 285–86
Lois, 210–13, 249–50, 275–76, 291
Lydia, 167–69
Lynn, 189–90, 193, 194, 253–54, 262, 291
Molly, 188, 193, 194, 206, 260–61, 134–36, 188, 194, 206, 255–57, 260–61, 284–85
Nan, 143, 148, 152, 154
Nora, 202–3, 290
Pam, 127, 153–54, 195, 261, 262, 263
Ricky, 92–94, 97, 118
Robin, 202–3, 215–17, 238
Sally, 249, 280–82, 290
Sarah, 196, 198, 249, 254, 280–82, 290
Val, 92–93, 118, 122
see also Jenny; Julia; Lorraine; Miriam

"cult of motherhood," 137–38
CWLU (Chicago Women's Liberation Union), 44–46, 50, 68, 71, 93, 163, 188–89
 Jane as member of, 46, 208–9

D & C (dilation and curettage), 35, 40, 56, 90, 106, 126, 127, 148, 152, 157, 158–59, 174, 196, 201, 211, 214, 237, 239, 256, 262, 267
Dalkon Shield, 141
Democratic National Convention (1968), 17, 18
Doe v. *Bolton,* 272, 273, 274
drivers, Jane, 108–9

Ehrenreich, Barbara, 283–84
Eisenstadt v. *Baird,* xv, 272
Emma Goldman's Women's Health Center, 278, 283
English, Deirdre, 283–84
Ergotrate, 102, 106, 107, 114, 115, 116, 126, 128

Feminine Mystique, The (Friedan), 13, 50, 73
feminists, 17, 24, 49, 97, 115, 125, 169, 194, 250, 267
First National Conference on Abortion Laws, 24
Freedom Summer, 7, 8
Friedan, Betty, 13, 24, 191

Governor's Commission on Abortion, N.Y. (1969), 72
Griswold v. *Connecticut* (1965), 34, 79, 272
Gurner, Rowena, 26*n*
gynecological exams, 195, 196

Hawaiian abortion reform bill (1970), 80, 116
Hurst, Jane, 88*n*
Hyde, Henry, 205
Hyde Amendment, xvi

Illinois, Northern, U.S. District Court for, 116–17
Illinois Citizens for the Medical Control of Abortion (ICMCA), 5, 24, 61, 62
Inner Circle, of Jane, 161–67
 meetings of, 161–62
 membership in, 152, 163
 secrecy of, 164, 166
intrauterine device (IUD), 141
It Changed My Life: Writings on the Women's Movement (Friedan), 24

Jane (The Abortion Counseling Service of Women's Liberation; ACS), ix, xvii-xx
 and abortion fatalities, 181–83, 184, 186, 187
 and abortions of teenagers, 144, 151, 155, 252

Jane (*cont.*)
betrayal of, by ex-member, 109
"burn-out" of members of, 213–16, 252–54, 261
California women's health group and, 198–99
Chicago Women's Liberation Union and, 209
contraception counseling at, 34–35, 77, 106
control of abortions as key issue for, 38–39, 41–43, 76, 84–85, 98, 100–102, 103, 120, 121, 131, 159, 160
cost of abortions through, 42–43, 75–76, 77, 100, 120, 131, 135, 149, 175, 178, 234
criteria for new members of, 70–71
Curette Caper of, 280
decision to fold, 278–80
Delores's death and, 184, 186, 188
doctors involved with, 37–38, 39–40, 53–60, 70, 76, 111, 149, 174, 176, 182, 195, 196, 265–67
and documentation of follow-up care, 264, 265–67
dynamics of group power at, 98, 118, 165, 166, 207, 215, 248, 255, 268
educational role of, 67–69, 137–40, 268–71
evolution from counseling to abortion service of, 122
expansion beyond neighborhood of, 105
as feminist service, 125, 140–41, 209
first public announcement about, 69
formation of, 15–30
Fronts of, 92, 94, 96, 97, 106, 107–8, 109, 126, 135, 142–43, 146, 174, 179, 183, 193, 210–11, 249, 256
and full-time midwives for miscarriages, 202–3
husbands' attitudes toward wives' involvement in, 170–71, 249
increased demand for abortions through, 95–96, 120, 256
increasing responsibility for abortions of, 121–22
and inducement of miscarriages, 148–58, 211–12
inner circle of, 161–67, 183, 206, 217, 245
Irene's involvement with, 197
isolation of, within women's movement, 208–9
and issue of pregnant counselors, 132–33
Jenny as go-between for Nick and, 92, 94, 164

Jenny as spokeswoman for, 117–18
Julia's abortion through, 98
Julia's growing leadership role in, 97
leadership of, 97, 98, 118
legal risks to, 31, 32, 46, 52, 70, 76–77, 87, 88, 91, 105, 108, 110, 122, 127, 164, 166, 177, 181, 183, 184, 186, 187, 190, 208, 233, 248
lesbian members of, 171–73
lives of members after, 284–92
Loan Fund of, 28, 29, 36–37, 40, 75, 76, 95, 107–8
Lorraine as counseling session leader of, 105–6
Lorraine as phone contact for, 29, 32–33
medical practice demystified by, 128, 129, 130
membership of, 46, 48, 74, 103, 105, 175, 176, 188–89, 194, 255
members lost by, 112–13, 248
members' loyalty to, 167
mutually beneficial contact between clergy and, 64, 204–5, 206
naming of, 27
Nan's involvement with, 143, 148, 152, 154
Nick as mainstay of abortion program of, 110
Nick's resistance to new assistants in, 119, 167
Nick's unlicensed status and, 109–11, 112–13
orientation sessions for new members of, 86–87, 103, 105, 123, 165–66, 181, 188–90, 191
pap tests offered at, 176–77
paramedic position at, 179, 190
personal sorrows in lives of members of, 259–60
places of, 92, 94, 96, 97, 136, 177, 193
and plans for women's health center, 278
police raid on, 91
positive abortion experiences through, 134, 144–47, 168, 236, 250, 257–59
preparatory work for abortions by members of, 126
as process, 108
publicizing services of, 44
restructuring of, 236–37
and resumption of pre-arrest work, 248
Ricky's apartment as Place for, 93–94
Roe v. *Wade* and, 276–77
role of drivers for, 108–9
salaried vs. voluntary jobs at, 179

Jane (*cont.*)
Sally's involvement with, 249, 280
Sally's ode to, 280–82
Sarah's involvement with, 196, 198
secret group within, 94, 98, 103, 118
self-exams and, 195–200, 268–69
as service for poor and black women, 175–76, 267–68
sense of responsibility felt by members of, 167, 187, 263, 275, 285
successful medical record of, 129
teamwork of, at abortions, 121
and temporary overturning of Illinois abortion statute, 117
threats made against, 82–84
training sessions of, 26–27, 105–6, 191–92
Val as a driver for, 93
Val's apartment as Front for, 92–93
younger members of, 213
Jenny, 3–6, 16–17, 18–19, 22, 27, 29, 30, 108, 119, 161
as abortionist, 157–60, 165, 174, 195
in arguments with Nick over abortion costs, 99–100, 116, 120, 131
"burn-out" of, 213–15, 251–53
as buyer of medical supplies, 116, 236
as co-leader, 98, 118, 161–62, 164–65
and feminist issue of women controlling abortions, 115
as go-between for Nick and Jane, 92, 94, 164
as Jane delegate to CWLU retreat, 45
as negotiator with doctors, 38–43, 76, 84–85, 98, 100–102, 131
as Nick's abortion assistant, 90–91
as Nick's apprentice, 113–14, 115, 116, 126–27
Nick's unlicensed status and, 109–11
participation of, in Nick's "house calls," 116
police interview of, 185–86
post-Jane life of, 287
and return to Jane work after burn-out, 232, 233
secret group created by, within Jane, 94
and speaking engagements, 117–18
as teacher of other Jane members, 127, 128, 129, 158, 167, 213

Journal of Obstetrics and Gynecology, 241
Judson Memorial Church, 61
Julia, 89, 109, 161, 165, 199, 217, 267
- abortion of, 98
- as abortionist, 195, 215, 253
- assistance at abortions by, 119–20, 136
- and counseling work for Jane, 120, 145, 146
- friendship between Deborah and, 118
- as Gail's "Big Sister," 192
- growing feminism of, 97
- and husband's attitude toward Jane work, 171
- leadership qualities of, 97, 118
- post-Jane life of, 289
- as role model for younger members, 213
- training of, 127–28, 129

Kaufman, Dr., *see* Nick

Lader, Lawrence, xiv, 24, 61
Lamm, Richard, 23–24
legislation of abortion, 22–23, 79, 116
- repeal vs. reform, 24, 80–81

Leunbach paste, 148–50
loan fund, Jane, 28, 29, 36–37, 40, 75, 76, 95, 107–8
long-term abortions, 153–57
Lorraine, 15–16, 27, 30, 31, 98, 159–60
- as counseling session leader, 105–6
- as counselor to member of police department, 76–77
- and Jane's last name, 47
- as Jane's phone contact, 29, 32–33
- Leunbach paste and, 149–51
- and meeting with "Nathan Detroit," 55–56
- as moderator of Speak-Out on Abortion, 68–69
- post-Jane life of, 287
- pregnancy of, as issue for Jane, 132–33

Maginnis, Pat, 22, 26*n*, 61
McCarthy, Eugene, 15
Marshall, Thurgood, 117
Medical Committee for Human Rights, 59
menstrual extractions (ME), 197–98, 200, 201
Michaels, George, xv, 81
Miriam, 19–20, 29, 30, 74, 97, 105, 119, 161, 195, 213, 232–33, 238, 255, 267
- as co-leader, 98, 118, 161–62, 164–65
- and counselees with advanced pregnancies, 157

Miriam (*cont.*)
counseling compromise proposed by, 113
and husband's attitude toward Jane work, 170
post-Jane life of, 288
as negotiator with Nick for more abortion control, 101–102
as Nick's assistant, 90–91
Nick's unlicensed status and, 109–11
miscarriages, 40, 148–58
full-time Jane midwives for, 202–3
hospital treatment of, 150–51, 154, 177–78
post-, counseling, 157
super coils technique in, 237–38, 239, 240, 241
and teenagers, 155, 252
Monica and Pat, 197, 198
Moody, Howard, xiii, 61, 62, 63, 64, 89, 99
Movement, The, 5, 10, 283
second-class status of women in, 8–9
Myers, Lonny, 24

NARAL (National Abortion and Reproductive Rights Action League), xii, 24, 61, 63
"Nathan Detroit," 54–57
and inducement of miscarriages, 148–50, 157
National Organization for Women (NOW), 13, 45, 67, 71, 73–74, 87–88, 163
Bill of Rights for Women of (1967), 22
New England Free Press, 140
New York abortion reform bill (1970), 80–81, 89–90, 116
New York Clergy Consultation Service on Abortion, xiii, 61, 89, 99
New Yorkers for Abortion Law Repeal, 80–81
New York Radical Women, 72
Nick (Dr. Kaufman), 53, 65, 74–75, 78, 82, 90–91, 92–94, 136, 200–201, 203
apprenticeship of, 110
arrest of Jane members and, 243
assistance by Jane members in abortions performed by, 90–91, 102, 111, 118–19, 136
competence of, 111, 112, 115, 130
and control over abortions, 84, 100–102, 120, 131
decline in abortions performed by, 174–75, 178
identity of, 83, 84, 85
Jane's first contact with, 40–43

Jenny's arguments with, 42–43, 85, 99–100, 116, 120, 131
Jenny's participation in house calls of, 116
as Jenny's teacher, 113–14, 115, 116, 121, 126–27
as mainstay of Jane's abortion program, 110
miscarriages as viewed by, 157
non-physician status of, 109–11, 112, 115, 159
as part of abortion team, 121
patients as viewed by, 85, 90, 101–2, 114, 120, 130, 174
self-protection efforts of, 41, 42, 84, 85, 92, 94, 98, 100, 102
as trainer of Jane's members, 127

Our Bodies, Ourselves (Boston Women's Health Collective), xii, 139–40, 141, 146, 188, 266

pap tests, 176–77, 195
paramedics, 179, 190
Pat and Monica, 197, 198
Phelps, Lana, 26*n*
"Philadelphia Story, The: Another Experiment on Women," 241–42
Planned Parenthood, 117, 140–141
Protestants, abortion position of, 64–65

Red Squad, the, 93–94
Redstockings, 72
reproductive freedom:
as civil rights issue, 14, 17, 20–21, 23, 24, 25
as empowering experience, x-xii, 36, 73
role of women's liberation movement in, xii-xiii, xvii
Reveille for Radicals (Alinsky), 19
Rockefeller, Nelson, 81
Rockefeller Chapel, 61, 62, 206
Roe v. *Wade,* ix, xv, xvi, 246–47, 251, 272, 273, 274, 275, 276

Sales, Kirkpatrick, 93*n*
self-exams, women's, 195, 196, 197, 198, 269
Society for Humane Abortion, 22
Speak-Out on Abortion, 67–69
Supreme Court, U.S., xiv-xv, xvi, 79, 80, 117, 246, 251, 272, 275, 276
Susskind, David, 17

teenage abortions, 102, 144, 151, 155, 252

Underground Railroad, xiii-xiv

vacuum aspirator, 197, 237
Voters Committed to Change, 5, 17
Vuitch, Milan, 32*n,* 66

Washington, D.C., abortion reform bill (1970), 116
Webster v. *Reproductive Health Services,* xvi
Westside Group, 9, 12, 68
Wilson, Harris, 61–65, 68, 204–6, 234
  as co-founder of Illinois Citizens for the Medical Control of Abortion, 61–62
  Illinois grand juries and, 205–6
Wisconsin abortion statute, 79–80
Witches, Midwives and Nurses (Ehrenreich and English), 283–84
Women and Their Bodies (class), 188, 268–69, 291
women's groups, 61, 232
  formation of, 9, 13–14
  self-help, 197
  in support of abortion repeal, 117
women's health issues, lack of lay information on, 26, 33, 138–40
women's liberation, xii-xiii, xvii, 35, 97, 191, 274
  abortion as issue of, 5–6, 16, 17, 21, 22, 25, 37, 45, 73, 81, 93, 115, 169
  agenda of radicals in, 71–73
  anti-hierarchy stance of, 199
  black vs. white agenda of, 211
Women's Radical Action Project (WRAP), 9, 12, 62

"Your Flag Decal Won't Get You Into Heaven Anymore," 280